T0301458

The Economic and Political Aftermath of the Arab Spring

The Economic and Political Aftermath of the Arab Spring

Perspectives from Middle East and North African Countries

Edited by

Carlo Altomonte

Associate Professor of Economics of European Integration, Bocconi University, Milan, Italy

Massimiliano Ferrara

Associate Professor of Mathematical Economics, Mediterranea University of Reggio Calabria, Italy

Edward Elgar

Cheltenham, UK • Northampton, MA, USA

Published by
Edward Elgar Publishing Limited
The Lypiatts
15 Lansdown Road
Cheltenham
Glos GL50 2JA
UK

Edward Elgar Publishing, Inc.
William Pratt House
9 Dewey Court
Northampton
Massachusetts 01060
USA

A catalogue record for this book
is available from the British Library

Library of Congress Control Number: 2013949822

This book is available electronically in the ElgarOnline.com
Economics Subject Collection, E-ISBN 978 1 78254 091 5

ISBN 978 1 78254 090 8

Typeset by Servis Filmsetting Ltd, Stockport, Cheshire
Printed and bound in Great Britain by T.J. International Ltd, Padstow

Contents

Contributors

Sergio Alessandrini, University of Modena and Reggio Emilia, Italy

Carlo Altomonte, Bocconi University, Milan, Italy

Ali H. Bayar, Université Libre de Bruxelles and EcoMod, Belgium

Maria Giovanna Bosco, ERVET and Bocconi University, Milan, Italy

Silvio Contessi, Federal Reserve Bank of St Louis, USA

Francesca de Nicola, World Bank, USA

Arian Farshbaf, University of Southern California and Gettysburg College, USA

Massimiliano Ferrara, Mediterranea University of Reggio Calabria and CRIOS, Bocconi University, Milan, Italy

Li Li, Federal Reserve Bank of St Louis, USA

Roberto Mavilia, MEDAlics, Reggio Calabria and CRIOS, Bocconi University, Milan, Italy

Marcella Nicolini, University of Pavia and Fondazione Eni Enrico Mattei, Milan, Italy

Jeffrey B. Nugent, IZA, Bonn; ERF, Cairo; University of Southern California, USA

Simona Porcheri, Fondazione Eni Enrico Mattei, Milan, Italy

Valeria Talbot, Italian Institute for International Political Studies, Italy

Hoda Youssef, European Bank for Reconstruction and Development, UK

MENA countries: economic and political perspectives in the aftermath of the Arab Spring – an introduction

Carlo Altomonte and Massimiliano Ferrara

The Middle East and North Africa (MENA) region's economies have always been characterized by economic volatility and social disparities.

A long history of state-driven development led to a rise in human development, reducing poverty, but it also exacerbated social exclusion. Notwithstanding the reforms introduced in the 1980s and 1990s, the problem of social exclusion has not been solved in the subsequent decades. Such reforms, indeed, included large-scale privatizations and reduction of barriers to trade and, together with the increase in oil prices, they stimulated growth in the Arab region, but only a small politically connected elite was able to access the benefits of the growth process. This same sense of economic exclusion and social injustice fuelled recent episodes of violence and protests characterizing the so-called Arab Spring.

Between 2010 and 2011 the first mass mobilizations overthrew the government in Egypt and in Tunisia, while a wave of popular protests spread all over the MENA countries, although with different intensities and outcomes. In the short term, the so-called Arab Spring has increased political uncertainty and instability in the region, further exacerbating those socioeconomic problems that were among the root causes of the protests, causing the economic outlook in the region to deteriorate. In the long term, however, the effects of the Arab Spring are still uncertain. They could offer an opportunity to begin a real process of political and economic reform in the region.

This uncertainty leads to a still weak actual macroeconomic trend, frail from many points of view.

I.1   THE POLITICAL PERSPECTIVE

Huntington (1996) attributed decisive importance to the role played by geography in the development and spread of democratic institutions. The

1

theorist of the clash of civilizations thesis also advanced his ideas on the development of democracy (Huntington, 1991). In his interpretation, the process of democratization developed through three consecutive waves: the first involving North America and Western Europe, the second concerning Southern Europe, Latin America and parts of Asia, and finally the third having its focus on Eastern Europe (basically the countries formerly belonging to the Soviet bloc). Huntington died in 2008 so he was not able to observe what, in the eyes of many analysts, seemed to act as a fourth wave of democracy in the Southern Mediterranean. However, it appears to be still too early to determine whether this process, largely exogenous, will be successful or whether it will fail.

In recent years in particular two phenomena have placed the democratic question at the centre of the Mediterranean political agenda:

- On the northern shore, the difficulties encountered on the path of the European integration, which now seems much more laborious and complex than twenty years ago. Some of the German media showed no hesitation in defining 'democracy as garbage' when the Berlin–Paris axis rejected Papandreou's idea of proposing a referendum to the Greek people on the European rescue plan.
- On the other side of the Mediterranean basin, riots broke out in December 2010 and quickly spread in North Africa and the Middle East under the inappropriate definition of 'Arab Spring' (a definition that we use for convenience only).

I.2 NORTH AFRICA

The key element in defining North Africa is the Sahara, a huge box of sand. If we try to turn the map upside down – as suggested by Braudel (1949) – it will seem to fall on us. In the era of globalization, we live the myth that the digital revolution and the development of the means of transport have made the world smaller and more homogeneous. But the desert escapes this over-simplification.

In the desert the springs – as we know them – never bloom. Similarly, the Arab Spring seems to have been too short as it soon degenerated into an endless autumn.

At the basis of the riots along the southern shore of the Mediterranean, there were several factors: the demographic explosion in the 1970s and 1980s that two/three decades later inevitably produced youth unemployment in the area; the closure of the relief valve of migration (towards Europe) on account of the global economic crisis; the development of new technologies that enabled the Mediterranean riots to spread with a few clicks, bypassing – as never before – the censorship of the regimes.

In addition, the riots did not have identical consequences throughout the area because of the intervention, in some territories, of external factors including the decisive involvement of foreign powers (for example, France in Libya). We could simplify the effects of the riots of the so-called Arab Spring in this way: large protests in Algeria, change of government in Morocco, removal or killing of the heads of state in Tunisia, Egypt and Libya. Nevertheless, the analysis of the phenomenon must be much more complex because we are registering a counter-revolution, where the aspirations for freedom (and democracy?) have been frustrated by the reaction of the military hierarchy who have always been at the helm of those states from the second half of the twentieth century onwards.

The situation never seems quiet even in the Maghreb but still there are two critical points concerning the north-eastern part of the continent. One year after Gheddafi's death, Libya is still trying to get out of the deadlock. If Libya is still a unified country, it is only because of the intervention of the foreign countries that helped the new government to face the contrasts between regions (Cyrenaica and Tripolitania were reunified in 1934 by Mussolini). In Egypt the political and institutional situation is unstable. After the 2011 revolution and the fall of Mubarak, Egypt was finally able to hold parliamentary elections but 2012 was marked by massive protests and riots against the government and President Morsi. In both cases, the coming months will tell us if we are approaching either stabilization or a new revolutionary/counter-revolutionary phase.

I.3   MIDDLE EAST

The group of countries which we usually refer to as the Middle East (Anglo-Saxon terminology) or Near East (French terminology) is the most heterogeneous in the Mediterranean area, not only from an economic point of view, but also from a political perspective.

In the space between the Dardanelles and Suez coexist two parliamentary republics (Israel and Turkey), a monarchy (Jordan), a dictatorship (Syria, officially an Islamic republic), a territory not yet internationally recognized as a state (Palestine) and a unique model of non-Western democracy (Lebanon).

According to the geopolitical perspective of the United States, this area corresponds to the western part of the Greater Middle East, the region of international security stretching from the eastern shores of the Mediterranean to Iran.[1] It is perhaps the region in which geopolitical interests seem to be more closely linked to economic ones. It is one of the regions with the most impact on the perspectives of global foreign policy.

In Syria a new world war is in progress, involving on one side the Assad regime, which has been very slowly losing control, and on the other side various and separate oppositions, having as their unique common goal Assad's defeat. The USA and Europe oppose the Syrian regime but China and Russia have protected it during the UN Security Council. Whereas among the Mediterranean countries Turkey and Jordan are supporting the rebels, contributing to the isolation of Syria, on the other side Iran, its eastern neighbour, is one of the Assad regime's main partners.

A few kilometres southwards, the conflict between Israel and Palestine is far from being solved. After the Second World War the creation of two states in the territory of historic Palestine was proposed. Today, 65 years from the creation of the State of Israel, peace – which will have to go through the recognition of a Palestinian state – is still a chimera. Israel and Palestine do not seem to be able to communicate without the intervention of other counties or international organizations. Moreover, Palestinian people are divided geographically. The historic Palestine is divided into three areas, the largest of which is formed by the young and rampant State of Israel, bordered by two non-communicating territories, the Gaza Strip and the West Bank. Only one third of the Palestinian people live in these two areas. Despite the acquisition of 'non-member observer state' status at the UN, the definition of the Palestinian National Authority is shifty. The idea of 'two peoples, two States' remains a dream.

The future of the Middle East will depend on the evolution of the conflicts in Syria and Palestine, which inevitably involve the neighbouring countries. Among them, Turkey follows the Mediterranean vocation of 'bridge-state' between Asia, Europe and Africa. It is the most populous nation of the area, and it aims to play a leading role in the geopolitical chessboard of the Great Sea.

I.4 SOUTHERN EUROPE

From a political point of view Southern Europe and the Balkans are living in a period of deceptive calm ready to degenerate into instability if the economic troubles are not adequately faced.

It is not easy to give a unifying political outlook on the northern shore of the Mediterranean basin. The Italian peninsula always separated, not only geographically, West from East, Latin civilization from a conglomerate of young states in which Greek-Orthodox, Muslim and Christian populations were experiencing a difficult coexistence.

Before becoming a sea, the Adriatic was for a long time a gulf, and before becoming a bridge, it was a trench dividing two ways of living, thinking and preaching. We are in the middle of a long path on which we have to understand where to go. The question is whether the Balkans are becoming a part of Europe or if a part of Europe is going to 'balkanize' itself.

Doubts are justified from the fact that the political process of European unification has begun to be questioned by public opinion in those countries (for example Italy) which were formerly the main promoters of the European Union and amongst its most enthusiastic supporters. The latest elections (in Italy and Greece) have also been seen as an opportunity for a kind of referendum for or against the European Union. A mutual distrust between the Northern and Southern European countries is currently developing. The stability of the Mediterranean northern shore's political panorama – Italy, Greece, Spain and Portugal – seems to be strictly connected to economic developments.

On the other hand, for the stability and the development of the process of European integration, the Balkans appear strategic on the perspective of a still distant but desirable Mediterranean integration. After Slovenia, Croatia will be the second of the six republics that were part of Yugoslavia to become a member of the EU (1 July 2013). The referendum of 2012 (67 per cent favourable) was significant because it demonstrated a desire to join the European Union, even if it was without any popular enthusiasm. The path to the European Union must necessarily first pass through the consolidation of recent national sovereignty. In Montenegro, for example, an official candidate for EU membership, the process of state building seems to be still in progress. Almost half of the citizens feel comfortable with the Serbian language rather than with the official Montenegrin one. At the basis of Balkan public life, with the constraints that arise in the political field, there is the question of the presence and coexistence of the majority and minorities, namely between different ethnicities, religions and cultures. The memory of the war is still too vivid. Macedonia, for example, acquired the status of official candidate for the European Union but is dealing with problems related to the presence of a large Albanian community. Three potential candidates for the European Union have similar problems to face: Albania, which is dealing with ethnic and religious conflicts; Serbia, which is dealing with the coexistence of Bosnian, Albanian and Kosovar minorities; and Bosnia-Herzegovina, where Croatian, Serbian and Muslim components are present. Kosovo, which has a large Serbian population in the north, declared itself independent in 2008, but is administrated by the UN and has still partial international recognition.

From a geopolitical point of view, the hegemonic influence of the

United States, acquired on the northern part of the Western Basin since the Second World War and consolidated in the Balkans with the outbreak of the Yugoslav Wars in the 1990s, does not seem to be questioned.

Since the mid-twentieth century, Europe has chosen to build its union starting from economic cooperation. The ECSC (European Coal and Steel Community, 1952) and EEC (European Economic Community, 1957) were followed by the EU (European Union, its current name since 1993). The question is whether Europe has chosen the right track or whether the discouraging perspectives suggest the need for uniform policies as a pre-empting basis for the desired economic development.

I.5   THE ECONOMIC PERSPECTIVE

A book on the economic perspectives of the MENA countries at this very moment aims at highlighting those critical areas for the future development and growth of the area. The macroeconomic indicators are characterized by a great deal of uncertainty, and in particular GDP growth and unemployment, together with energy-related issues, represent the most relevant challenge in the medium term.

If we add that Gulf Cooperation Council countries (GCC) entered the scene as major players in the resetting of the political scenario of the Arab Spring countries, the uncertainty is even greater, as illustrated in the first chapter of this book. In particular, Valeria Talbot, in this political scenario assessment, describes the differentiated GCC countries' attitudes towards the events in Egypt, Tunisia and Libya.

Figure I.1 shows that the overall trend of per capita income in the MENA region has already recovered, after a slight contraction in 2009–10. The situation is very heterogeneous when considering the countries that are involved in the Arab Spring, though Libya, in particular, suffering a severe drop in 2011, immediately recovered in 2012. In general, however, the overall trend has recovered (see Figures I.1 and I.2).

The growth rate of the region remained very volatile after the drop experienced between 2007 and 2009, and it is expected to remain below long-term trends, as seen from Figures I.3 and I.4.[2] This is mainly due to weak global demand, high food and fuel commodity prices and continued socio-political tensions and uncertainty.

Sluggish growth is not enough to stabilize the employment trend, with a population change that is expected to recover its long-term evolution (see Figure I.5).

Unemployment is thus increasing in many of the countries that experienced the Arab Spring (Figure I.6), with Egypt and Tunisia facing the most

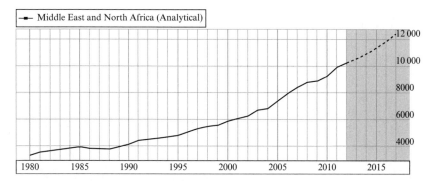

Note: GDP based on PPP per capita (current international dollars per capita).

Source: IMF *World Economic Outlook*, October 2012.

Figure I.1   Evolution of MENA region's GDP

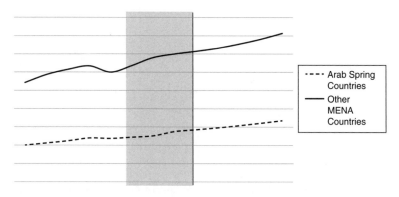

Note: ª Arab Spring countries include Algeria, Egypt, Iraq, Jordan, Kuwait, Lebanon, Libya, Morocco, Oman, Syria, Tunisia and Yemen, where data are available, while other MENA countries include Bahrain, Djibouti, Iran, Israel, Malta, Qatar, Saudi Arabia and United Arab Emirates. The definition of MENA countries follows the World Bank: http://web.worldbank.org/WBSITE/EXTERNAL/COUNTRIES/MENAEXT/0,,menuPK:247619~pagePK:146748~piPK:146812~theSitePK:256299,00.html.

Source: IMF *World Economic Outlook*, October 2012.

Figure I.2   Recent evolution of GDP in MENA countries: Arab Spring countriesª vs. others

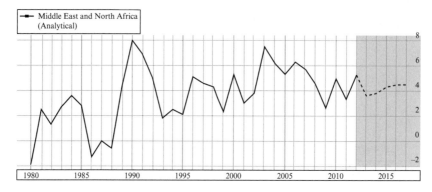

Note: Data represent GDP per capita in PPP.

Source: IMF *World Economic Outlook*, October 2012.

*Figure I.3   Evolution of MENA region's real GDP growth (annual
              percentage change)*

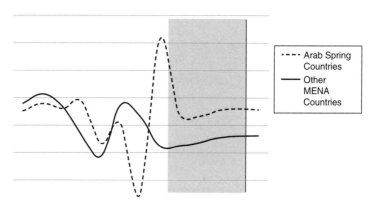

Note: Data represent real GDP growth, weighted average for each group of countries
(weights based on GDP).

Source: IMF *World Economic Outlook*, October 2012.

*Figure I.4   Recent evolution of GDP growth rate in MENA countries:
              Arab Spring countries vs. others*

difficult situation in this regard, and it is expected to reach 2010 levels only
in 2017.

Rising unemployment implies increasing deterioration of the business
climate and job opportunities, as well as rising discrimination against

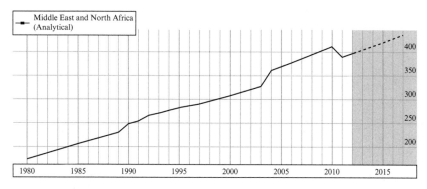

Source: IMF *World Economic Outlook*, October 2012.

Figure I.5 Evolution of MENA region's population (millions of people)

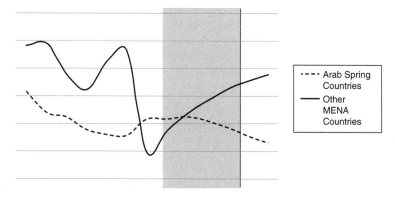

Note: Data represent unemployment rate, weighted average for each group of countries (weights based on GDP).

Source: IMF *World Economic Outlook*, October 2012.

Figure I.6 Recent evolution of unemployment rate in MENA countries: Arab Spring countries vs. others

women in the area. The specific relationship between trade, female labour and entrepreneurship is tackled in the empirical study by Contessi, de Nicola and Li (Chapter 4), who find that women are more likely to be business owners in female labour-abundant countries when they face fewer *de jure* constraints and operate in industries with a higher concentration of female workers.

Rising commodity prices and high unemployment are also driving an

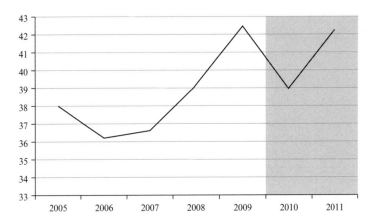

Note: Data represent government expenditure, as a percentage of GDP, average for the group of countries considered.

Source: IMF *World Economic Outlook*, October 2012.

Figure I.7   Recent evolution of government expenditure in Arab Spring countries

increase in government spending on wages and subsidies in the whole region (see Figure I.7), an instrument that can help in the short term, but that is not sustainable in the long term if a growth-lifting strategy is not employed.

Inflation has increased sharply since 2010, but it is expected to slow down in the near future (see Figure I.8) and stabilize in the majority of countries (see Figure I.9).

The current account balance is also expected to deteriorate, as depicted in Figure I.10. The MENA countries have been traditionally seen to be under-trading with each other, with the typical pattern of trade becoming much more like a hub and spoke structure with Europe in the middle. But in the recent past, as Asian economies became dominant in the international scenario, things have been changing slightly; the decline in the over-trading of MENA countries with the EU and the US has been accompanied by the decline in under-trading among MENA countries themselves and also with Asian countries, as illustrated in the trade discussion of Arian Farshbaf and Jeffrey Nugent (Chapter 2).

Moreover, the deterioration of external competitiveness of the region is also confirmed by the deterioration of Foreign Direct Investment (FDI) attractiveness since the beginning of the Arab Spring for the whole MENA region, a negative trend that inverted the positive, although volatile, trend

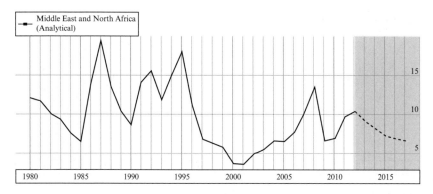

Source: IMF *World Economic Outlook*, October 2012.

Figure I.8   Evolution of MENA region's inflation rate (average consumer prices; annual percentage change)

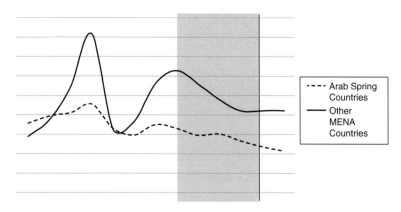

Note: Data represent inflation rate (annual % change CPI), weighted average for each group of countries (weights based on GDP).

Source: IMF *World Economic Outlook*, October 2012.

Figure I.9   Recent evolution of inflation in selected Arab countries

of previous years (see Figure I.11) and worsened the impact of the global economic crisis (see Figure I.12).

FDI plays a role in providing fresh capital, external financing possibilities, know-how and technologies to the host countries; these benefits potentially lead to spillovers of various kinds, but they also contribute to labour creation, therefore the linkage with employment-related issues is

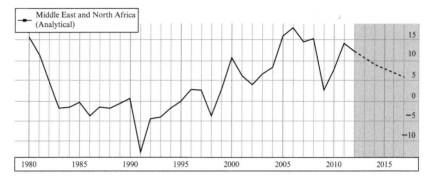

Source: IMF *World Economic Outlook*, October 2012.

*Figure I.10   Evolution of MENA region's current account balance
(percentage of GDP)*

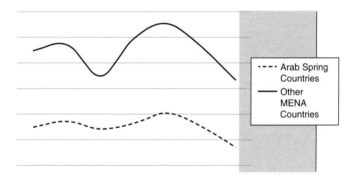

Note: Average performance of the countries belonging to each group.

Source: UNCTAD Database, UNCTADStat.

*Figure I.11   Evolution of FDI inflows, as percentage of world's total in
MENA countries*

self-evident, and is discussed in the chapter on productivity, labour and
FDI by Sergio Alessandrini (Chapter 3).

The financial scenario was heavily affected by the political turmoil in the
area, with investors acting cautiously as long as the scenario was unstable.
However, the increase in the consolidated CDS[3] for the Middle East region
has slowed down in the last year, signalling a positive consideration of
financial markets of the first signs of restored political stability in many
MENA countries (see Figures I.13 and I.14).

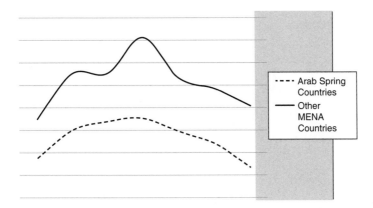

Note: Data are expressed at current prices and current exchange rates, total inflows in each region.

Source: UNCTAD Database, UNCTADStat.

Figure I.12 Evolution of FDI inflows, in millions of US dollars

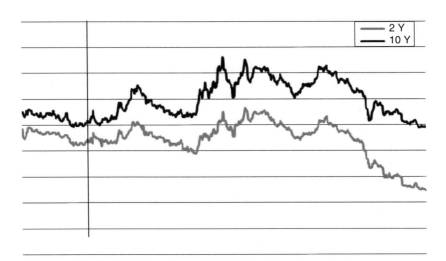

Source: Bloomberg.

Figure I.13 Evolution of Middle East 2 years and 10 years CDS

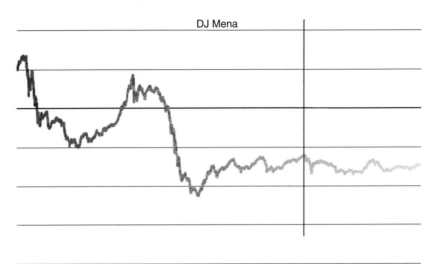

Source: Bloomberg.

Figure I.14   Evolution of Dow Jones Index for the MENA region

The macroeconomic outlook just depicted thus highlights that recovery still appears quite slow and fragile in the region, and the full rehabilitation of MENA economies depends largely on the path of socio-economic reforms that will be undertaken in the near future.

Some positive signals in this perspective came from the recent economic summit that took place in Riyadh in January 2013 and represented the first economic summit of Arab leaders since the Arab Spring started. During the 3rd Arab Economic Summit, indeed, traditional issues such as the pan-Arab free trade area and support for SMEs in the area were coupled with completely new topics inspired by the Arab Spring. These include the urge to tackle unemployment or the problem of 'non-existent' job opportunities for a young, highly educated new generation or the importance of the untapped potential of Arab women who are increasingly educated and eager to make their contribution to the economic success of the region. Other crucial topics for the development of the region were redefined and substantiated, such as environmentally sustainable development.

These new themes and important priorities for the future of the MENA regions' countries are the focus of this book. Considering the problem of youth unemployment, Farshbaf and Nugent find that the young workforce who have very few prospects in their home countries could prove crucial in improving the classical problem of under-trading of the region. Focusing on the untapped potential of Arab women, Contessi, de Nicola and Li propose a gender study in the realm of international trade. Since MENA countries stand out in international comparisons for *de jure* obstacles to female employment and entrepreneurship, they analyse female labour participation and find that women are more likely to be business owners in female labour-abundant countries when they face fewer *de jure* constraints and operate in industries with a higher concentration of female workers. The problem of high unemployment in the region in general is also addressed by Alessandrini (Chapter 3), who discusses the contribution of foreign capital inflows to domestic employment and labour productivity. Using the input–output matrix, the author finds strong and significant positive effects from the backward spillovers of FDI on productivity and employment.

As far as environmental issues of sustainable development are concerned, Nicolini and Porcheri (Chapter 6) describe the actual energy scenario and stress the importance of the Arab Spring in deterring and postponing large investments in the area. Bayar and Youssef (Chapter 5) go further by considering the way in which energy is produced, distributed and used and the way it affects the social, economic and environmental dimensions of any development efforts. Since climate also depends on energy production, CO_2 emissions and the use of alternative energies are also investigated.

Finally, in the last chapter of this book, Bosco and Mavilia discuss long-term growth and innovation, drawing attention to the fragility of any growth policy that focuses only on trade integration, but is based on risible figures for R&D expenditure and human capital formation.

NOTES

1. G8 definition. A wider definition includes the countries from the Atlantic shore of the Maghreb to Central Asia.
2. Note that the negative peak of 2011 and the positive peak of 2012 for Arab Spring countries in Figure I.4 is mainly driven by the performance of Syria.
3. A CDS is a swap designed to transfer the credit exposure of fixed-income products between parties. The buyer of a credit default swap receives credit protection, whereas the seller of the swap guarantees the creditworthiness of the debt security. In doing so, the risk of default is transferred from the holder of the fixed-income security to the seller of the swap. For example, the buyer of a credit default swap will be entitled to the par value of the contract by the seller of the swap, should the third party default on payments. By purchasing a swap, the buyer is transferring the risk that a debt security will default.

REFERENCES

Braudel, F. (1949), *La Méditerranée et le Monde Méditerranéen à l'Epoque de Philippe II*, Paris: Librairie Armand Colin.

Huntington, S. (1991), *The Third Wave: Democratization in the Late Twentieth Century*, Norman, OK: University of Oklahoma Press.

Huntington, S. (1996), *The Clash of Civilizations: Remaking of World Order*, New York: Simon & Schuster.

1. Gulf monarchies' role in the new MENA region*

Valeria Talbot

1.1 INTRODUCTION

The emergence of the Gulf Cooperation Council (GCC) monarchies (Bahrain, Kuwait, Oman, Qatar, Saudi Arabia and United Arab Emirates) as a major player in the Middle East and North Africa (MENA) region is one of the most interesting outcomes of the Arab Spring. Nevertheless, the Gulf monarchies' presence in the region is not new. Over the last decade relations between the GCC and Southern Mediterranean states[1] have intensified at both political and economic levels. Islam has been a major driver of the progressive Gulf expansion in the region. Gulf monarchies, in particular Saudi Arabia, have financed religious groups and activities in MENA countries in order to support political Islam, mainly Salafi-inspired groups (Maestri, 2012). Since the 1980s the charities of the Gulf states have operated inside the GCC as well as outside. In the economic field, GCC foreign direct investment (FDI), which grew between 2003 and 2008 as a consequence of the oil boom registered in those years, played a key role in fostering economic growth in MENA countries. At the regional level, Gulf monarchies – led by Saudi Arabia and Qatar – particularly engaged in the resolution of the Israeli–Palestinian conflict, sponsoring several – albeit unsuccessful – peace initiatives. The Arab awakening and the deep regional transformations that it has engendered have pushed the Gulf monarchies to assume a more dynamic and assertive stance in the area in order to protect their interests and avoid a wave of unrest that could endanger their own stability.

1.2 GULF MONARCHIES FACE THE ARAB UPRISINGS

GCC countries were taken by surprise by the outbreak of uprisings in North Africa and the overthrow of old friendly regimes in Tunisia and

Egypt. Uncertainty about future developments in those countries and upsetting consequences on the regional context provoked deep concern in the GCC rulers, the most conservative of the Arab world. In a fast-changing regional scenario, the main interest of the Gulf monarchies was to avoid the spread of unrest to the Arabian peninsula as well as to stabilize the Arab region, trying to influence transformations and developments in the Arab countries where revolts and protests had erupted. However, although the GCC appears as a conservative bloc interested in maintaining the status quo by managing instability, it is not a monolithic bloc and different positions exist internally. Undoubtedly Saudi Arabia is the most conservative monarchy, while Qatar has adopted a more progressive and pragmatic approach driven by a mix of aspirations in terms of international prestige, religious motivations and economic interests. Qatar backed the Muslim Brotherhood in North Africa, financing, for example, the victory of the Ennahda party in Tunisia, despite the fact that Qatari rulers embrace the conservative Wahhabi interpretation of Islam (Beaumont, 2012).

The Gulf monarchies' response to the Arab uprisings was not homogeneous, at least on the surface. On one hand, they assumed a reactionary stance: this was the case in the crisis in Bahrain, where Saudi Arabia and United Arab Emirates, under the aegis of the GCC, intervened militarily to repress the revolt and to avoid a potential spillover effect. Alongside military intervention, a conspicuous economic package worth $20 billion was approved to sustain both Bahrain and Oman – where less intense protests broke out as well – by financing long-term projects in infrastructure and housing sectors. A conservative attitude was also adopted towards the other two Arab monarchies outside the GCC, fearing that a possible agenda of reforms in Jordan and Morocco could have emboldened demands for a political opening at home, unlocking a Pandora's box and endangering the stability of the Gulf regimes.

On the other hand, the GCC backed regime change in Libya and is in favour of power handover in Syria, although this does not mean support for the people's demands for democratic reforms. In both cases the Arab Spring provided the Gulf monarchies – especially Saudi Arabia and Qatar – with an opportunity to expand their influence in the MENA region. In particular, 'the crisis in Libya gave Doha the opportunity to play a more proactive role in line with the ambition to increase its weight at the international level' (Talbot, 2011). Qatar was the first Arab country to recognize the Libyan Transitional National Council (TNC) government as the 'sole legitimate representative' of the Libyan people; it also provided financial aid – almost $300 million – and contributed, along with the United Arab Emirates, to patrolling the no-fly zone by deploying aircraft. As for Syria,

Saudi Arabia and the other Gulf monarchies have an interest in backing Syrian opposition against the regime of Bashar al-Assad. Indeed, the Syrian crisis appears to have become the main fault line of the Iranian–Saudi confrontation for supremacy in the Middle East. This confrontation has both geopolitical and religious dimensions. From a geopolitical point of view, since the fall of Saddam Hussein and given the prevalence of the Shia majority in new Iraq, Teheran has gained weight and leverage, progressively shifting in its own favour the regional balance of power. Therefore for Riyadh the overthrow of the Syrian regime, Iran's main regional ally, would contribute to reduce the Iranian influence in the Middle East. As for the religious dimension, that is, the clash between Sunnis and Shias for religious pre-eminence in the Muslim world, it has assumed greater importance in Saudi–Iranian rivalry since the 'Shia revival' (Nasr, 2006) in the aftermath of the Iraq war, at the same time becoming one of the main thorny issues in Middle Eastern affairs.

In the GCC annual summit in December 2011, Saudi Arabia proposed for the first time to form a tighter political and economic union among GCC monarchies in response to the Arab awakening and to a fast-changing strategic landscape (Riedel, 2012). Only Bahrain, due to well-known deep political and economic reliance on the Saudi monarchy, reacted positively, while Qatar, Kuwait, Oman and the United Arab Emirates were more circumspect. Although no agreement has been reached until now, the Saudi initiative has to be considered as a further attempt of Riyadh to build walls around the Gulf monarchies to make them immune from the 'reform virus' inoculated by the Arab Spring. Aside from the sporadic protests of the Shia minority in Eastern regions – where the largest part of the Saudi oilfield is located – the kingdom has not experienced serious political turmoil so far. In March 2011, soon after the fall of the regimes in Tunisia and Egypt and the outbreak of the civil war in Libya, the Saudi monarchy allocated two $130 billion economic packages to buy off any potential domestic discontent. As long as the *rentier* state works, Saudi Arabia and the other rich Gulf monarchies could maintain social control and domestic stability. However, under pressure of demographic growth and increasing domestic energy consumption, it is questionable how long the Saudi *rentier* state will be able to preserve wealth, social satisfaction and political consensus. Furthermore, the high dependence of the Saudi economy on oil production, notwithstanding the economic diversification attempts in recent years, makes it excessively exposed to oil price fluctuations. Indeed, 'high oil prices are necessary to sustain the domestic political system and the patronage that fuels it, as well as the kingdom's hegemony in the region' (Jones, 2011).

1.3   A CLUB OF ARAB MONARCHIES?

Another 'attempt at stabilization', this time within the Arab monarchies outside the GCC, originated at the organization's summit in May 2011. The GCC proposed, once again under Saudi impulse, to offer membership to Jordan and Morocco. This move was seen as part of the strategy of Saudi Arabia – backed by the United Arab Emirates and Bahrain, whereas Kuwait, Oman and Qatar had some reservations – to create a 'Sunni monarchy club' (Boukhars, 2011) and to preserve this bloc from the wind of reform that was blowing over the region. According to some analysts, it was also an attempt to counterbalance Iran's growing influence in the region and 'to find a long-term solution to regional uncertainty and regional balance of power' (Fakir, 2011).

The GCC decision generated different reactions both in Jordan and Morocco. In the Hashemite Kingdom, which shares a border with Saudi Arabia, along with deep political and economic ties, many saw the GCC initiative as a good opportunity to tackle their country's deep economic problems (large budget deficit, unemployment, poverty, low growth, lack of energy sources, rising energy costs, and so on). Nevertheless, reformist and liberal forces feared that putting Jordan more and more under the Saudi umbrella could affect any reform process in the country. The same concern was shared by many in Morocco, where a timid reform process was started from above since the approval by referendum of some constitutional amendments in July 2011.

However, in a first stage, neither the timing of the accession process nor the kind of status they would be awarded – full membership (including the future monetary union) or partial membership (only of some GCC institutions) – was clearly defined. In July 2011 talks started to evaluate Jordan's requirements for membership. Indeed, Jordan, thanks to its geographic proximity to Saudi Arabia and to its smaller economy and population, is better positioned than Morocco to become a member state. In addition, Amman has shown greater interest in joining the organization than Rabat, which, despite longstanding relations with the Gulf states, has closer political and economic ties with the European Union. Joining the GCC does not seem to be a priority for Morocco, although membership could bring important economic advantages. In October 2011, at the meeting of GCC ministers of foreign affairs in Jeddah, a five-year economic development assistance programme to help Jordan and Morocco was approved. In December a $5 billion fund ($2.5 billion for each country) was established to support development projects in both countries, even though it was not clear whether and when they would join the organization.[2] Actually, there is no consensus among Gulf monarchies to include Jordan and Morocco in the club,[3] despite some benefits they could bring in terms of strategic depth, investment opportunities, large population and military force in the case of Morocco.

Economic benefits of a possible GCC enlargement would be even more significant for Rabat and Amman. From an economic point of view, both Morocco and Jordan (both net oil-importing countries) could take great advantage from GCC membership. Indeed, this would increase the flow of foreign direct investment, trade and labour mobility and boost tourism and manufactured exports to the Gulf region. However, the process might not be straightforward and is likely to take a long time because of the deep differences in economic structures, GDP and GDP per capita, budget deficit, and population size for Morocco, which, with its 32 million people, is more highly populated than Saudi Arabia (27 million).

1.4 SAUDI ARABIA AND EGYPT: RESHAPING RELATIONS

Prior to the fall of President Mubarak, Egypt and Saudi Arabia, the two leading Arab countries, enjoyed long-lasting and positive relations and cooperated on several regional dossiers. However, the vacuum of power and political instability which followed the end of Mubarak's regime has impacted negatively on bilateral relations. Saudi Arabia was really concerned about political developments in Egypt and the emergence of forces that could have adopted hostile regional policies and, even worse, have tried to export unrest to the Arabian peninsula. This double concern has characterized the Saudi attitude towards Egypt since the popular uprising in January 2011. But at the same time pragmatic and opportunistic reasons have emerged. Indeed, the Saudi kingdom has been aware of the importance of Egypt's political stability for the entire region and the preservation of the status quo in the GCC monarchies.

Due to its geo-strategic location, demographic weight (more than 80 million people) and leading role in regional issues and balance of power, Egypt represents a keystone in the Southern Mediterranean region architecture, and its stability is crucial for the Gulf regimes. Indeed, no Gulf country would want to see an Egyptian political and economic collapse that would negatively impact not only internally but also externally. The victory of the Muslim Brotherhood party in Egyptian elections was not welcomed by Saudi rulers, as tensions have long existed between the Saudi kingdom and Muslim Brotherhood. At the same time, Saudi Arabia distrusted the Muslim Brotherhood's political agenda, fearing possible interference in its domestic affairs. On the other side, strategic and economic reasons suggested that good relations should be maintained with whoever ruled Egypt, considering that mutual benefits would come from keeping cooperation alive.

Eighteen months of ups and downs have characterized Saudi–Egyptian relations, which reached the lowest point in April 2012 when Riyadh withdrew its ambassador from Cairo after a diplomatic crisis over the detention of an Egyptian human rights activist in the kingdom. Although harshly affected, bilateral ties did not break up and a rapprochement between Saudi Arabia and Egypt occurred in July when the newly elected Egyptian President Mohammed Morsi paid a visit to Saudi Arabia. The choice of the Saudi kingdom for Morsi's first official visit was a sign of continuity in Egypt's foreign policy as well as of pragmatism. Egypt needs Saudi economic and financial aid along with Gulf investments to recover its economy, boost economic growth and reduce high unemployment.[4] Saudi Arabia, for its part, had the assurance that political developments in Egypt would not compromise GCC security. Furthermore, for Saudi rulers, fostering Egyptian economic recovery is a means to sustain the most populous Arab country's political stability in a regional environment in great turmoil.

Yet two other aspects have to be taken into account in Saudi–Egyptian rapprochement. First, Egyptians are the biggest expatriate community – about 1.6 million – in Saudi Arabia and remittances from the Saudi kingdom, which accounted for 13 per cent of the $7.8 billion total in the fiscal year to June 2009, are a significant source of revenues for the Egyptian economy.[5] Second, Riyadh needs the support of the biggest Arab country for its 'Sunni project',[6] which implies the strengthening of Sunni Muslims all over the Arab world, as the division between Sunnis and Shias has been emerging as one of the main fault lines of the new Middle East. In conclusion, it seems that for Riyadh it does not matter who 'is in power in Cairo, as long as its interests are maintained'.[7]

1.5   GCC FINANCIAL AID TO THE ARAB SPRING COUNTRIES

In the wake of the G8 summit in Deauville in May 2011, where international donors promised $38 billion to the Arab Spring countries, GCC monarchies pledged significant financial aid. Egypt was supposed to receive the largest share. In particular, United Arab Emirates (UAE) pledged $3 billion, Saudi Arabia committed to provide $4 billion in the form of soft loans, deposits and grants, while Qatar promised $10 billion through investments and projects.[8]

However, more than a year later only a small part of the promised financial aid arrived in Egypt and in the other Arab Spring countries. GCC states, along with other international financial sponsors, were suspicious of the ongoing political instability, and uncertainty regarding the transition process – above all in Egypt and Libya – made them very cautious. Domestic stabilization was considered as a necessary precondition for any financial aid package and investment. Only in May 2012 was a first Saudi aid package worth $500 million provided to Egypt. A month later Saudi Arabia deposited $1 billion in the Egyptian central bank and transferred $500 million to buy Egyptian T-bonds.[9] Further aid worth $430 million was also approved for projects. After Morsi's visit, it is likely that the Saudi monarchy will provide more funding as long as the Egyptian government remains aligned to Riyadh's interest. Saudi Arabia is also the main shareholder in the Islamic Development Bank which signed a $1 billion cooperation agreement to support Egypt's food and energy sectors at the beginning of July 2012.[10] Previously, in June, the Saudi kingdom donated $500 million to the UN World Food Programme Egypt to support development projects in the country. In spite of enduring uncertainty, it seems that pragmatism has prevailed in the Saudi approach towards Cairo, as well as in the other GCC monarchies: helping the Egyptian economy to recover and sustaining its development would benefit Gulf monarchies and the region as a whole.

Along with Saudi Arabia, Qatar has proved to be the more active GCC state in the region in the wake of the Arab uprisings. Thanks to its natural gas wealth, Qatar is trying to play a significant economic role as well as to establish itself as a prominent player in the Middle East and North Africa. In the light of the Qatari investment diversification strategy around the world, MENA countries could be profitable both economically and in terms of political leverage. The victory of the Muslim Brotherhood in Egypt and the emergence of affiliated parties in Tunisia and Morocco gave Qatar an opportunity to reinforce ties with these countries – unlike Saudi Arabia, Qatar kept up good relationships with the Muslim Brotherhood – as well as to increase its political and economic influence in North Africa.

In August 2012 the Qatari monarchy announced a $2 billion deposit for Egypt's central bank – a first tranche worth $500 million had already been deposited – to boost Egyptian foreign reserves, which dramatically decreased since the previous year's uprising. Qatar's interest in Egyptian economic recovery extends to many sectors, from energy infrastructure to real estate and tourism, and investments in a number of projects have been announced. Indeed, Qatar Petroleum International committed $362 million in a $3.7 billion oil refinery project in the Cairo periphery.[11] Furthermore, Qatar invested $544 million in real estate projects in Cairo and Sharm el-Sheikh.[12] At the beginning of September, Qatar announced it would invest

$18 billion in tourism and industry projects along Egypt's Mediterranean coast over the next five years. The projects include $8 billion for gas, power and iron and steel plants at the northern entrance to the Suez Canal and $10 billion for a giant tourist resort on the Mediterranean coast.[13]

Cooperation in the economic and investment fields was also strengthened with Tunisia. During the visit of the Qatari crown prince, Sheikh Tamim bin Hamad al Thani, to the North African country in mid-July 2012 several agreements and memoranda of understanding were signed,[14] covering a wide range of sectors (development, justice, oil, energy). Furthermore, Qatar is financing the Omar al-Mukhtar housing project, which will provide more than 600 housing units together with shops and parks, and will promote the development of the Sidi Hussein district of Tunis. Previously, in April, a $500 million Qatari loan, at a 2.5 per cent interest rate, arrived in Tunisia's central bank.[15] Qatar also showed interest in resuming long delayed plans to build a $2 billion oil refinery to increase the country's refining capacity.

Qatar's new wave of investments also extends to Morocco where it created a $2 billion joint venture to fund development projects. In addition, the sovereign funds of Qatar, the United Arab Emirates and Kuwait invested $2.5 billion in a new fund, Wissal Capital, established by Morocco's Tourism Investment Authority, aiming at developing tourism in the North African country.[16]

1.6   GCC MONARCHIES' ECONOMIC ROLE IN THE SOUTHERN MEDITERRANEAN

The slow return of FDI flows from GCC monarchies to the Southern Mediterranean countries represents a positive sign, although it is unlikely that investments will quickly recover to the oil-boom levels of the previous decade. Indeed, during the 2003–08 oil boom, the Southern Mediterranean countries benefited from the GCC monarchies' big investments which contributed to regional countries' economic growth (see Table 1.1). A strong rise in oil prices provided Gulf monarchies with a substantial surplus which was invested in new, and diversified, destinations in Southern Mediterranean countries – previously the region was not considered by GCC investors which preferred the US and Europe – where a more favourable business environment existed thanks to the start of economic reform and liberalization processes (Talbot, 2010).

Figures provided by the Anima/MIPO Observatory show that in 2003–08 Gulf monarchies ranked second after Europe as a source of investment in the Southern Mediterranean countries. Indeed, they provided 28.6 per

Table 1.1   Percentage real GNP growth in MENA and GCC countries

	Average	Projections						
	2000–2006	2007	2008	2009	2010	2011	2012	2013
Algeria	4.1	3.0	2.4	2.4	3.3	2.5	3.1	3.4
Bahrain	6.1	8.4	6.3	3.1	4.5	1.8	2.0	2.8
Egypt	4.4	7.1	7.2	4.7	5.1	1.8	1.5	3.3
Jordan	6.3	8.2	7.2	5.5	2.3	2.5	2.8	3.0
Kuwait	6.8	4.5	5.0	−5.2	3.4	8.2	6.6	1.8
Lebanon	3.0	7.5	9.3	8.5	7.0	1.5	3.0	4.0
Libya	4.6	7.5	5.4	−0.1	2.5	−61.0	76.3	21.0
Morocco	4.9	2.7	5.6	4.9	3.7	4.3	3.7	4.3
Oman	3.8	5.3	12.9	1.1	4.0	5.5	5.0	4.0
Qatar	11.2	18.0	17.7	12.0	16.6	18.8	6.0	4.6
Palestinian Territories	−0.1	5.4	7.1	7.4	9.8	9.9	6.2	5.6
Saudi Arabia	3.9	2.0	4.2	0.1	4.6	6.8	6.0	4.1
Syria	4.0	5.7	4.5	5.9	3.4	–	–	–
Tunisia	4.6	6.3	4.5	3.1	3.1	−0.8	2.2	3.5
UAE	8.2	6.5	5.3	−3.3	0.9	4.9	2.3	2.8

Source: International Monetary Fund, *Regional Economic Outlook Update: Middle East and Central Asia*, Washington, April 2012.

cent, that is to say 65.8 billion euros, of the total amount of FDI – 229.8 billion euros – attracted by those countries, while 37.3 per cent came from Europe (Abdelkrim and Henry, 2009). Gulf monarchies invested above all in Mashreq countries, which attracted $41.46 billion, corresponding to 63 per cent of total GCC FDI to the Southern Mediterranean region (Table 1.2), while the Maghreb received a smaller amount, $15.38 billion (23.3 per cent). Egypt had the lion's share, attracting $25.58 billion (38.8 per cent), followed by Jordan with $7.5 billion, Tunisia with $5.7 billion, Syria $5 billion, Algeria $4.8 billion, Morocco $3.9 billion, and Lebanon $2.9 billion.

Lastly, Libya and the Palestinian Territories received $854 and $392 million respectively. United Arab Emirates was the main investor, allocating $35.7 billion in FDI. Kuwait ranked second with $11.6 billion, followed by Saudi Arabia with $11 billion, Qatar with $4.1 billion and Bahrain with $3.1 billion (Table 1.2). However, in 2008–10 FDI from GCC declined as a consequence of the international economic financial crisis (see Table 1.3).

In the last decade the United Arab Emirates has emerged as the largest Arab FDI exporter. In 2000–11 FDI outflows from the Emirates amounted

Table 1.2 Announced FDI from GCC countries to the Southern Mediterranean countries in 2003–08 (millions of euros)

Origin	Destination countries										
	Maghreb				Mashreq					Other Med.	Total
	Algeria	Morocco	Tunisia	Libya	Egypt	Jordan	Lebanon	Palest.	Syria	Turkey	
Bahrain	143	592	132		229	1497			452	66	**3111**
Kuwait	2081	730	296	55	3009	1584	1257		1533	1148	**11693**
Qatar		54	403	223	1503	762		339	669	230	**4183**
Saudi Arabia	736	439	80	12	2993	1345	493	53	1250	3667	**11068**
UAE	1939	2110	4795	564	17848	2313	1218		1111	3852	**35750**
Total	**4899**	**3925**	**5706**	**854**	**25582**	**7501**	**2968**	**392**	**5015**	**8963**	**65805**

Source: Abdelkrim and Henry (2009, p. 153).

Table 1.3 Main announced FDI from GCC to the Southern Mediterranean countries in 2008–10 (millions of euros)

Origin	Destination countries									
	Maghreb				Egypt	Mashreq				Total
	Algeria	Morocco	Tunisia	Libya		Jordan	Lebanon	Palest.	Syria	
Bahrain		327	11	325					83	**746**
Kuwait		34			193	129	287		87	**730**
Oman	67			55						**122**
Qatar			386	111	420	18		58	68	**1061**
Saudi Arabia		88			387	44		12	44	**575**
UAE		160	92	157	627	719	124		82	**1961**
Total	**67**	**609**	**489**	**648**	**1627**	**910**	**411**	**70**	**364**	**5195**

Source: ANIMA (2011).

to $56.1 billion, surpassing Kuwait and Saudi Arabia, which invested $48.5 billion and $33.5 billion respectively, according to UNCTAD (n.d.) (Table 1.4).

Broadly speaking, since 2003 GCC investment outflows worldwide have progressively expanded, with a peak of $45 billion in 2007. A new strong rise in oil prices since the end of 2010, due to several factors – the Arab uprisings, the stopping of Libya's oil production and tensions over the Iranian nuclear programme – gave Gulf monarchies a large investable surplus that enhanced FDI from GCC. This more than doubled in 2011, reaching $21 854 million compared to $10 505 million in 2010, according to UNCTAD (Table 1.4). On the other hand, there was a drop in GCC FDI inflows of 35 per cent in 2011, from $39 869 million in 2010 to $25 960 million (Table 1.5).

According to the 2012 UNCTAD Report, 'GCC countries are still recovering from the suspension of large-scale projects in previous years' (UNCTAD, 2012), and cancelled or suspended projects in construction (one of the main sectors for investment) in the Middle East and North African countries were estimated at $1.74 trillion.

As for Southern Mediterranean countries, the international financial and economic crisis, first, and then the outbreak of the Arab uprisings, political turmoil and social unrest contracted FDI inflows (Table 1.6) – including those from GCC – with the only exception of Algeria and Morocco for 2011. A gradual recovery is expected in 2012, as there are some positive signs. The oil wealth of Gulf monarchies, combined with a more stable and safer political environment in some Arab Spring countries, are supposed to create a favourable environment for a new wave of FDI from the Gulf to the Southern Mediterranean countries. At the same time, the need to diversify Gulf countries' economies and reduce their dependence on the hydrocarbon sector is likely to create new business opportunities not only at home, to become more attractive for foreign investors in the longer term, but even in other MENA countries.

The GCC states rely on abundant energy resources, sound finances and banks, and strong public finances. Yet their dependence on oil makes them vulnerable to oil price volatility. To compensate for this problem, the GCC states have adopted strategies to diversify their economies and enhance the private sector through investment in manufacturing, infrastructure and services, in particular finance, tourism, trade-related services, health and education. Nevertheless, the energy sector remains the main source of revenues. The GCC countries possess 40 per cent of the world's proven oil reserves and 25 per cent of gas reserves. According to the Organization for Arab Petroleum Exporting Countries (OAPEC), in 2011 Saudi Arabia's oil revenues increased to $289 billion from $184.4 billion in 2010, while

Table 1.4   GCC: FDI outflows (millions of dollars)

	2000	2001	2002	2003	2004	2005	2006	2007	2008	2009	2010	2011	2000–11
Bahrain	10	216	190	741	1036	1135	980	1669	1620	–1791	334	894	7034
Kuwait	–303	–242	–78	–5016	2581	5142	8240	10156	8521	8737	2069	8711	48518
Oman	–2	55	0	153	250	234	275	243	329	406	317	572	2832
Qatar	18	17	–21	88	438	352	127	5263	2400	3772	1863	6027	20344
Saudi Arabia	1550	39	2020	473	78	53	1257	13139	1080	6526	3907	3472	33594
UAE	424	214	413	991	2208	3749	10892	14568	15800	2723	2015	2178	56175
GCC total	1696	299	2524	–2569	6591	10665	21772	45038	29750	20373	10505	21854	168498
% world total	0.12	0.04	0.40	–0.46	0.92	1.21	1.56	2.10	1.60	1.85	0.79	1.50	1.13

Source: UNCTAD (n.d.).

Table 1.5 GCC: FDI inflows (millions of dollars)

	2000	2001	2002	2003	2004	2005	2006	2007	2008	2009	2010	2011	2000–11
Bahrain	364	80	217	517	865	1049	2915	1756	1794	257	156	781	7838915
Kuwait	16	–175	4	–68	24	234	122	123	56	145	81	399	961
Oman	83	5	122	494	229	1538	1688	3125	2928	2211	2045	788	15256
Qatar	252	296	624	625	1199	2500	3500	4700	6700	8722	5534	–87	34565
Saudi Arabia	183	504	453	778	1942	12097	18293	24318	38223	35514	28105	16400	176810
UAE	–506	1184	1314	4256	10004	10900	12806	14187	13700	4003	3948	7679	83475
GCC total	**391**	**1894**	**2734**	**6602**	**14262**	**28318**	**39324**	**48209**	**63401**	**50852**	**39869**	**25960**	**321816**
% world total	*0.03*	*0.23*	*0.44*	*1.18*	*1.99*	*2.91*	*2.69*	*2.44*	*3.74*	*4.56*	*3.20*	*1.70*	*2.23*

Source: UNCTAD (n.d.).

30

Table 1.6   FDI inflows to Mediterranean countries (millions of dollars)

	2003	2004	2005	2006	2007	2008	2009	2010	2011	2003–11
Algeria	634	882	1081	1795	1662	2594	2746	2264	2571	**16 229**
Egypt	237	2157	5376	10 043	11 578	9495	6712	6386	−483	**51 501**
Jordan	443	816	1774	3268	2622	2826	2413	1651	1469	**17 282**
Lebanon	2977	1993	2791	2675	3376	4333	4804	4280	3200	**30 429**
Libya	143	357	1038	2064	3850	3180	3310	1909	0	**15 851**
Morocco	2314	895	1653	2450	2803	2487	1952	1574	2519	**18 647**
Pal. Terr.	18	49	47	19	28	52	301	180	214	**908**
Syria	180	275	500	659	1242	1467	1514	1850	1059	**8746**
Tunisia	1283	1540	7281	3312	1616	2758	1688	1513	1143	**22 134**
Total	**8229**	**8964**	**21 541**	**26 285**	**28 777**	**29 192**	**25 440**	**21 607**	**11 692**	**181 727**
Maghreb	4374	3674	11 053	9621	9931	11 019	9696	7260	6233	**72 861**
Mashreq	3855	5290	10 488	16 664	18 846	18 173	15 744	14 347	5459	**108 866**

Source: UNCTAD, *World Investment Report 2012.*

the United Arab Emirates earned $85.9 billion, Kuwait $79.6 billion, and Qatar $27.3 billion.[17] High oil prices combined with oil production that is expected to be higher than in 2011 – Saudi Arabia is maintaining high output levels to satisfy any shortfall due to sanctions on Iran – will contribute to support robust public spending. With the exception of Bahrain, GCC states will continue to experience large fiscal and current account surpluses, around 13 per cent and 24 per cent of GDP respectively in 2012.[18]

In 2011 GDP growth in GCC countries reached 8 per cent. According to the International Monetary Fund (IMF), Qatar and Kuwait were the strongest performers with growth rates upgraded to 18.8 per cent (exceeding the peak of 18.0 per cent in 2007) and 8 per cent, followed by Saudi Arabia with a growth of 6.8 per cent, Oman with 5.5 per cent, and United Arab Emirates with 4.9 per cent (Table 1.1). Only Bahrain witnessed a significant decrease, from 4.5 per cent in 2010 to 1.8 per cent, as a consequence of unrest and enduring political tensions (IMF, 2012a). In 2012 GDP growth is expected to average 5.3 per cent, according to new projections released by the IMF (IMF, 2012b).

As in the last decade's oil boom, GCC monarchies' economic wealth and growth – fostered by the new wave of high oil prices – could produce benefits for the whole MENA region and contribute once again to the growth of Southern Mediterranean countries. New investment projects in construction and energy infrastructure foreseen in the medium and long term in GCC countries could also serve as a driver for new investment opportunities in other Arab countries. However, although it is unquestionable that FDI flows from GCC states boosted the economic growth of their Mediterranean neighbours in the last decade, the explosion of economic and social contradictions showed that the GCC model of economic diversification based on real estate and financial services proved not to be appropriate for Mediterranean economies and did not contribute to the improvement of the social and economic context in those countries. Therefore, new investments from the GCC should be aimed at creating new job opportunities, as unemployment remains one of the most urgent problems to be addressed, as well as to support economic sustainability.

1.7   CONCLUSION

Economic, political and religious dimensions are strictly intertwined in the Gulf monarchies' new dynamism in the Southern Mediterranean. A mix of concern, pragmatism and aspiration for a more prestigious regional and international status, repression inside and support for regime change outside, characterized their reaction to the Arab Spring. Gulf rulers proved to be very active in pursuing their own interests – that is, preventing unrest at home, expanding their influence outside – although their goals have not always been easily achieved. GCC activism is more striking if compared with the low profile of other international players – that is, the US and European Union – more focused on their domestic political and economic problems. In an era of international economic crisis, capital from the rich Gulf monarchies is the lifeblood for Southern Mediterranean economies. So if the economic role they could play in boosting economic stabilization and growth of MENA countries is unquestionable, questions arise about their role in political issues. Being among the most conservative countries in the world, Gulf monarchies are unlikely to promote democratic changes in the MENA region and their political and social systems – whose sustainability in the long run has to be proven – contrast with the transformation process enhanced by the Arab awakening and Arab people's expectations for democratic change. However, democracy as a result of the transition process in the Arab Spring countries is just one of the possible long-term options and a greater influence of Gulf monarchies in Southern Mediterranean political developments does not seem to foster democracy.

NOTES

*   This chapter is the result of research concluded in September 2012.
1.   Algeria, Egypt, Jordan, Lebanon, Libya, Morocco, Syria, Tunisia, Palestinian Territories.
2.   'GCC creates $5 billion support fund for Jordan and Morocco', *The Daily Star*, 21 December 2011.
3.   'Morocco nowhere near to join the GCC', *Morocco World News*, 30 November 2011.
4.   10.4 per cent in 2011 according to the International Monetary Fund official data, although unofficial estimates are much higher.
5.   'Mursi bolsters Saudi ties, prepares to bolster government', *Mist News*, 16 July 2012.
6.   Al-Qassemi, Sultan, 'Morsy to renew the Brotherhood–Saudi relationship', *Egypt Independent*, 19 July 2012.
7.   Ibid.
8.   'UAE pledges US$3 billion in assistance to Egypt', *Almasryalyoum*, 5 July 2011.
9.   'Saudi Arabia approves $430 mln in new aid to Egypt', *Reuters*, 8 June 2012.
10.   'Egypt signs $1 bln finance for food, energy', *Reuters*, 1 July 2012, www.reuters.com.
11.   'Economics, politics underpin Qatar aid to North Africa', *Zawya*, 16 August 2012.
12.   Ibid.
13.   'Qatar says to invest $18 bln in Egypt economy', *Zawya*, 6 September 2012.
14.   'Qatar, Tunisia sign agreements', *Gulf Times*, 17 July 2012.
15.   'Tunisia: 500 million dollar loan from Qatar', *ANSAmed*, 19 April 2012.
16.   'Economics, politics underpin Qatar aid to North Africa', *Zawya*, 16 August 2012.
17.   'Arab oil income at record high in 2011', *Emirates 24/7*, 31 July 2012.
18.   Samba, *The GCC 2012: Flash Economic Update*, Report Series, March 2012.

REFERENCES

Abdelkrim, S. and P. Henry (2009), 'Foreign direct investment in the Med countries in 2008', Anima Investment Network, study no. 3, March.

ANIMA (2011), 'La Méditerranée entre croissance et révolution', Invest in Med, study no. 21, March, available at www.animaweb.org.

Beaumont, P. (2012), 'How Qatar is taking on the world', *The Guardian*, 7 July.

Boukhars, A. (2011), 'The monarchy club', *Bitterlemons-international.org*, **18**(9), 23 June.

Fakir, I. (2011), 'Morocco, the GCC's Maghreb protector?', *The Daily Star*, 14 October.

IMF (2012a), *Regional Economic Outlook: Update*, Middle East and Central Asia Department, April, Washington, DC: IMF.

IMF (2012b), *World Economic Outlook*, October, Washington, DC: IMF.

Jones, T.C. (2011), 'Saudi Arabia versus the Arab Spring', *Raritan*, **31**(2), 46.

Maestri, E. (2012), 'The Gulf in the Southern Mediterranean', in Nathalie Tocci, Elena Maestri, Soli Özel and Serhat Güvenç (eds), 'Ideational and material power in the Mediterranean. The role of Turkey and the Gulf Cooperation Council', GMF-IAI Mediterranean Paper Series, June, pp. 1–9.

Nasr, V. (2006), *The Shia Revival: How Conflicts Within Islam Will Shape the Future*, New York: W.W. Norton.

Riedel, B. (2012), 'Saudi Arabia's more perfect union', *The National Interest*, 18 May.

Talbot, V. (2010), 'GCC economic presence in the Mediterranean and the outlook for EU–GCC Cooperation', GMF-IAI Mediterranean Paper Series, December.

Talbot, V. (2011), 'Gulf States' political and economic role in the Mediterranean', in *IEMed Mediterranean Yearbook 2011*, Barcelona, p. 102.

UNCTAD (n.d.), UNCTAD database, available at: http://unctadstat.unctad.org/ReportFolders/reportFolders.aspx?sCS_referer=&sCS_ChosenLang=en.

UNCTAD (2012), *World Investment Report*, UNCTAD.

2. Does MENA trade too little, both within the region and with other regions? If so, why, and if not, why not?

Arian Farshbaf and Jeffrey B. Nugent

2.1 INTRODUCTION

The Euro–Med partnership has been at least in part motivated by the desire in Europe to decrease the amount of migration (much of it illegal) from Africa and the Middle East by strengthening trade both within the Southern Mediterranean region and between it and Europe. This strategy led to the offers by the EU of Association status and to a lesser extent by EFTA of Free Trade Agreements (FTAs) to countries from these regions. The desire to contribute to Middle East peace was another objective of both Europe and the United States in offering trade arrangements to the countries of the Middle East and North Africa (MENA) region. These offers were often accompanied by financial support, technical assistance and other programs designed to help these countries to be more productive and to trade more among each other so as to become a stronger trading bloc.

These agreements required gradual elimination of tariffs on each other's goods without affecting the external tariffs of either set of countries on trade with other regions. Although in this way they provided MENA countries with improved access to large markets, from the perspective of the MENA countries involved they were far from what might have been hoped for. In particular, the markets for goods in which MENA countries may have had comparative advantage, such as agricultural products and textiles, remained quite closed to MENA exporters. Other benefits such as FDI have also remained rather disappointing to MENA countries as a result of the competition arising from several Central and Eastern European countries which simultaneously have been gaining full accession to the EU and in the process have been required to undertake more substantial institutional changes than in the MENA countries.

Among the factors that have been cited as contributing to these somewhat disappointing results are allegedly: (1) the comparative failure of most MENA countries to strengthen property rights and liberalize their regulations sufficiently to attract substantial FDI inflows relative to the Central and East European countries; (2) the 'hub and spokes' problem that provided less incentive for both European and other investors to invest in MENA countries than in European countries to establish plants that would serve all countries both in the EU as well as in the MENA countries with Association status;[1] and (3) the continuance of very autocratic governance that undermines policy credibility (since without the usual checks and balances of multi-party democracies with independent judiciaries, policies are changeable according to the changing whims of autocratic leaders).

To the surprise of much of the world, however, and stimulated by high-level corruption and their unusually strong youth bulge, in many of these MENA countries in the last year or two there have arisen political uprisings, which in some cases at least have led to revolutionary regime changes. In view of the trend toward regime change and the continuing pressure to generate suitable jobs for their citizens, this would seem to be an appropriate time for a thorough rethinking of their entire economic, social and political orientation by MENA countries, and as a result also that of Europe and much of the rest of the world with respect to MENA. Clearly, this reassessment on behalf of all parties should include an evaluation of MENA's trade with its various trade partners and vice versa, and reconsideration of the strategies that the MENA countries on the one hand, and Europe and other developed countries on the other, might employ in struggling to alleviate the youth bulge and other tension-creating conditions of the Arab Spring.

Even though some MENA countries had begun to make some substantial economic reforms in the early 1990s, because of their remaining relatively high tariffs and non-tariff barriers (NTBs), inefficient customs and logistics at the ports and border crossings, even in the late 1990s MENA countries were frequently identified as important 'under-traders', both with the rest of the world and (especially) among themselves. It was because of this (but no doubt also because of strategic considerations) that European countries and to a lesser extent the United States began to offer incentives to some MENA countries to participate in free trade arrangements. Also, despite earlier rather failed attempts at economic integration within the region,[2] most Arab countries of the MENA region signed an agreement in 1997 to gradually put into effect the Greater Arab Free Trade Association (GAFTA). This agreement called for the elimination in steps of tariffs as well as NTBs on the vast majority of goods among the Arab countries which had signed the agreement. It began to come into effect in 2005 for 14 of the countries and in 2009 for Algeria but full implementation is still some years away.

The offers of Association with the EU were taken up first by Turkey in 1995, by Tunisia in 1998, by neighboring Israel in 2000, Morocco in 2000, Jordan in 2002, Kuwait in 2003, Egypt in 2004 and Algeria in 2005. Between 2000 and 2007 Egypt, Jordan, Lebanon, Morocco and Tunisia took up special trade arrangements with EFTA. Similarly, Jordan signed trade agreements with the US in 2001, which became fully effective in 2010, as did Bahrain and Morocco (effective 2006) and Oman (effective 2009). Given their recent vintage and only gradual elimination of the various trade barriers, it will be some time before the effects of some of these arrangements can be evaluated, but one would expect at least some of the effects of some of the earlier arrangements to have become discernible by now.

The purpose of this chapter is to make use of bilateral trade data from virtually all countries in the world for the years 1960 to 2005 to evaluate progress of MENA countries in their exports to, and imports from, the world and especially the EU, US, fast-growing China and with the MENA countries themselves, that is, intra-regional trade. Is it true that they were under-traders prior to the late 1990s? Are they still under-traders? If they still are under-traders, can some possible explanatory factors be identified? Conversely, if they are not, we would like to find some clues as to what may have changed to bring this about. Further, we wish to determine the extent to which the answers to these questions may vary depending on the definition of the MENA region as well across different sub-groups of MENA countries. In any case, a major motive for the study is to provide a basis for discussion of various alternative ways in which these countries could take better advantage of trade and other mechanisms to generate income growth and additional employment opportunities for their citizens.

The remainder of the chapter is organized as follows: a brief review of relevant literature is presented in section 2.2. Section 2.3 makes use of the data to generate trends in world trade and the shares of countries of MENA and other regions in this trade as well as the shares of MENA countries in the trade of these other regions over the period 1965–2005 in five-year intervals. Section 2.4 identifies the data sources and the empirical strategy. Section 2.5 presents and interprets the empirical results. Section 2.6 concludes, containing both some immediate conclusions derived from the chapter as well as other suggestions for boosting trade within MENA as well as between MENA and the EU and other regions.

2.2   BACKGROUND AND RELEVANT LITERATURE

Mention has already been made of the MENA region as a whole as an under-trading region, especially with respect to intra-regional trade. In one of the earliest studies examining both intra-regional and extra-regional trade of Arab countries as a whole, Al-Atrash and Yousef (2000) showed that among all other regions identified (which included the Andean Pact countries, Australia–New Zealand, MERCOSUR, East Asia, NAFTA and the EU) the Arab region was the only one not to have its share of intra-regional trade grow significantly over time from 1970 to 1998. The authors also pointed out that, despite the unusually low tariff rates in the GCC countries, the Arab region's tariff rates averaged among the highest tariff regions in the world, suggesting the potential for economic integration programs.

However, since countries, and therefore regions comprising several countries, vary in population size, income levels and physical characteristics, such as whether or not the countries are contiguous, landlocked, sharing the same language and legal systems, and so on, the determination of whether a region under-trades is usually based on the extent to which the region's actual trade differs from what might be predicted for it based on the standard factors included in gravity models. Gravity models have long been the workhorse of international trade flows, Leamer and Levinsohn (1995) having referred to the gravity model as 'providing some of the clearest and most robust empirical findings in economics'. When Al Atrash and Yousef (2000) applied a standard gravity model to bilateral trade data for 61 countries for 1996 (actually based on 1995–97 averages), they found that the Arab region traded significantly less than would be predicted by the gravity model (especially with respect to imports), and exported significantly less than predicted to the rest of the world. Intra-Arab trade was estimated to be about 15 per cent lower than what the gravity model predicted. This finding further supported their recommendation for further trade liberalization within the region. Indeed, they concluded: 'Greater regional integration, in a way that is compatible with multilateral liberalization, could contribute to growth not only by increasing trade and allowing regional producers to benefit from economies of scale, but also by encouraging foreign direct investment and the deepening of capital markets' (Al-Atrash and Yousef, 2000, p. 18). When they disaggregated the Arab countries into three regions, GCC, Maghreb and Mashreq (Egypt, Jordan, Lebanon, Sudan and Syria), they found that the Mashreq region was in fact a slight over-trader with respect to the world as a whole but the Maghreb and GCC sub-regions were serious under-traders.

An even more prominent demonstration of under-trading among Arab countries, or in this case the somewhat broader MENA region, was provided in the IMF's *World Economic Outlook* of 2002 (Chapter 3, Table 3.3). This table was based on an application of a standard gravity model and slightly more recent bilateral trade data (1995–99). It showed MENA to be the largest under-trader among the regions studied, with actual trade 49 per cent below that which could be predicted by the gravity model (compared to 44 per cent for South Asia and 11 per cent for South America). While it traded 24 per cent less than predicted with advanced industrial countries, the largest trade shortfalls were with respect to both intra-regional trade (74 per cent below the predicted level) and other developing countries (60 per cent below the predicted level). While its intra-regional trade shortfall of 74 per cent was slightly lower than that of South Asia, at 76 per cent, South Asia's shortfall could partly be blamed on the unusually bad political relations among the countries of that region during that period of time and the high rate of military, political turbulence within these countries.

This is not to say that all existing gravity model-based estimates for Arab or MENA countries demonstrate that MENA trades too little either intra-regionally or extra-regionally. This is because existing studies differ in terms of the number of MENA as well as non-MENA countries covered, the time period, the specific gravity model determinants used, the estimation procedure and the ways in which missing or 0 data are treated.[3]

Yet to our knowledge a majority of such studies, and especially the more comprehensive ones, indicate that MENA countries do under-trade, especially with respect to intra-regional trade. For example, with an unusually comprehensive dataset, Miniesy et al. (2004), making use of data for a series of years between 1970 and 1992 for 186 countries, demonstrated that actual intra-regional trade for MENA was between 45 per cent and 68 per cent of that trade which would be predicted by an especially inclusive gravity model. Combined with a fairly large coefficient of their FTA dummy variable (designed to estimate the effect on bilateral trade when both countries are members of the same FTA), this study, too, suggested that trade liberalization within the MENA region could, potentially at least, do much to reduce the under-trade gap with respect to intra-regional trade. An especially large estimate of the extent of under-trading in one part of the MENA region, namely the West Bank and Gaza, was provided by Bannister and Erickson von Allmen (2001). They demonstrated that, while this territory neither over- or under-traded with Israel, thanks in large part to the restrictions on its trade imposed by Israel, it under-traded by almost 80 per cent with respect to the rest of the world.

Given that oil exports of MENA are not likely to be 'under-traded', Iqbal and Nabli (2007) used a gravity model applied to non-oil exports. Of all the MENA countries, only Jordan and Morocco did not under-export non-oil products, and three MENA countries (Algeria, Iran and Egypt) were identified as the three largest non-oil under-exporters to the world. Overall, they found that MENA countries export on average only about one third of the levels of non-oil products that would be predicted for them on the basis of a very simple gravity model.

While the claim that overall trade is good for growth and development is rarely challenged, the argument that intra-regional trade is necessarily good for growth has frequently been challenged. Traditional customs union theory *à la* Viner (1950) suggested that FTAs and customs unions give rise to two effects at the same time, trade creation effects which are welfare-improving, but also trade diversion effects which are welfare-reducing. Depending on the detailed circumstances of the countries involved (the magnitude of the tariff rates, the price elasticities of demand and supply, and so on), it is certainly possible that the trade diversion effects can outweigh the trade creation effects. Yet, taking into consideration some of the more dynamic and non-traditional effects of FTAs, such as those on FDI, skills generation and technological spillovers, scale economies, increased competition within domestic economies, and the possibility of greater product varieties as long as intra-regional trade is promoted within a rather open economy setting, it would seem unlikely that it could have negative effects on growth and development and therefore long-term welfare.

Yet clearly the determination of what, if anything, should be done about under-trade, be it intra-regional or inter-regional, should depend to a large extent on the reasons for, or factors lying behind, under-trading. Bhattacharya and Wolde (2010) extend a traditional gravity model with country-specific indicators from survey data reflecting the degree of severity of other obstacles to business that could affect imports and exports. These include transport costs and the time required to complete customs procedures. An important advantage of their study is the use of more recent data (2005–07). When they apply the standard gravity model, their results indicate that MENA countries do not under-trade in the case of imports but do under-trade by as much as 85 per cent in the case of exports. But when they apply an 'augmented' gravity model that includes country-specific scores for the degree of severity of transport and customs constraints, the shortfalls below predicted trade are reduced substantially. Specifically, they conclude that if MENA countries were to reduce the transport constraints from their present levels that are above the world average to the world average, MENA exports could be increased by 10 per cent and imports by 11 per cent. An important disadvantage of the use of the survey data in the analysis, however, stems from the fact that such data were available for a relatively small number of MENA countries and were also unavailable for many other countries, reducing the size and representativeness of the sample.

A somewhat similar tack was taken by Peridy (2005) in his *ex ante* evaluation of the likely benefits of the aforementioned Greater Arab Free Trade Agreement (GAFTA). He concluded that, because MENA countries did not differ sufficiently in terms of factor endowments, especially those located close to each other, the trade creation effects of GAFTA, even when fully implemented, would be rather small. Notably, however, in what they claim to be the first post-evaluation of the effects of GAFTA on trade, Abedini and Peridy (2008) concluded that intra-regional trade had grown by somewhere between 16 per cent and 24 per cent as a result of GAFTA but that the EU-FTAs with some Arab countries of MENA had had no significant effects on trade.[4] Once again, the gravity model used in this study included some rather non-traditional factors such as expectations and sunk costs but the results were relatively robust to different specifications and estimation techniques. Moreover, the findings of the gravity model were not dissimilar to the direct data aggregates showing that, during the period under study (1988–2005), trade of GAFTA countries both with each other and with the other countries grew faster than that of the world as a whole. Since the data used were in current prices and reflect the rather dramatic rise in oil prices from their lows of the late 1980s to the highs of 2005, one would like to know the extent to which these results would have been affected had it not been for the oil price increases.[5]

2.3 TRENDS IN WORLD TRADE AND SHARES OVER TIME FOR MENA AND OTHER REGIONS

In the tables and graphs to be presented in this section as well as in our empirical estimates, we make use of the following definitions of the MENA region: (1) Arab or MENA defined as the sum of the following three sub-regions of Arab countries, the Maghreb (Algeria, Libya, Morocco and Tunisia), Gulf (Bahrain, Kuwait, Oman, Qatar, Saudi Arabia and the United Arab Emirates) and Mashreq (Egypt, Iraq, Jordan, Lebanon, Sudan, Syria and Yemen); (2) MENA2 defined as Arab plus Djibouti and three non-Arab countries (Iran, Israel and Turkey); (3) MENA3, which is MENA2 but excluding Israel.

Table 2.1 shows the changing import and export values and shares of the Gulf, Maghreb and Mashreq sub-regions of Arab, followed by MENA as a whole, China, EFTA and EU in world imports and exports at five-year intervals between 1965 and 2005. Prior to 1975 several countries in the MENA region did not exist as countries (Bahrain, Oman, Qatar and

Table 2.1 *Shares of different MENA and other regions in world trade,*
1965–2005

Group	Year	Sum of import	Sum of export	Share of world import	Share of world export
Gulf	1965	2969.43	674.92	1.75	0.40
Gulf	1970	4761.44	1303.37	1.60	0.44
Gulf	1975	50730.14	11380.55	6.05	1.36
Gulf	1980	152597.17	50460.93	7.89	2.61
Gulf	1985	65850.07	42757.07	3.49	2.27
Gulf	1990	91257.69	46521.50	2.74	1.40
Gulf	1995	102924.04	65342.69	2.16	1.37
Gulf	2000	165004.60	73803.44	2.61	1.17
Gulf	2005	345370.25	199705.37	3.34	1.93
Maghreb	1965	2475.55	1666.97	1.46	0.98
Maghreb	1970	4462.45	2742.78	1.50	0.92
Maghreb	1975	13741.27	13400.79	1.64	1.60
Maghreb	1980	43193.18	24957.95	2.23	1.29
Maghreb	1985	29336.36	21801.43	1.56	1.16
Maghreb	1990	35421.47	27945.36	1.07	0.84
Maghreb	1995	33864.17	31819.20	0.71	0.67
Maghreb	2000	51803.49	33144.21	0.82	0.52
Maghreb	2005	106119.16	65602.59	1.03	0.63
Mashreq	1965	2323.58	2234.81	1.37	1.32
Mashreq	1970	2981.28	2448.37	1.00	0.82
Mashreq	1975	12737.39	12510.40	1.52	1.49
Mashreq	1980	41539.20	26056.98	2.15	1.35
Mashreq	1985	20402.07	22547.03	1.08	1.20
Mashreq	1990	23620.09	23589.40	0.71	0.71
Mashreq	1995	13302.36	25273.01	0.28	0.53
Mashreq	2000	33865.70	38329.79	0.54	0.61
Mashreq	2005	61131.10	80375.61	0.59	0.78
MENA	1965	7768.56	4576.70	4.58	2.70
MENA	1970	12205.17	6494.52	4.10	2.18
MENA	1975	77208.80	37291.74	9.20	4.45
MENA	1980	237329.55	101475.86	12.27	5.25
MENA	1985	151041.16	87105.53	8.01	4.62
MENA	1990	150299.24	98056.26	4.52	2.95
MENA	1995	150090.58	122434.91	3.14	2.56
MENA	2000	250673.79	145277.44	3.96	2.30
MENA	2005	512620.51	345683.57	4.96	3.35
MENA2	1965	10137.04	6732.20	5.98	3.97
MENA2	1970	16250.01	10231.66	5.46	3.44
MENA2	1975	100563.32	55854.73	11.99	6.66
MENA2	1980	260494.77	125775.74	13.47	6.50

Table 2.1 (continued)

Group	Year	Sum of import	Sum of export	Share of world import	Share of world export
MENA2	1985	178 973.72	116 946.40	9.49	6.20
MENA2	1990	193 501.11	153 179.76	5.82	4.61
MENA2	1995	206 478.35	196 669.24	4.33	4.12
MENA2	2000	336 695.38	244 662.80	5.32	3.87
MENA2	2005	682 806.15	543 878.15	6.61	5.26
MENA3	1965	9733.86	5971.30	5.74	3.52
MENA3	1970	15 530.20	8895.26	5.22	2.99
MENA3	1975	98 861.83	52 383.21	11.78	6.24
MENA3	1980	255 885.09	119 790.67	13.23	6.19
MENA3	1985	173 544.68	110 003.32	9.20	5.83
MENA3	1990	182 536.82	139 386.31	5.49	4.19
MENA3	1995	189 272.87	170 672.72	3.97	3.58
MENA3	2000	304 528.22	212 840.84	4.81	3.36
MENA3	2005	639 771.95	505 575.79	6.19	4.89
China	1965	958.28	1269.84	0.57	0.75
China	1970	1398.56	1747.44	0.47	0.59
China	1975	5027.10	6004.66	0.60	0.72
China	1980	15 325.26	18 690.98	0.79	0.97
China	1985	23 188.55	36 606.80	1.23	1.94
China	1990	58 808.43	36 286.35	1.77	1.09
China	1995	162 515.71	106 761.16	3.40	2.24
China	2000	357 614.87	294 368.76	5.65	4.65
China	2005	928 823.78	746 472.94	8.99	7.22
United States	1965	28 020.53	21 960.11	16.52	12.95
United States	1970	45 146.14	40 811.21	15.17	13.72
United States	1975	112 992.11	101 429.65	13.47	12.09
United States	1980	238 427.59	247 919.84	12.33	12.82
United States	1985	228 234.21	348 174.86	12.10	18.46
United States	1990	400 693.49	503 339.66	12.05	15.14
United States	1995	628 217.45	754 496.19	13.16	15.81
United States	2000	846 738.59	1 228 438.07	13.38	19.41
United States	2005	960 043.10	1 720 247.81	9.29	16.65
EFTA	1965	28 208.94	32 928.50	16.63	19.42
EFTA	1970	44 164.96	49 872.07	14.84	16.76
EFTA	1975	107 362.74	124 431.21	12.80	14.83
EFTA	1980	246 681.87	268 099.39	12.76	13.86
EFTA	1985	239 865.28	240 748.15	12.72	12.77
EFTA	1990	460 092.14	498 226.36	13.84	14.99
EFTA	1995	592 518.36	587 901.55	12.41	12.32
EFTA	2000	706 432.76	710 918.65	11.16	11.23
EFTA	2005	1 059 222.17	1 082 612.67	10.25	10.48

Table 2.1   (continued)

Group	Year	Sum of import	Sum of export	Share of world import	Share of world export
EU	1965	50174.19	53921.75	29.59	31.80
EU	1970	93753.22	96888.12	31.51	32.56
EU	1975	257175.09	259949.22	30.66	30.99
EU	1980	550839.80	628589.99	28.48	32.51
EU	1985	533820.52	536317.20	28.31	28.44
EU	1990	1112486.59	1117762.62	33.46	33.62
EU	1995	1401375.77	1390535.54	29.36	29.13
EU	2000	1636467.28	1672673.59	25.86	26.43
EU	2005	2724121.43	2754115.15	26.36	26.65

UAE) and the data for Yemen (then separated into North and South) were also missing. Hence, the 1965 and 1970 figures for the Gulf and MENA are underestimates of the totals.[6] Therefore the jumps in Gulf and MENA trade and shares in world trade from 1970–75 are overestimates. For this reason, in examining trends for MENA and its shares in world trade, it is more appropriate to start with 1975. Although there are some fluctuations, the shares of Gulf, Maghreb, Mashreq and MENA were all generally falling over this period, making it seem that the MENA under-trading phenomenon has been increasing over time. However, as can easily be seen, the shares of the US, EFTA and the EU were also declining and in some cases more sharply than for MENA regions and again for both imports and exports. Not surprisingly, the shares of China were growing quite sharply, as the shares of the rest of the world (not shown in the table) were getting worse over time. Even though these statistics are in nominal values, it is clear from the world totals that this was a period of explosive growth in world trade.

Table 2.2 presents the shares of various regions in the imports and exports of MENA and MENA2 for MENA2, the EU, US, China and all other countries (Other) over the same period of time. The rows labeled 'Total' immediately above the world total represent the total values of MENA and MENA2 imports and exports.

These figures reveal the importance of the relative price of oil and the importance of the three most important increases in that price from 1965 to 1975, 1975–80 and from 1995–2005, and the sharp reductions in oil prices 1980–95. For this reason, we deem it relevant to control for the relative price of oil in MENA region shares in the empirical analysis below. Reading down from the top of the table, the entries represent the share of MENA2 in the imports and exports of MENA and MENA2, followed

Table 2.2 World and MENA and MENA2 trade and shares of other regions in that trade, 1965–2005

Region	Year	MENA[a]		MENA2[b]	
		Import	Export	Import	Export
MENA2 %	1965	5.69	9.12	5.11	7.52
MENA2 %	1970	4.65	8.54	4.04	6.34
MENA2 %	1975	5.61	10.13	4.98	8.89
MENA2 %	1980	4.92	8.98	5.10	10.36
MENA2 %	1985	8.70	11.18	10.59	12.70
MENA2 %	1990	9.73	12.09	9.38	11.68
MENA2 %	1995	10.24	12.14	9.74	10.11
MENA2 %	2000	8.55	12.80	8.00	10.78
MENA2 %	2005	11.53	16.61	11.56	14.18
EU %	1965	53.69	43.32	50.53	41.04
EU %	1970	54.81	41.79	49.24	39.17
EU %	1975	39.32	38.34	38.77	35.44
EU %	1980	34.60	38.28	34.00	37.02
EU %	1985	33.55	36.05	33.10	34.35
EU %	1990	28.52	36.16	30.33	35.08
EU %	1995	29.61	42.87	33.68	45.37
EU %	2000	28.11	41.11	30.89	43.87
EU %	2005	25.48	35.67	28.77	37.34
US %	1965	3.50	13.96	5.17	17.34
US %	1970	1.68	10.25	3.19	14.53
US %	1975	9.73	12.89	10.38	14.83
US %	1980	14.67	12.46	13.99	11.67
US %	1985	5.39	10.13	6.86	10.05
US %	1990	13.27	10.86	12.67	10.27
US %	1995	9.58	12.56	10.72	12.65
US %	2000	12.11	11.32	13.86	11.08
US %	2005	12.18	8.92	12.50	7.80
China %	1965	1.22	1.73	0.96	1.18
China %	1970	0.60	1.90	0.45	1.21
China %	1975	0.23	1.15	0.18	0.90
China %	1980	0.20	0.96	0.20	0.81
China %	1985	0.16	0.97	0.17	0.82
China %	1990	0.34	1.72	0.31	1.50
China %	1995	1.32	3.25	1.20	2.49
China %	2000	3.78	4.17	3.94	3.96
China %	2005	5.78	7.87	5.98	7.57
Other %	1965	35.89	31.86	38.23	32.92
Other %	1970	38.26	37.53	43.08	38.76
Other %	1975	45.11	37.50	45.69	39.94

Table 2.2 (continued)

Region	Year	MENA[a]		MENA2[b]	
		Import	Export	Import	Export
Other %	1980	45.61	39.33	46.71	40.15
Other %	1985	52.19	41.67	49.28	42.08
Other %	1990	48.13	39.17	47.32	41.47
Other %	1995	49.25	29.17	44.65	29.38
Other %	2000	47.45	30.61	43.31	30.30
Other %	2005	45.02	30.94	41.19	33.12
Total	1965	7768.56	4576.70	10137.04	6732.20
Total	1970	12205.17	6494.52	16250.01	10231.66
Total	1975	77208.80	37291.74	100563.32	55854.73
Total	1980	237329.55	101475.86	260494.77	125775.74
Total	1985	115588.50	87105.53	143521.06	116946.40
Total	1990	150299.24	98056.26	193501.11	153179.76
Total	1995	150090.58	122434.91	206478.35	196669.24
Total	2000	250673.79	145277.44	336695.38	244662.80
Total	2005	512620.51	345683.57	682806.15	543878.15
World total	1965	169590.00	169590.00	169590.00	169590.00
World total	1970	297530.00	297530.00	297530.00	297530.00
World total	1975	838920.00	838920.00	838920.00	838920.00
World total	1980	1933800.00	1933800.00	1933800.00	1933800.00
World total	1985	1885900.00	1885900.00	1885900.00	1885900.00
World total	1990	3324600.00	3324600.00	3324600.00	3324600.00
World total	1995	4773500.00	4773500.00	4773500.00	4773500.00
World total	2000	6328800.00	6328800.00	6328800.00	6328800.00
World total	2005	10333000.00	10333000.00	10333000.00	10333000.00

Notes:
a. This narrow definition of MENA consists strictly of the following Arab countries: Maghreb (Algeria, Libya, Morocco and Tunisia), Gulf (Bahrain, Kuwait, Oman, Qatar, Saudi Arabia and United Arab Emirates) and Mashreq (Egypt, Iraq, Jordan, Lebanon, Sudan, Syria and Yemen).
b. This is a broad definition of MENA that also includes neighboring non-Arab countries (Iran, Israel and Turkey).

by the shares of the EU, US, China and all other countries in MENA and MENA2 imports and exports. For each of the columns, we see some increases in the shares of both MENA2 and China in that trade, declines, but from very high levels, in the EU shares and more mixed patterns in the shares of both the US and Other, in some cases differing between imports and exports. Hence, even though the share of MENA trade in total world trade had been on the decline from 1975 to 2005 (though with some volatility), the share of MENA2 countries in that trade reflected an at least moderate increase.

Appendix Table 2A.1 shows the shares of each of these same regions in the imports and exports of each MENA country, again over the same period. Recalling the aforementioned common claim that MENA countries also under-trade with each other, in the sense that the intra-regional trade has typically been shown to be less than what would be predicted on the basis of standard gravity models of international trade, we turn first to the shares of MENA2 in the imports and exports of each country. For most of the individual MENA countries (especially, Algeria, Egypt, Libya, Oman, Qatar, Syria, Yemen and Iran) the MENA2 shares in both imports and exports increased over time. In most of the other countries of the region there was an upward trend of MENA2 in either imports or exports but not both. In Lebanon there was virtually no trend in the MENA and MENA2 shares in either imports or exports and in Iraq and Turkey an inverted-U pattern over time can be observed, in the case of Iraq with a sharp peak in 1995 (presumably due to the effect of international sanctions on Iraq's trade). The MENA2 shares were generally high in Lebanon (for exports), Oman (for imports) and for Bahrain.[7]

Not surprisingly, given the various different locations, productive structures, and special trading arrangements, Appendix Table 2A.1 reveals some important differences across the individual MENA countries with respect to the trends of other regions in their imports and exports. While most MENA2 countries experienced declining shares of imports and exports with the EU, Tunisia was an exception as there these shares were actually increasing. Similarly, while the shares of the US in exports and imports of most countries were declining, for Algeria, Egypt, Iraq, Jordan, Morocco and Saudi Arabia the US shares in exports were rising over the 1965–2005 period.[8] As already indicated, the share of China was generally rising and especially so for exports (especially for Oman, Sudan, UAE, Yemen and Iran) but was falling in Egypt. The shares of other countries (Other) were generally falling in most countries, but for exports were rising in Iraq and Oman.

Because of the small numbers of observations across time, these trends may not be statistically significant and even if they were, it would be difficult to explain them with any degree of certainty. For this reason, we turn in the next section to our quantitative analysis based on various types and applications of gravity models which allow us to identify both levels and over time changes in the extent of MENA under-trading, after controlling for as many as possible of the various factors which have been found to affect bilateral trade flows and shares.

2.4   EMPIRICAL MODEL AND DATA

The purpose of this section is to identify the forms of the gravity that will be used, the data sources and the estimation procedure. We make use of both a 'Benchmark' gravity model and a couple of broader versions we call 'Expanded Gravity' models which include other factors such as a variety of free trade arrangements, armed conflicts and relative factor endowments that are seldom included in the traditional gravity models. The Benchmark model largely contains only various proxies for 'mass' (measured by GDP of the countries of origin and destination, respectively) and other trade cost factors such as the geographic distance between the countries, the extent to which they are 'closed' to international trade based on some explicit criterion or index, whether or not they are landlocked, and whether they share the same legal origins, language and geographic borders. These are all factors which should be expected to affect the transportation and transaction costs in trade between pairs of countries. But, given the aforementioned observation from Table 2.2 concerning the important influence of real oil prices on the level and quite possibly also the direction of trade (at least for MENA countries), even in our Benchmark specification we include the real price of oil along with its interaction with a dummy for an oil exporter. The names and identities of these and all other variables included in our empirical model are listed in Table 2.3. Very important for the analysis is the addition of region-specific dummy variables used to identify the extent to which MENA countries and specific trade partners under- or over-trade relative to what would be expected on the basis of the gravity models, as well as time trends and their interactions with the region variables to determine the extent to which the degree of under- or over-trading varies over time.

The most important data is that for bilateral trade, M_{ij} representing imports from country of origin i by country of destination j, and exports X_{ij} by country of origin to country of destination j. As with all the other measures identified in Table 2.3, the primary source is given in the table, most of which was in turn obtained from the IMF's Direction of Trade Statistics (DOTS), supplemented with data from Barbieri et al. (2009) and Barbieri's International Trade Dataset. The data are recorded in current US dollars.[9] An important advantage of this compiled data is that it has been widely used and certain adjustments have been made to make sure that the reported trade flow from importer to exporter and vice versa match. Some of the missing data were also completed using other sources.

The source labeled 'CEPII' in Table 2.3 means that it was compiled by Keith Head, Thierry Mayer and John Ries (2010) in a data set called

Table 2.3   Variables included in the empirical model

Name	Measure or Form	Units	Source
Arab Maghreb Union Trade agreement among Algeria, Morocco, Tunisia	amu	0,1	Our construction
Conflict	conflict	0,1	Our construction based on MIDB
Common border	contig	0,1	CEPII
Common legal origin	comleg	0,1	CEPII
Common official language	Comlang_off	0,1	CEPII
Distance between countries	L_dist		CEPII
European Union	eu_o, eu_d	0,1	Our construction
FTA (Common membership)		0,1	Our construction
GDP of origin country	l_gdp_o,		Penn World Tables
GDP of destination country	l_gdp_d		Penn World Tables
Gulf Cooperation Council (FTA)	gcc	0,1	Our construction
Landlocked	Landl_o, landl_d	0,1	Wikipedia Online Encyclopedia
Region			
Maghreb (AMU +Libya)	magh	0,1	Our construction
Mashreq (Egypt, Iraq, Jordan, Lebanon, Syria, Yemen)	mash	0,1	Our construction
MENA (Broadest definition)	MENA2	0,1	Our construction
MENA (Narrower) (Israel excluded)	MENA3	0,1	Our construction
MENA (Still narrower) excluding	Arab	0,1	Our construction
Oil exporter	oilexp	0,1	Our construction
Oil price (real)	oilp		International Energy Agency
Openness	Openk_o, openk_d		Penn World Table
Resource endowment measures			Based on PWT
a. Difference in GDP per capita			and WB's WDI
b. Difference in share of agriculture in GDP			
c. Difference in share of fuel in exports			
Time (year index)	Prd (1965–2005)	1–9	Our construction
Trade (Bilateral) X, M	lM, lX	current US Dollars	Dyadics Trade Data, from Correlates of War (COW)

CEPII used in their paper: 'The erosion of colonial trade linkages after independence'.[10]

Bilateral conflict data ('conflict' in Table 2.3) used for constructing the Conflict dummy variables used in this chapter is based on the Correlates of War's (COW) 'Militarized Interstate Disputes' data set (MIDB). It is a binary variable that takes 1 if the reported 'hostility level' by MIDB – which ranged between 1 to 5 – is greater than 3 at the time of trade among the pair of countries. We constructed other variations of this conflict variable but the one that seems relevant and showed statistically significant influence in our empirical results is the one that captures relatively high levels of hostility (4 or 5) with the time of conflict coinciding with the year in which the trade is recorded (and not a few years ahead or before).

Because of the large number of country pairs for which no trade is recorded and substantial heterogeneity in the data, the estimation proce-dure used is the Poisson pseudo-maximum-likelihood (PPML) technique proposed by Silva and Tenreyro (2006) to avoid the potential biases that could be created by these problems. Silva and Tenreyro (2006) compare the results of this technique with others through Monte Carlo simulations which provide justification for this estimation method. The other popular estimation methods that were included in their evaluation included: simple OLS, which obviously ignores a large number of observations due to inability to include zero-trades in a log-function; augmented OLS, which adds a positive number to zero-trades so they can be included in a logarith-mic function; non-linear least squares, which can be 'very inefficient in the presence of heteroskedasticity' and finally the Tobit method following the work of Eaton and Tamura (1994). Silva and Tenreyro's simulation results conclude that the PPML method outperforms others in the presence of zero-trades and more importantly heterogeneity, which is characteristic of trade data. Under the assumption that the conditional variance is pro-portional to the conditional mean ($E[y_i|x] = \exp(x_i\beta) \propto V[y_i|x]$), the coef-ficient β can be estimated from the following set of first-order conditions in a consistent manner 'even if the data are not Poisson at all', and even if y_i is not an integer:

$$\sum_{i=1}^{n} [y_i - \exp(x_i\tilde{\beta})]x_i \qquad (2.1)$$

In the above equation y_i is the value of bilateral trade and x_i is either of our independent variables that appear in gravity models. In particular, $y_i \in \{M_{ij}, X_{ij}\}$ and $x_i \in \{\log(GDP_i), \log(GDP_j), \log(distance), landlocked_i, landlocked_j, Region_{ij}, FTAs, \ldots\}$. In turn, $Region_{ij} \in \{MENA2, MENA3, MENA\text{-}EU, MENA\text{-}US, \ldots\}$ is a binary variable indicating whether the country of origin and destination belong to a specific set of country relationships whose under- or over-trading behavior we would like to examine. For example MENA-EU is 1 if the country of origin is in the MENA region and the country of destination is a member of European Union. It should be mentioned that despite its seeming complexity, the estimated coefficients can be interpreted in the same way one would interpret those from a standard gravity equation in the log-form

$$\ln T_{ij} = \alpha_0 + \alpha_1 \ln GDP_i + \alpha_2 \ln GDP_j + + \alpha_3 \ln Dist_{ij} + \cdots$$

where T_{ij} is the bilateral trade among countries i and j.

As indicated above, to mitigate the influence of measurement errors, random shipping accidents and erratic weather, the bilateral trade measures we use for each of the years under study are actually three-year averages, that is, 1964–66 for 1965, 1969–71 for 1970, and so on. The time trends are captured by the variable 'prd' which is coded 1–9, where it is 1 if for the year 1965 and 9 for 2005.

2.5 EMPIRICAL RESULTS

Our empirical results, based on applying the data set obtained from the sources indicated in Table 2.3 and estimated by the PPML method explained in the previous section, are presented in Tables 2.4–2.13. These tables investigate the extent of under- or over-trading of MENA countries with each other, with the EU, Asian and Pacific and US regions. In each case we distinguish between MENA imports (M) and exports (X). We also investigate the extent of differences according to the different definitions of MENA and for sub-regions within MENA. In each table the dependent variable is the average level (in natural logs) of bilateral trade between country i and country j during the three years closest to the year in question, 1965, 1970, . . . , 2005.

We begin in Table 2.4, with preliminary estimates of the extent of intra-regional under- or over-trading among MENA countries making use of the Benchmark version of the gravity model. The first two columns present the PPML estimates of bilateral trade where the definition of MENA is the broadest one (MENA2). The corresponding results with alternative definitions (MENA3) and Arab (or MENA) are presented in the last several columns of the table.

Notice that most of the coefficients vary only slightly, if at all, across the corresponding estimates for imports and then again across those for exports. They do vary somewhat, though not a great deal, between imports and exports. Since, because of the large numbers of observations, all

Table 2.4 Benchmark model comparing MENA2, MENA3 and Arab

Variable	M	X	Variable	M	X	Variable	M	X
l_dist	-0.604	-0.629	l_dist	-0.603	-0.628	l_dist	-0.603	-0.627
l_gdp_o	0.919	0.890	l_gdp_o	0.920	0.892	l_gdp_o	0.921	0.892
l_gdp_d	0.815	0.846	l_gdp_d	0.816	0.847	l_gdp_d	0.816	0.848
comleg	0.149	0.167	comleg	0.149	0.168	comleg	0.148	0.165
comlang_off	0.334	0.309	comlang_off	0.332	0.307	comlang_off	0.334	0.311
contig	0.520	0.466	contig	0.520	0.466	contig	0.520	0.466
mena2	**-0.338**	**-0.491**	**mena3**	**-0.200**	**-0.368**	**arab**	**-0.211**	**-0.374**
openk_o	0.006	0.005	openk_o	0.006	0.005	openk_o	0.006	0.005
landl_o	-0.412	-0.463	landl_o	-0.409	-0.460	landl_o	-0.408	-0.459
landl_d	-0.459	-0.347	landl_d	-0.456	-0.343	landl_d	-0.455	-0.342
oilp	0.003	0.002	oilp	0.003	0.002	oilp	0.003	0.002
prd	-0.148	-0.147	prd	-0.148	-0.148	prd	-0.148	-0.148
oilp_oilexp	-0.006	0.000	oilp_oilexp	-0.006	0.000	oilp_oilexp	-0.006	0.000
oilexp_o	0.267	0.288	oilexp_o	0.265	0.286	oilexp_o	0.264	0.284
_cons	-9.587	-9.391	_cons	-9.618	-9.425	_cons	-9.628	-9.445
N	175225	175225		175225	175225		175225	175225
Pseudo R2	0.9112	0.9126		0.9112	0.9125		0.9112	0.9125

Note: Dependent variable in all regressions is the natural log level of bilateral trade.

Table 2.5 Benchmark model with MENA3 with alternative productive structure controls

Variable	M	X	Variable	M	X	Variable	M	X
l_dist	−0.566	−0.729	l_dist	−0.616	−0.622	l_dist	−0.602	−0.626
l_gdp_o	0.955	0.864	l_gdp_o	0.917	0.906	l_gdp_o	0.917	0.905
l_gdp_d	0.850	0.814	l_gdp_d	0.807	0.851	l_gdp_d	0.814	0.847
comleg	0.127	0.122	comleg	0.106	0.111	comleg	0.149	0.158
comlang_off	0.323	0.341	comlang_off	0.291	0.255	comlang_off	0.317	0.304
contig	0.698	0.411	contig	0.531	0.502	contig	0.515	0.485
mena3	**−0.304**	**−0.385**	**mena3**	**−0.133**	**−0.223**	**mena3**	**−0.028**	**−0.371**
openk_o	0.006	0.004	openk_o	0.004	0.006	openk_o	0.006	0.005
landl_o	−0.465	−0.672	landl_o	−0.377	−0.505	landl_o	−0.398	−0.398
landl_d	−0.315	−0.382	landl_d	−0.512	−0.343	landl_d	−0.461	−0.347
lgdpc_diff	**0.100**	**0.076**	**agry_diff**	**0.003**	**0.005**	**fuelx_o**	**−0.002**	**0.003**
oilp	0.003	0.001	oilp	0.003	0.002	oilp	0.003	0.002
prd	−0.174	−0.166	prd	−0.145	−0.164	prd	−0.151	−0.156
oilp_oilexp	−0.005	0.005	oilp_oilexp	−0.005	0.000	oilp_oilexp	−0.005	−0.001
oilexp_o	0.133	−0.081	oilexp_o	0.343	0.349	oilexp_o	0.331	0.283
_cons	−11.568	−8.208	_cons	−9.311	−9.668	_cons	−9.534	−9.570
N	64955	64955		94029	94029		124434	124434
Pseudo R2	0.9181	0.92		0.9224	0.9253		0.9089	0.9122

53

Table 2.6   Benchmark model with MENA2 and MENA3 and their interactions with time (prd)

Variable	1965	1965	1975	1990	Variable	1965	1975	1990
	M	X	X	X		X	X	X
l_dist	−0.604	−0.629	−0.629	−0.624	l_dist	−0.628	−0.628	−0.623
l_gdp_o	0.920	0.891	0.892	0.899	l_gdp_o	0.892	0.893	0.900
l_gdp_d	0.815	0.846	0.848	0.858	l_gdp_d	0.848	0.849	0.859
comleg	0.149	0.167	0.167	0.155	comleg	0.168	0.168	0.155
comlang_off	0.334	0.308	0.303	0.278	comlang_off	0.307	0.302	0.276
contig	0.520	0.466	0.466	0.489	contig	0.467	0.467	0.490
mena2	**−1.029**	**−1.315**	**−1.295**	**−0.333**	**mena3**	−1.275	−1.256	−0.086
mena2_prd	**0.098**	**0.117**	**0.116**	**0.008**	**mena3_prd**	0.130	0.128	−0.003
openk_o	0.006	0.005	0.005	0.005	openk_o	0.005	0.005	0.005
landl_o	−0.412	−0.463	−0.461	−0.466	landl_o	−0.460	−0.458	−0.463
landl_d	−0.459	−0.347	−0.345	−0.332	landl_d	−0.343	−0.341	−0.328
oilp	0.003	0.002	0.002	−0.007	oilp	0.002	0.002	−0.007
prd	−0.148	−0.148	−0.142	−0.019	prd	−0.149	−0.143	−0.019
oilp_oilexp	−0.006	0.001	0.001	−0.003	oilp_oilexp	0.001	0.001	−0.003
oilexp_o	0.261	0.281	0.278	0.396	oilexp_o	0.278	0.275	0.393
_cons	−9.587	−9.391	−9.493	−10.448	_cons	−9.425	−9.527	−10.483
N	175225	175225	157585	96117	N	175225	157585	96117
Pseudo R2	0.9113	0.9126	0.9117	0.9164	Pseudo R2	0.9125	0.9117	0.9164

Table 2.7 Benchmark model with MENA3, Conflict, LGDPC_Diff and FTA Controls with and without Prd

Variable	M	X	M	X
l_dist	−0.541	−0.681	−0.546	−0.690
l_gdp_o	0.952	0.859	0.858	0.767
l_gdp_d	0.849	0.809	0.807	0.770
comleg	0.124	0.122	0.070	0.074
comlang_off	0.333	0.354	0.404	0.416
contig	0.674	0.386	0.747	0.438
mena3	−0.396	−0.331	−0.473	−0.407
openk_o	0.005	0.004	0.003	0.002
ftaw_comm	0.109	0.194	−0.016	0.103
w_eu_o	−0.037	0.058	−0.231	−0.133
gafta	0.213	0.070	−0.131	−0.268
amu	−0.145	−0.186	−0.398	−0.390
gcc	0.338	0.125	0.348	0.140
lgdpc_diff	0.107	0.088	0.071	0.059
landl_o	−0.414	−0.630	−0.462	−0.651
landl_d	−0.311	−0.379	−0.441	−0.508
conf_0_0_a	0.041	−0.608	0.047	−0.614
oilp	0.003	0.001	0.004	0.002
prd	−0.177	−0.170		
oilp_oilexp	−0.005	0.005	0.000	0.010
oilexp_o	0.136	−0.065	−0.177	−0.392
_cons	−11.776	−8.578	−10.727	−7.581
N	64 954	64 954	64 954	64 954
Pseudo R2	0.9115	0.9205	0.9115	0.9135

coefficients are statistically significant at the 1 per cent level at least, standard errors are not reported. The signs of the coefficients of all the standard gravity measures are as expected. The effects of GDP for the countries of origin and destination are both positive, as are those of common legal tradition, common official language and common border (*contig*), and the de facto trade openness ratio *openk*. The effects of distance and landlocked are, on the other hand, negative. The signs in front of the coefficient of the MENA2, MENA3 and Arab are all negative and significant, indicating that, as suggested in much of the literature mentioned above, MENA is an under-trader with respect to intra-regional trade. For all three definitions of MENA they are larger under-traders on intra-regional exports than intra-regional imports. Not surprisingly, the shortfall in intra-regional trade is greatest for the broadest definition that includes not only the fairly

Table 2.8   Benchmark and extended gravity models with MENA3–EU trade

Variable	M	X	Variable	M	X
l_dist	−0.601	−0.629	l_dist	−0.536	−0.673
l_gdp_o	0.922	0.891	l_gdp_o	0.956	0.859
l_gdp_d	0.817	0.850	l_gdp_d	0.847	0.808
comleg	0.148	0.174	comleg	0.121	0.122
comlang_off	0.331	0.296	comlang_off	0.338	0.351
contig	0.524	0.457	contig	0.672	0.386
mena3_eu	0.069	−0.185	**mena3_eu**	**0.698**	**2.269**
			mena3eu_prd	**−0.031**	**−0.384**
openk_o	0.006	0.005	openk_o	0.005	0.004
			ftaw_comm	0.117	0.203
			w_eu_o	−0.037	0.094
			gafta	−0.026	−0.169
			amu	−0.342	−0.367
			gcc	0.211	−0.012
			lgdpc_diff	0.103	0.084
landl_o	−0.404	−0.459	landl_o	−0.400	−0.633
landl_d	−0.452	−0.333	landl_d	−0.311	−0.370
			conf_0_0_a	0.009	−0.646
oilp	0.003	0.002	oilp	0.003	0.001
prd	−0.149	−0.148	prd	−0.177	−0.166
oilp_oilexp	−0.006	0.000	oilp_oilexp	−0.006	0.002
oilexp_o	0.258	0.298	oilexp_o	0.121	0.040
_cons	−9.672	−9.435	_cons	−11.822	−8.643
N	175 225	175 225		64 954	64 954
Pseudo R2	0.9112	0.9125		0.9184	0.9212

large non-Arab countries of Turkey and Iran but also Israel, with which international relations have not always been peaceful. The exact percentages of shortfalls in percentage terms in this and all subsequent tables can be calculated from the coefficient by the formula $100 \cdot [e^{coeff} - 1]$ but as long as the coefficient is no more than .3 or .4, the corresponding percentage shortfall will be a little more than 100 times that coefficient. For example, the coefficient of −0.338 in the first column of the table indicates a shortfall of intra-MENA2 imports of close to 40 per cent relative to the level of trade expected by the given gravity model.

Among the other variables, note that oil price (*oilp*) and the dummy for oil exporter (*oilexp*) have positive and significant effects but the interaction of *oilp* with oil exporter *oilexp* has negative effects on imports (M) but

Table 2.9   Benchmark gravity model with MENA2 and MENA3 trade with the world

MENA2 and World	Coef.	Coef.	MENA3 with World	Coef.	Coef.
	M	X		M	X
l_dist	−0.603	−0.627	l_dist	−0.603	−0.627
l_gdp_o	0.916	0.888	l_gdp_o	0.916	0.889
l_gdp_d	0.816	0.849	l_gdp_d	0.816	0.849
comleg	0.152	0.171	comleg	0.152	0.171
comlang_off	0.326	0.296	comlang_off	0.324	0.295
contig	0.515	0.459	contig	0.514	0.460
mena2_o	−0.113	−0.115	mena3_o	−0.131	−0.112
openk_o	0.005	0.005	openk_o	0.005	0.005
landl_o	−0.415	−0.464	landl_o	−0.415	−0.462
landl_d	−0.451	−0.334	landl_d	−0.450	−0.333
oilp	0.003	0.002	oilp	0.003	0.002
prd	−0.147	−0.147	prd	−0.147	−0.148
oilp_oilexp	−0.006	0.000	oilp_oilexp	−0.006	0.000
oilexp_o	0.280	0.301	oilexp_o	0.284	0.302
_cons	−9.567	−9.395	_cons	−9.564	−9.406
N	175225	175225	N	175225	175225
Pseudo R2	0.9112	0.9125	Pseudo R2	0.9112	0.9125

small positive effects on exports (X). The coefficient of time (*prd*) is also negative.

What happens to the extent of within-region under-trading when one controls for resource endowment differentials between countries? To answer this question, Table 2.5 presents the corresponding results, where MENA3 is the definition of MENA, but when three different measures of resource endowment differentials are employed. These are GDP_{PC} differences in the first two columns, differences in the agriculture-GDP shares in the next two columns and the differences in fuel shares in trade in the last two columns. Because of missing data for the construction of these resource endowment differentials between the trading partners, the numbers of observations available for use in generating these results are considerably smaller than in Table 2.4. Nevertheless, the results for the corresponding variables are with perhaps a couple of exceptions very similar to those in Table 2.4. An exception is the change in the sign of the coefficient of oil exporter for exports (in the X column) from positive in Table 2.4 to negative in Table 2.5. The coefficients for *fuelx_o* in the last

Table 2.10   *Benchmark gravity model with endowment differences and MENA3–EU trade flows*

	Using GDPPC Differences			Using Agric–GDP Share Differences	
	Coef.	Coef.		Coef.	Coef.
	M	X		M	X
l_dist	−0.565	−0.725	l_dist	−0.617	−0.622
l_gdp_o	0.961	0.886	l_gdp_o	0.915	0.904
l_gdp_d	0.851	0.816	l_gdp_d	0.808	0.852
comleg	0.125	0.116	comleg	0.108	0.114
comlang_off	0.324	0.352	comlang_off	0.287	0.248
contig	0.692	0.392	contig	0.528	0.498
mena3_o	0.197	0.631	mena3_o	−0.075	−0.083
openk_o	0.006	0.005	openk_o	0.004	0.006
landl_o	−0.448	−0.619	landl_o	−0.380	−0.508
landl_d	−0.313	−0.381	landl_d	−0.509	−0.337
lgdpc_diff	0.097	0.065	agry_diff	0.003	0.006
oilp	0.003	0.001	oilp	0.003	0.002
prd	−0.176	−0.171	prd	−0.144	−0.164
oilp_oilexp	−0.006	0.002	oilp_oilexp	−0.005	0.000
oilexp_o	0.079	−0.298	oilexp_o	0.352	0.359
_cons	−11.644	−8.458	_cons	−9.286	−9.650
N	64955	64955	N	94029	94029
Pseudo R2	0.9182	0.921	Pseudo R2	0.9225	0.9253

two columns of Table 2.5 would seem to indicate that being a large oil exporter reduces the shortfall in expected intra-regional imports but not intra-regional exports.

How has the degree of intra-MENA trading been changing over time and to what extent would the result be sensitive to a different starting date for determining this? As noted above, an important reason for the different starting points is that several of the Gulf countries were not countries until 1971 and hence their trade could not be included until 1975. Another is the fact that the Iran–Iraq conflict was going on during the 1980s and Yemen was also not a unified country for several of the early periods. The results of Table 2.6 show that once again there is little change in the effects of the standard gravity measures. What is very striking, however, is that for both imports and exports the MENA dummies are associated with very large negative coefficients but with positive coefficients for the MENA-*prd* interaction terms, suggesting that the intra-regional trade shortfalls for both imports and exports were very large at the beginning of the period but have

Table 2.11 *Benchmark gravity model with subregional trade within MENA*

	Coef.		Coef.		Coef.	
	M	X	M	X	M	X
l_dist	-0.602	-0.626	-0.602	-0.626	-0.602	-0.626
l_gdp_o	0.922	0.894	0.921	0.893	0.921	0.893
l_gdp_d	0.817	0.850	0.817	0.850	0.817	0.850
comleg	0.150	0.169	0.150	0.169	0.150	0.168
comlang_off	0.329	0.300	0.330	0.302	0.329	0.303
contig	0.521	0.467	0.521	0.468	0.521	0.467
mash_mash / magh_magh / gcc_gcc	0.447	0.488	-0.585	-0.677	-0.019	-0.232
openk_o	0.006	0.005	0.006	0.005	0.006	0.005
landl_o	-0.405	-0.453	-0.406	-0.454	-0.406	-0.455
landl_d	-0.451	-0.334	-0.452	-0.336	-0.452	-0.336
oilp	0.003	0.002	0.003	0.002	0.003	0.002
prd	-0.149	-0.149	-0.149	-0.149	-0.149	-0.149
oilp_oilexp	-0.006	0.000	-0.006	0.000	-0.006	0.000
oilexp_o	0.264	0.284	0.264	0.284	0.264	0.284
_cons	-9.657	-9.497	-9.647	-9.485	-9.651	-9.482
N	175225	175225	175225	175225	175225	175225
Pseudo R2	0.9112	0.9124	0.9112	0.9124	0.9112	0.9124

Table 2.12 Benchmark gravity model with intra-MENA subregional trade flows

	Mashreq–GCC Trade Coef. M	Mashreq–GCC Trade Coef. X	Maghreb–Mashreq Trade Coef. M	Maghreb–Mashreq Trade Coef. X	Mashreq–Maghreb Trade Coef. M	Mashreq–Maghreb Trade Coef. X
l_dist	-0.602	-0.626	-0.602	-0.626	-0.602	-0.626
l_gdp_o	0.922	0.894	0.921	0.893	0.921	0.893
l_gdp_d	0.817	0.850	0.817	0.850	0.817	0.850
comleg	0.151	0.169	0.150	0.168	0.150	0.169
comlang_off	0.328	0.300	0.330	0.303	0.330	0.301
contig	0.521	0.467	0.521	0.466	0.521	0.467
mash_gcc / magh_gcc / mash_magh	0.472	0.201	-0.271	-2.163	-0.713	-0.496
openk_o	0.006	0.005	0.006	0.005	0.006	0.005
landl_o	-0.404	-0.453	-0.406	-0.454	-0.406	-0.454
landl_d	-0.451	-0.334	-0.452	-0.336	-0.452	-0.335
oilp	0.003	0.002	0.003	0.002	0.003	0.002
prd	-0.149	-0.149	-0.149	-0.149	-0.149	-0.149
oilp_oilexp	-0.006	0.000	-0.006	0.000	-0.006	0.000
oilexp_o	0.264	0.284	0.264	0.283	0.263	0.283
_cons	-9.660	-9.494	-9.650	-9.485	-9.649	-9.490
N	175225	175225	175225	175225	175225	175225
Pseudo R2	0.9112	0.9124	0.9112	0.9124	0.9112	0.9124

Table 2.13   Expanded gravity model with MENA3 trade with Asia Pacific and US regions

MENA3–Asia Pacific Trade			MENA3–US Trade		
	Coef.	Coef.		Coef.	Coef.
	M	X		M	X
l_dist	−0.537	−0.676	l_dist	−0.538	−0.678
l_gdp_o	0.956	0.865	l_gdp_o	0.953	0.860
l_gdp_d	0.848	0.808	l_gdp_d	0.849	0.809
comleg	0.125	0.124	comleg	0.123	0.121
comlang_off	0.333	0.354	comlang_off	0.332	0.352
contig	0.671	0.381	contig	0.672	0.384
mena3_pac	−1.098	−0.452	mena3_us	0.327	1.890
mena3pac_prd	0.198	0.137	mena3us_prd	−0.039	−0.325
openk_o	0.006	0.004	openk_o	0.005	0.004
ftaw_comm	0.121	0.209	ftaw_comm	0.115	0.199
w_eu_o	−0.023	0.079	w_eu_o	−0.030	0.065
gafta	−0.041	−0.127	gafta	−0.063	−0.165
amu	−0.332	−0.336	amu	−0.343	−0.356
gcc	0.198	0.027	gcc	0.178	−0.009
lgdpc_diff	0.106	0.086	lgdpc_diff	0.106	0.086
landl_o	−0.405	−0.619	landl_o	−0.410	−0.625
landl_d	−0.306	−0.371	landl_d	−0.307	−0.375
conf_0_0_a	0.002	−0.644	conf_0_0_a	−0.003	−0.654
oilp	0.003	0.001	oilp	0.003	0.001
prd	−0.180	−0.174	prd	−0.177	−0.169
oilp_oilexp	−0.005	0.005	oilp_oilexp	−0.005	0.004
oilexp_o	0.094	−0.132	oilexp_o	0.133	−0.049
_cons	−11.840	−8.665	_cons	−11.816	−8.621
N	64 954	64 954	N	64 954	64 954
Pseudo R2	0.9184	0.9208	Pseudo R2	0.9182	0.9206

been declining since then. In most cases it would seem that the extent of intra-MENA under-trading would be largely eliminated by *prd*= 9, which is 2005. When the starting date is only 1990, the initial shortfalls are shown to be much smaller but, accordingly, the steepness of the offsetting upward trends is also smaller.

Table 2.7 presents the results for the extended gravity model in which not only is the GDP$_{PC}$ measure of resource endowment differences added but so too are the dummy variable for *conflict* and several FTA dummies, the most important being *ftaw_comm*, for when both partners are members of the same major FTA at the time of the trade, *w_eu_o*, when one of the partners is a MENA country with an association agreement with the EU and the other partner is an EU country, and GAFTA, when both members are members of GAFTA at the time of the trade. Because the participation in these FTAs has grown over time, this table presents results with and without the time trend variable *prd*. Notice that the effects of most of the additional variables are as expected, the effect of the difference in GDP_{PC} positive in each of the columns, the effects of both *ftaw_comm* and *GAFTA* positive in the first two columns, *conflict* negative for exports but surprisingly positive for imports. Not surprisingly, for those who have followed the sub-regional FTAs in MENA, one sees the effects of GCC to be positive and of AMU to be negative. The effects of the association agreements are negative in three of the four columns, and especially for imports. The fact that the negative values of the coefficients of the MENA3 dummy variables are now larger than in Table 2.6 would seem to suggest that if it were not for GAFTA and the GCC, whose effects are estimated to be fairly substantial, the shortfall in intra-MENA trade would have been larger than indicated in Table 2.6. Not surprisingly, given the strength of the time trend effects that we have seen in the preceding tables, whether or not *prd* is included in the specification has some influence on some of the other coefficients as well.

While the preceding tables have revealed large but declining intraregional shortfalls, Table 2.8 turns to the application of MENA trade with the world as a whole. This table makes use of the benchmark gravity model but applies it with MENA2 in the first two columns and MENA3 in the last two columns. As such this table is comparable to the intra-MENA trade in Table 2.4 above. For both imports and exports MENA has on average been an under-trader with the outside world, but the extent of such under-trading of some 12 to 15 per cent is much smaller than the 20–50 per cent intra-MENA under-trading revealed in Table 2.4. Another interesting observation is that while MENA without Israel (MENA3) is a greater under-trader with the rest of the world in regard to imports, its level of under-trading remains almost at the same level in exports without Israel.

How would these results be affected by the addition of alternative measures of resource endowments to the benchmark gravity model when MENA3 is the definition of MENA? As can be seen by comparing the coefficients for *MENA3_o* between columns in Table 2.9 and between Tables 2.8 and 2.9, the answer would seem to be quite a bit. In particular, when differences in GDP_{PC} are used as the measure of resource endowment differences, MENA3 becomes an over-trader with the world rather than an under-trader. Yet, when differences in the shares of agriculture are used as the measure, MENA3 remains an under-trader, though a somewhat smaller one than indicated in the last two columns of Table 2.8. The counterpart to this is that the positive effects of the endowment differences on trade are larger when the GDP_{PC} differences are used than when it is the agricultural share differences.

Table 2.10 employs first the Benchmark Gravity model and then in the latter two columns the more comprehensive extended gravity model, in the latter case also including the MENA3-EU*prd interaction term, in this case trying to identify any under-trading between MENA countries and EU members. From the first two columns it can be seen that there is a shortfall in exports from MENA3 to the EU, but not in the case of imports. With the additional controls and the *MENA3_eu*prd* interaction term, the level effect is positive but the interaction effect negative for both imports and exports. The latter findings seem to suggest that early in the period studied (1965–2005) MENA and the EU were trading much more than would have been expected on the basis of gravity considerations but that this has been declining with time. The declining share of the EU in MENA trade reported in Tables 2.1 and 2.2 may have prepared us for this rather striking finding. As noted by the last two columns of the table, the association agreement may have helped MENA exports somewhat in recent years, but it does not seem to have increased MENA imports from the EU. These findings might well be due to the omission from the analysis of colonial ties which have often been demonstrated to be positive on trade. One could expect that the positive effect of colonial ties between most MENA3 countries and an EU member would have been strongest in the early years, especially soon after independence, but declining in strength over time.

Table 2.11 presents the estimation results for the evolution of over- or under-trading between MENA3 countries on one hand and Asia Pacific and the United States on the other hand. These results, along with the previous ones from MENA–EU trade, point to an obvious trend in international trade, the increasing importance of Asian economies in global trade. In particular, we can observe that the decline in the over-trading of MENA countries with the EU and the US has been accompanied by the decline in under-trading among MENA countries themselves and also that with Asian countries. The left panel in Table 2.11 indicates a relatively high level of under-trading in imports of MENA3 from Asia Pacific countries in the early periods. This under-trading has been improving by about 21 per cent on average over each period and somewhere after the fifth period it turned into an over-trading. Both exports and imports equations point to relatively high levels of over-trading in recent periods among MENA and Asia Pacific countries. On the other hand, the right panel in Table 2.11 tells a story for MENA–US trade relations which is very similar to those with the EU. Although MENA3–US started with an over-trading status in early periods – with a higher magnitude for exports – this over-trading has been subject to decline over periods. Our estimations show that for MENA3's imports from the US, this over-trading ceased and turned into under-trading with the turn of the millennium (after year 2000) while their exports to the United States did so in earlier periods.

Our measure of '*conflict*' among countries appears with the expected sign in most of the regression settings in Table 2.11, indicating that military conflicts that coincide with the time of trading do have significant and relatively large deterrence impacts, almost as large as the impact of being landlocked, on bilateral trade. As mentioned in section 2.4, our examination of the variations of this variable indicates that only severe conflicts/hostilities and those occurring at the same time as the trade (and not a few years before or after) appear to have significant and negative impact on bilateral trade of the countries.

Tables 2.12 and 2.13 turn attention to sub-regions within MENA, namely Maghreb, GCC and Mashreq. Table 2.12 presents results obtained from applying the Benchmark Gravity model to both imports and exports in such a way as to measure to what extent the degree of under- or over-trading varies from one sub-region to another. In this case, we see major differences, with almost 50 per cent over-trading within the Mashreq sub-region but over 60 per cent under-trading within the Maghreb and slight under-trading within the GCC. The second of these results is consistent with the earlier finding in Table 2.7 concerning the negative effect of the AMU (the special trade agreement among three of the four Maghreb countries, that is, without Libya) as well as widespread recognition that this agreement had not been seriously implemented or enforced. The large positive coefficient for Mashreq is consistent with the findings of others cited above. One can also notice how very similar across the different estimates are all the other parameter values, though once again with at least slight differences between those for imports and exports.

Finally, Table 2.13 presents the estimates obtained by applying the same Benchmark Gravity model testing for under-trading between the three sub-regions. In this case the difference in these coefficients is even larger than in Table 2.12. The only trade flows that are larger than predicted by the gravity model are those between Mashreq and GCC countries, especially on the import side. In the other two cases, the degrees of under-trading are very large and significant. All the other coefficients are very similar across the columns for imports as well as for exports.

In general, our empirical analyses from MENA countries' intra- and inter-regional trade behavior relative to what is predicted by our augmented gravity model points to improved trade relations among these countries and also towards Asian countries, probably at the expense of trade relations with the EU and the US (despite all the preferential trade agreements that the latter group of countries have signed with some MENA countries). As shown in Tables 2.8 and 2.9, most of our estimates have revealed MENA to be an under-trader. An exception, however, is in the first two columns of Table 2.9 in which the GDP$_{PC}$ differences are used as the measure of resource differences between countries.

2.6 CONCLUSION

The purpose of this section is not to repeat all the findings, but rather to draw implications from these findings to suggest priorities for further study and especially possible policy actions both within the MENA countries and within the EU and other regions. As indicated in section 2.1, because of the alarmingly high youth unemployment rates throughout much of the MENA region and the difficult economic situation in much of Europe, and the fragile new democracies that may perhaps be emerging in Arab Spring countries, some policy initiatives and re-thinking of old policies and institutional arrangements deserve serious consideration both in the MENA region and in Europe and America.

The implications we derive are organized in the following four categories.

Implications for Trade Policy

First, and most importantly, on no side of the Mediterranean (North, South or East) should policy makers do anything to use protectionism as a means of boosting domestic production and employment at the expense of imports. On the contrary, further steps should be taken to identify the specific barriers to greater trade both intra-MENA and between MENA and the EU. Among the further steps that should be undertaken in Europe and especially the EU to the benefit of the MENA countries with Association status in the EU would be to liberalize the rules of origin and other non-tariff barriers that would improve the opportunities for the relevant export sectors in the MENA region such as agriculture, textiles and petrochemicals to export to Europe. Doing so would allow FDI and technology to be transferred in industries which are increasingly not the ones which should be encouraged in Europe but in which European management and engineering could play a very useful role in upgrading technology and efficient management in MENA countries.

Second, and especially if the benefits of access to the European and US markets can be improved, greater efforts should be made to increase the number of MENA countries with Association status in the EU as well as with special trading arrangements with EFTA members and the United States. Given the superior trade and investment effects arising in the Central and Eastern European countries in the wake of more substantial institutional changes than in the MENA countries obtaining Association Agreements with the EU, consideration should be given to strengthening the institutional requirements for acceptance by the EU.

Third, in order to mitigate the hub and spokes disadvantage that MENA countries associated with the EU face in the absence of a rather perfectly functioning GAFTA, more should be done within MENA (perhaps with EU assistance) to strengthen GAFTA. Enforcement of existing agreements on rules should be strengthened and trade disputes within the region handled both expeditiously and fairly.

Fourth, in view of the large growth gap between slow-growing Europe and America (the traditional markets for MENA trade) and rapidly-growing China, India and much of Asia, efforts should be made within MENA to take advantage of special trading arrangements with Asian countries within which the numbers of FTAs and other special trading arrangements have been proliferating, but largely excluding MENA countries. Trade infrastructure may need to be re-oriented in such a way as to facilitate this trade, as has recently been the case with large Chinese investments in Egypt and Morocco.

Labor Market Policies

The variation in the degree of rigidity of labor laws and regulations within the MENA region is very considerable, in general with some of the North African countries having some of the most rigid regulations in the world and the GCC countries some of the least rigid ones according to Doing Business, IMF and other sources (see, especially, Campos and Nugent, 2011). These differences are to a large extent the result of GCC countries having relatively few nationals and thus being highly dependent on foreign workers, and the North African countries being almost entirely reliant on nationals but with worker rights being of some political importance.

There might well be gains to be made by reducing the differences across countries of the region. For GCC and other MENA countries heavily dependent on foreign labor, some tightening of regulations in GCC countries could have the effect of increasing the willingness of GCC nationals and the nationals from other MENA countries to take jobs in the private sector. The lack of willingness of nationals to take private sector jobs in these countries is an increasingly serious problem given the growing numbers of nationals without employment and the already excessive staffing in and low productivity of nationals in the public sector. At the same time, GCC and other MENA countries should be strongly discouraged from their continuing tendency to offer extremely attractive salaries and benefits to nationals employed in the public sector (Al-Sheikh and Erbas, 2012).

On the other hand, for the North African and Mashreq countries with relatively high indexes of labor law rigidities, efforts should be made to liberalize these regulations. Using a large cross-country, cross-firm data set based on the same World Bank Enterprise Surveys used by Contessi et al. (Chapter 4, this volume), Nugent and Wu (2012) have recently illustrated the surprisingly large extent to which the elimination of labor regulations in countries with very rigid labor regulations could lead to extra hiring based on responses to hypothetical questions about the extent to which firms would change their employment levels in the event of the elimination of existing labor regulations. At the same time, as shown by Li and Nugent (2012) based on Enterprise Survey data for Egypt and Morocco, lay-offs can sometimes outnumber hires in the responses of firms to the hypothetical elimination of existing labor regulations, and workers and government officials have reason to be concerned about the possible effect of such measures on lay-offs and unemployment.

Hence, to make such liberalization of labor laws more politically acceptable and economically efficient, there is reason to believe that such liberalization efforts should be coupled with increased unemployment insurance and 'flexicurity'. Flexicurity is the approach that has proven to be relatively successful in Denmark and other Northern European countries. Flexicurity combines unemployment insurance with incentives for those laid off to engage in retraining and active job search so that even unemployment spells can turn out to increase welfare and efficiency.

Another important benefit from liberalization of labor regulations is to encourage more firms and workers to work in the legal or formal sector of the economy rather than outside the law in the informal sector. As Elbadawi and Loayza (2008) have indicated, this would have the effect of increasing the efficiency of firms, especially in the long run, since formal firms have major advantages over informal firms in access to capital, technology and skilled labor. In addition, encouraging firm formality can also make it easier for governments to collect the taxes that are rightfully owed them.

Assistance Programs to New Countries Agreeing to Association Status with the EU

In the past the EU has provided technical assistance and other programs to those MENA countries agreeing to the conditions for Association status with the EU. The EU has been relatively non-demanding in the conditions for accepting such countries. Since, even despite having gained Association status with the EU, MENA countries seem to have been not very successful in their ability to attract FDI, it would seem quite clear that MENA countries could benefit by being more forcefully encouraged and taught how to undertake the kinds of reforms that would encourage FDI and technology transfer. More could be learned about what has and has not worked from the technical assistance programs of the EU tied to their MENA partners. Two such programs which seem to have been especially successful have been the Design Institute that EU assistance helped create in Egypt and the technical assistance to the Tunisian auto parts firms that EU firms offered in response to Tunisia's willingness to liberalize imports of European cars conditional on the willingness of EU firms to buy auto parts from Tunisia.

Peace Initiatives

Several of our results underscore the importance of avoiding conflict and strengthening and reinitiating the peace initiatives, some of which have been allowed to remain dormant for far too long. Of special importance in this respect is that the under-trading within MENA2 (that includes Israel) was substantially greater with respect to both imports and exports than for MENA3, which is identical except that it excludes Israel. Table 2.4, which reported results obtained from the benchmark model, showed that this minor change in how the region is defined made for a difference in under-trading of well over 14 per cent. Table 2.6 reveals that in addition to the static difference between the two coefficients (MENA2 and MENA3), the positive coefficient for interaction term MENA2*prd is also smaller than the corresponding MENA3*prd term. This is despite the fact that in general Israel is a large trader with the world as a whole for a country of its size. Note that in Table 2.8 (again with the benchmark model) MENA2's under-importing is less than MENA3's under-importing. Israel's GDP$_{PC}$ is considerably higher than that of all MENA3 countries outside the GCC, and GDP$_{PC}$ differences contribute positively to bilateral trade flows as indicated by the positive coefficients for *lgdppc_diff* in Table 2.5 (column 1), all columns of Table 2.7, the first two columns of Table 2.9 and the last two columns of Table 2.10. Finally, since conflicts have been observed between Israel and Egypt, Jordan and Syria during some of the years covered in this study, and our conflict variable in the exporting country leads to an over 60 per cent increase in under-exporting, the trade consequences of conflict for MENA countries have been serious. The conflicts among Iraq and Iran and Iraq and Kuwait and elsewhere in the region have also taken their toll. The magnitudes of these economic consequences underscore the importance of treating the current threats of additional conflict between Israel and Iran, Syria and the Gulf States and other countries.

Last but not least, it should be recalled that Israeli occupation of the Palestinian territories has led to the virtual exclusion of that rather centrally located region from international trade of any kind and the protection wall and security at border crossings into Israel have also greatly reduced the trade of the Palestinian territories with Israel. In the light of the extent to which high unemployment rates, especially youth unemployment rates, have contributed to unrest in the region, and Palestinian youth unemployment is near the highest in the world, it is quite clear that the virtual exclusion of the West Bank and Gaza from trade is a major contributor not only to under-trading in the MENA region but also to social tension and instability.

Clearly, the under-trading resulting from the virtual exclusions of Israel from trade with MENA3 countries and of the West Bank and Gaza from trade with virtually any country, are sources of considerable economic inefficiency and social and political frictions. Although very small in scale, as documented in Abdel Latif and Nugent (2012), the provision of free access to US markets in the Qualified Industrial Zones (QIZ) arrangements between Israel and both Egypt and Jordan has led to significant trade between both these countries and Egypt. Consider by contrast how much more has been accomplished in terms of both trade and peace by the much stronger inducement to trade, institutional change and peace that has been arising out of the EU's conditional offers of admission to the EU to the states of Eastern Europe, several of which had previously been engaged in conflict.

NOTES

1. While the EU countries would be the 'hub' with access both to EU hub countries and each of the MENA countries with association agreements, the MENA countries were 'spokes' because, until such time as a strong and fully enforced GAFTA would come into effect, the output from an investment in one MENA country would not have free access to the market of another.
2. Among the rather dormant or failed trade arrangements within the region were the Arab Common Market, the Arab Maghreb Union, and the Regional Cooperation for Development (among Iran, Turkey and Pakistan). Factors responsible for their failure include their very incomplete implementation, lack of enforcement of the rules, and periodic frictions among countries involved in these arrangements.
3. For example, with a very small number of countries, both MENA and non-MENA, Ekholm et al. (1996) produced an estimate suggesting that MENA was not an under-trader.
4. The failure of the EU–MENA association agreements to increase trade was attributed to the exclusion of agricultural products from this agreement and the decrease of the

trade preference advantage of MENA products in Europe after the phasing out of quotas and other barriers with the termination of the Multi-Fiber Agreement.
5. The closest that the authors come to dealing with this issue is that they use time fixed effects along with country of origin and destination fixed effects. Other shortcomings in this excellent study are that the sample is limited to only 56 countries, indeed only 35 countries outside of GAFTA, and the fact that for many of these countries no data is available whatsoever for three, four or more years. Their preferred estimates are based on a dynamic model in which it is change in bilateral trade that is estimated with lagged values of the dependent variables included and the Arellano, Bond and Bover version of GMM used to deal with the resulting endogeneity and to increase the efficiency of the estimates.
6. While data was also missing for some other parts of the world for these years, for most regions the omissions were of minor importance.
7. Because of the small size of Bahrain and its proximity to various other ports in Iraq, Kuwait, Qatar and Saudi Arabia, it is possible that some of Bahrain's trade with MENA2 should have been classified as transit trade (simply arriving in transit from another port where the import should have been registered).
8. In the case of Egypt, Jordan and Morocco this may have been the result of special trade arrangements with the US, FTAs with the US in the case of Jordan and Morocco, and the Qualified Industrial Zones (QIZ) arrangement in the case of Egypt, all finalized after 2000.
9. For a detailed description of data construction procedures see: Correlates of War Project Trade Data Set Codebook, Version 2.0, available online at: http://corre latesofwar.org.
10. http://www.cepii.fr/anglaisgraph/bdd/gravity.htm.

REFERENCES

Abdel Latif, Abla and Jeffrey B. Nugent (2012), 'A quiz on the QIZs of Jordan and Egypt: have they achieved their objectives?', Working Paper, Economic Research Forum.
Abedini, Javad and Nicolas Peridy (2008), 'The Greater Arab Free Trade Area (GAFTA): an estimation of its trade effects', *Journal of Economic Integration*, **23**(4).
Al-Atrash, J. and Tarik M. Yousef (2000), 'Intra-Arab trade: is it too little?', IMF Working Paper 00/10, Washington, DC: International Monetary Fund, Economic Commission for Western Asia.
Al-Sheikh, Hend and S. Nuri Erbas (2012), 'The oil curse and labor markets: the case of Saudi Arabia', ERF Working Paper no. 697.
Bannister, Geoffrey J. and Ulric Erickson von Allmen (2001), 'Palestinian trade: performance, prospects and policy', in Rosa A. Valdivieso et al. (eds), *West Bank and Gaza: Economic Performance, Prospects and Policies: Achieving Prosperity and Confronting Demographic Challenges*, Washington, DC: International Monetary Fund.
Barbieri, Katherine, Omar M.G. Keshk and Brian Pollins (2009), 'Trading data: evaluating our assumptions and coding rules', *Conflict Management and Peace Science*, **26**(5), 471–91.
Bhattacharya, Rina and Hirut Wolde (2010), 'Constraints on trade in the MENA Region', IMF Working Paper 10/31, International Monetary Fund.
Campos, Nauro F. and Jeffrey B. Nugent (2011), 'The determinants of labor

market protection legislation in the Middle East and North Africa since 1970', paper presented at the 86th annual conference of the Western Economic Association, San Diego, California, July.

Eaton, Jonathan and Akiko Tamura (1994), 'Bilateralism and regionalism in Japanese and US trade and investment flows', *Journal of the Japanese and International Economies*, **8**(4), 478–510.

Ekholm, K., J. Torstensson and R. Torstensson (1996), 'The economies of the Middle East peace process: are there prospects for trade and growth?', *The World Economy*, **19**(5), 555–74.

Elbadawi, Ibrahim and Norman Loayza (2008), 'Informality, employment and economic development in the Arab world', *Journal of Development and Economic Policies*, **10**, 25–75.

Head, Keith, Thierry Mayer and John Ries (2010), 'The erosion of colonial trade linkages after independence', *Journal of International Economics*, **81**(1), 1–14.

International Monetary Fund (IMF) (2002), *World Economic Outlook*, Washington, DC: IMF.

Iqbal, Farrukh and Mustapha K. Nabli (2007), 'Trade, foreign direct investment and development in the Middle East and North Africa', in M.K. Nabli (ed.), *Breaking Barriers to Higher Economic Growth: Better Governance and Deeper Reforms in the Middle East and North Africa*, Washington, DC: World Bank.

Leamer, Edward E. and J.A. Levinsohn (1995), 'International trade theory: the evidence', in G. Grossman and K. Rogoff (eds), *The Handbook of International Economics*, vol. III. Amsterdam: Elsevier-North Holland.

Li, Yunsun and Jeffrey B. Nugent (2012), 'What can be learned about the employment effects of labor market deregulation from the answers to hypothetical questions about it to firms? Evidence from Egypt and Morocco', paper presented at the Annual Conference of the Western Economic Association, San Francisco, 30 June.

Miniesy, Rania, Jeffrey B. Nugent and Tarik M. Yousef (2004), 'Intra-regional trade integration in the Middle East: past performance and future potential', in Hassan Hakimian and Jeffrey B. Nugent (eds), *Trade Policy and Economic Integration in the Middle East and North Africa: Economic Boundaries in Flux*, London: Routledge, pp. 41–65.

Nugent, Jeffrey B. and Yanyu Wu (2012), 'How would firms adjust employment if labor market regulations were eliminated? Evidence from the enterprise surveys', paper presented at the Western Economic Association International, June.

Peridy, Nicolas (2005), 'Towards a Pan-Arab Free Trade Area: assessing trade potential effects of the Agadir Agreement', *The Developing Economies*, **43**(3), 329–45.

Silva, J. and S. Tenreyro (2006), 'The log of gravity', *Review of Economics and Statistics*, **88**(4), 641–58.

Viner, Jacob (1950), *The Customs Union Issue*, New York: Carnegie Endowment for International Peace.

Zarrouk, Jamel (2000), 'The Greater Arab Free Trade Area: limits and possibilities', in Bernard Hoekman and Jamel Zarrouk (eds), *Catching up with the Competition: Trade Opportunities and Challenges for Arab Countries*, Ann Arbor, MI: University of Michigan Press.

APPENDIX

Table 2A.1 Shares of MENA2, EU, US, China and other countries in imports and exports of each MENA country

Country	Year	MENA2 % Import	MENA2 % Export	EU % Import	EU % Export	US % Import	US % Export	China % Import	China % Export	Other % Import	Other % Export	Total Value Import	Total Value Export
Algeria	1965	1.23	2.29	87.20	86.88	0.78	3.15	0.00	0.00	10.79	7.67	765.95	666.87
Algeria	1970	1.80	2.08	69.37	66.14	0.97	8.27	0.79	1.02	27.07	22.49	1136.94	1219.89
Algeria	1975	0.29	1.28	35.77	57.22	30.59	15.04	0.72	0.36	32.63	26.09	4734.06	6011.08
Algeria	1980	0.07	1.26	28.09	57.61	47.90	7.11	0.00	0.45	23.94	33.57	14364.58	10556.82
Algeria	1985	1.91	2.65	57.39	56.17	18.25	6.56	0.08	0.39	22.36	34.22	13295.32	9793.71
Algeria	1990	3.34	4.06	59.77	54.24	20.96	11.67	0.06	0.30	15.88	29.72	13589.10	9620.62
Algeria	1995	5.86	5.89	66.39	59.22	15.38	13.13	0.19	2.34	12.18	19.42	11749.85	10797.46
Algeria	2000	6.66	5.25	65.55	58.01	12.11	11.54	0.11	2.51	15.56	22.69	23081.51	9061.28
Algeria	2005	5.76	7.83	53.71	59.18	22.57	5.44	0.75	6.64	17.21	20.92	47997.10	23489.97
Bahrain	1965											0.00	0.00
Bahrain	1970											0.00	0.00
Bahrain	1975	13.99	55.56	11.59	17.20	14.24	7.74	1.86	3.07	58.32	16.43	807.46	1187.35
Bahrain	1980	28.46	60.18	5.09	12.63	0.73	7.83	0.00	0.50	65.72	18.86	2266.71	3391.97
Bahrain	1985	31.78	50.39	7.21	19.64	5.99	7.67	1.26	0.40	53.76	21.89	1502.88	3061.11
Bahrain	1990	19.12	56.30	8.66	15.09	4.95	7.43	0.00	0.66	67.26	20.52	1813.72	3563.19
Bahrain	1995	19.93	47.77	6.40	19.89	5.16	8.38	0.67	1.43	67.83	22.52	2818.70	3611.19
Bahrain	2000	18.81	36.18	12.56	25.81	10.72	12.84	2.98	3.32	54.93	21.85	3220.77	3522.71
Bahrain	2005	35.43	44.40	12.18	22.22	8.16	5.46	1.98	3.49	42.24	24.43	5570.29	7059.93
Egypt	1965	5.56	7.66	18.46	23.16	2.80	20.59	7.03	2.91	66.14	45.68	641.82	916.00
Egypt	1970	6.46	6.57	19.96	27.36	2.45	5.88	1.81	1.96	69.32	58.22	978.89	780.64
Egypt	1975	6.39	9.04	21.68	28.85	1.85	19.31	2.95	0.95	67.14	41.86	1782.49	3919.84
Egypt	1980	6.35	2.67	59.86	38.66	9.61	20.23	1.64	0.66	22.55	37.79	5947.19	4634.62
Egypt	1985	3.48	4.10	47.37	39.58	1.41	13.74	0.10	0.45	47.65	42.13	5986.43	5202.89

Country	Year												
Egypt	1990	8.27	4.30	51.86	34.45	8.02	14.92	0.11	1.18	31.75	45.14	5426.26	8715.83
Egypt	1995	17.61	5.94	50.22	41.09	10.98	19.91	0.22	2.66	20.97	30.40	5959.62	11105.69
Egypt	2000	16.76	8.65	51.56	38.80	14.08	18.13	1.95	5.65	15.65	28.77	6353.14	20564.33
Egypt	2005	26.54	13.77	41.42	35.23	14.54	11.34	2.19	7.39	15.31	32.27	15275.32	30748.22
Iraq	1965	6.52	6.08	60.74	27.88	2.08	12.18	0.55	3.92	30.10	49.93	1009.18	435.80
Iraq	1970	8.89	8.87	68.38	38.43	0.27	3.63	0.52	4.54	21.95	44.53	1119.21	504.04
Iraq	1975	10.11	3.30	53.94	25.73	0.28	8.81	0.00	1.62	35.67	60.53	8089.72	4201.25
Iraq	1980	7.32	6.15	43.26	36.02	1.52	5.82	0.40	1.00	47.49	51.01	31733.45	12444.18
Iraq	1985	13.51	16.36	42.55	29.63	4.22	4.46	0.06	1.34	39.66	48.21	11640.60	10523.55
Iraq	1990	15.57	17.83	24.02	32.36	28.67	10.80	0.63	0.55	31.11	38.46	11327.61	6513.54
Iraq	1995	96.73	60.92	0.27	5.69	0.00	0.03	0.13	0.05	2.87	33.31	466.99	665.44
Iraq	2000	7.30	10.73	33.37	33.02	38.92	0.35	3.97	10.56	16.44	45.34	16309.70	3414.17
Iraq	2005	5.84	56.04	22.86	14.71	49.67	11.69	2.14	3.49	19.48	14.08	19422.06	12914.52
Kuwait	1965	2.01	10.24	63.77	33.61	3.42	20.68	0.00	0.00	30.81	35.47	1493.07	319.22
Kuwait	1970	0.97	10.47	58.28	29.11	1.27	13.59	0.00	0.00	39.48	43.48	2128.00	610.04
Kuwait	1975	5.25	5.40	34.41	28.16	1.46	18.31	0.04	3.34	58.85	46.02	8617.59	2350.02
Kuwait	1980	5.29	4.77	26.29	26.77	2.74	14.82	0.22	2.11	65.46	51.35	19032.64	6390.65
Kuwait	1985	9.47	7.97	37.07	26.01	2.18	9.17	0.21	2.29	51.07	55.24	9080.07	5936.81
Kuwait	1990	8.90	9.75	24.79	29.59	7.57	12.11	0.52	1.61	58.23	46.58	8260.38	3642.91
Kuwait	1995	2.96	15.22	13.44	38.31	11.76	16.22	1.00	1.98	70.84	27.92	12487.58	7731.05
Kuwait	2000	2.98	21.03	13.80	32.19	14.39	12.14	1.69	2.32	67.14	28.98	20632.41	7349.42
Kuwait	2005	3.89	18.48	10.34	33.44	11.91	14.16	3.16	5.65	70.71	29.03	38735.54	15340.30
Lebanon	1965	44.25	25.03	38.94	33.83	3.58	12.21	0.24	4.89	13.00	27.93	167.70	486.62
Lebanon	1970	59.66	15.47	22.25	35.52	4.43	12.15	0.00	1.01	13.67	35.23	316.27	531.29
Lebanon	1975	79.13	8.69	10.88	41.08	2.89	20.48	0.00	1.63	7.11	29.75	1212.08	1801.33
Lebanon	1980	79.13	16.01	7.49	41.76	3.58	8.92	0.00	0.00	9.80	33.31	945.89	3396.00
Lebanon	1985	65.76	12.92	13.83	46.52	4.53	7.63	0.00	0.00	15.88	31.99	436.65	2031.61
Lebanon	1990	49.65	19.81	21.84	38.29	4.92	4.42	0.01	0.95	23.58	36.19	503.87	2443.60
Lebanon	1995	51.54	10.16	18.73	48.78	4.81	9.89	0.06	1.29	24.85	28.43	756.56	6568.98
Lebanon	2000	42.76	15.02	21.19	44.24	8.36	7.38	0.66	2.74	27.03	28.60	880.26	6198.13
Lebanon	2005	67.88	24.93	9.96	42.30	3.85	5.40	0.40	5.97	17.91	21.40	2369.80	9442.79

Table 2A.1 (continued)

Country	Year	MENA2 %		EU %		US %		China %		Other %		Total Value	
		Import	Export	Import	Export	Import	Export	Import	Export	Import	Export	Import	Export
Libya	1965	1.91	3.68	54.81	53.85	3.32	17.35	0.00	1.52	39.96	23.60	993.10	315.30
Libya	1970	0.34	8.17	66.88	45.91	3.03	14.02	0.00	1.94	29.76	29.95	2521.66	545.61
Libya	1975	1.31	5.53	35.14	54.28	20.54	4.11	0.00	0.32	43.01	35.76	6396.85	3441.03
Libya	1980	3.51	1.47	28.09	58.98	37.44	6.38	0.01	0.17	30.94	33.00	23780.49	6678.48
Libya	1985	8.12	2.61	60.72	48.53	0.40	6.27	0.25	0.60	30.52	42.00	11836.31	5461.30
Libya	1990	6.85	11.27	64.12	51.04	0.00	1.26	0.03	0.89	29.01	35.55	12517.03	5561.52
Libya	1995	10.54	16.62	80.55	63.92	0.00	0.00	0.76	0.71	8.15	18.75	9407.74	5145.49
Libya	2000	9.10	16.46	85.15	63.27	0.00	0.49	0.18	1.50	5.57	18.27	13985.09	4016.15
Libya	2005	9.68	17.39	76.16	53.62	5.19	1.06	2.95	4.56	6.02	23.37	31914.40	8746.24
Morocco	1965	2.39	2.23	71.14	54.18	1.28	12.15	1.68	2.70	23.53	28.74	548.95	440.20
Morocco	1970	2.96	2.36	65.94	55.24	1.82	11.39	1.10	1.62	28.18	29.40	603.11	680.95
Morocco	1975	4.54	6.70	59.46	51.73	0.62	7.75	0.36	1.11	35.03	32.71	1778.65	2539.16
Morocco	1980	3.12	19.38	60.29	50.26	1.45	6.57	0.50	0.91	34.63	22.88	2804.93	4211.19
Morocco	1985	7.86	21.87	56.40	44.47	1.71	6.13	0.63	1.42	33.41	26.12	2556.77	3848.57
Morocco	1990	10.11	15.40	61.27	50.47	2.12	6.23	0.31	1.60	26.18	26.31	5539.90	6964.36
Morocco	1995	6.58	12.73	72.19	58.04	3.50	6.79	0.54	2.02	17.18	20.43	7315.40	8228.83
Morocco	2000	4.77	16.28	67.61	58.35	5.61	5.55	0.72	2.61	21.29	17.22	8298.84	11593.04
Morocco	2005	3.85	16.32	72.60	51.24	3.06	3.37	1.81	5.35	18.68	23.73	15494.96	20339.15
Oman	1965											0.00	0.00
Oman	1970											0.00	0.00
Oman	1975	0.42	24.18	45.56	33.96	3.70	9.62	0.00	1.14	50.32	31.10	1568.73	671.78
Oman	1980	0.92	22.84	7.75	29.51	12.02	5.78	0.00	1.05	79.31	40.82	3018.12	1706.67
Oman	1985	0.61	22.59	3.02	31.30	1.09	5.77	0.00	0.36	95.28	39.98	4655.06	3101.35
Oman	1990	8.52	27.75	6.74	24.63	5.44	9.41	2.14	0.42	77.16	37.80	5868.36	2663.98
Oman	1995	1.99	30.36	2.73	28.09	5.88	6.54	8.83	0.90	80.57	34.11	5451.46	4222.96
Oman	2000	2.14	35.69	1.95	19.09	2.77	5.37	32.20	2.53	60.94	37.33	10135.59	5040.19

Country	Year												
Oman	2005	8.24	31.46	3.18	24.22	3.34	6.75	23.39	2.36	61.85	35.21	17824.05	9663.74
Qatar	1965											0.00	0.00
Qatar	1970											0.00	0.00
Qatar	1975	1.14	13.93	55.24	35.08	24.61	12.60	0.00	1.50	19.02	36.89	1557.16	406.80
Qatar	1980	2.52	8.10	39.84	38.61	4.21	11.58	0.72	1.58	52.71	40.13	5934.87	1407.04
Qatar	1985	2.75	9.69	43.44	41.07	0.19	6.98	0.22	0.56	53.40	41.69	3467.82	1066.30
Qatar	1990	6.50	13.01	1.36	36.62	1.64	9.74	0.70	1.01	89.79	39.61	3208.45	1647.82
Qatar	1995	7.15	19.01	1.36	35.63	2.52	11.04	2.29	1.53	86.68	32.78	3571.58	1849.60
Qatar	2000	7.10	18.10	1.05	36.03	3.44	10.41	3.17	3.59	85.24	31.86	10483.57	3218.50
Qatar	2005	5.86	16.38	6.14	40.02	1.83	10.34	1.84	2.38	84.32	30.89	24377.53	10494.04
Saudi Arabia	1965	4.42	19.06	34.87	29.29	7.72	21.06	0.00	0.00	52.99	30.59	1476.36	355.70
Saudi Arabia	1970	1.04	18.55	47.57	22.93	0.80	18.22	0.00	0.00	50.59	40.31	2633.44	693.33
Saudi Arabia	1975	3.36	24.22	38.55	20.72	9.82	17.38	0.00	0.11	48.27	37.57	31578.37	4153.50
Saudi Arabia	1980	3.89	4.38	35.50	31.03	13.46	20.48	0.02	0.85	47.14	43.26	100081.59	29488.06
Saudi Arabia	1985	10.31	5.21	20.13	29.74	6.42	17.27	0.07	0.89	63.07	46.89	31566.25	23230.07
Saudi Arabia	1990	8.67	5.80	17.81	29.07	21.04	16.89	0.16	1.87	52.32	46.37	51013.29	23813.90
Saudi Arabia	1995	10.27	7.33	18.86	35.82	15.78	21.46	0.98	2.82	54.12	32.57	56402.10	27317.82
Saudi Arabia	2000	7.94	7.28	17.83	35.20	17.51	20.78	2.66	0.00	54.06	36.74	81659.86	28069.80
Saudi Arabia	2005	10.73	10.60	16.19	30.50	16.89	14.95	7.40	7.74	48.79	36.20	171457.20	58884.36
Sudan	1965	9.39	4.91	33.14	40.50	3.35	7.10	7.37	3.39	46.75	44.10	208.84	191.60
Sudan	1970	8.29	8.45	25.63	33.31	4.21	3.12	5.75	4.33	56.11	50.79	308.58	282.18
Sudan	1975	7.07	13.38	48.12	33.59	2.07	9.25	8.63	4.87	34.11	38.90	434.16	954.21
Sudan	1980	28.94	24.68	32.01	32.64	2.49	8.12	8.11	3.34	28.45	31.22	751.71	1559.66
Sudan	1985	25.99	23.37	24.57	33.18	1.87	12.34	0.17	2.05	47.42	29.07	482.55	899.35
Sudan	1990	18.56	34.14	31.62	31.94	2.74	3.57	10.72	2.91	36.36	27.43	572.91	1302.97
Sudan	1995	28.59	35.79	29.80	30.96	3.93	3.80	12.48	3.63	25.20	25.82	597.24	1259.87
Sudan	2000	12.25	20.26	10.12	30.71	0.11	1.26	41.55	12.39	35.96	35.37	1769.54	1451.46
Sudan	2005	7.66	29.49	4.10	16.73	0.25	1.94	47.88	20.71	40.12	31.14	5464.43	6693.03
Syria	1965	33.24	18.70	40.77	31.98	1.35	6.98	5.67	2.78	18.96	39.55	296.04	204.79
Syria	1970	25.30	19.35	41.02	24.81	0.77	3.52	6.14	2.81	26.77	49.51	258.33	350.22
Syria	1975	24.86	11.02	56.16	33.36	0.57	6.69	1.87	2.77	16.55	46.17	1218.94	1633.77

Table 2A.1 (continued)

Country	Year	MENA2 % Import	MENA2 % Export	EU % Import	EU % Export	US % Import	US % Export	China % Import	China % Export	Other % Import	Other % Export	Total Value Import	Total Value Export
Syria	1980	10.32	27.12	57.38	32.72	1.28	5.47	2.29	1.41	28.74	33.28	2160.96	4022.52
Syria	1985	8.12	30.86	31.89	29.34	0.15	6.27	0.31	0.79	59.54	32.74	1855.84	3889.63
Syria	1990	18.22	16.49	24.57	37.90	1.40	11.51	0.11	1.37	55.70	32.74	4087.14	2239.39
Syria	1995	25.46	15.91	63.83	39.42	1.83	7.76	0.05	4.40	8.83	32.51	3543.48	4108.74
Syria	2000	27.47	13.87	62.13	40.44	3.13	5.28	0.20	4.90	7.08	35.51	5079.52	4400.80
Syria	2005	61.43	44.07	31.86	22.93	3.13	1.09	0.16	6.47	3.42	25.45	11244.56	15811.50
Tunisia	1965	7.16	5.81	68.28	58.09	2.98	16.31	1.49	0.65	20.08	19.13	167.55	244.60
Tunisia	1970	15.15	2.05	53.90	56.29	1.49	17.44	0.00	0.05	29.45	24.16	200.74	296.33
Tunisia	1975	11.04	7.73	55.46	63.67	3.37	6.78	0.72	0.54	29.42	21.29	831.71	1409.52
Tunisia	1980	5.14	11.63	73.02	60.76	2.79	5.90	0.55	0.56	18.50	21.15	2243.18	3511.46
Tunisia	1985	9.01	7.03	63.22	59.21	0.82	5.86	1.50	1.41	25.44	26.48	1647.96	2697.85
Tunisia	1990	10.73	8.79	61.81	56.61	0.90	5.15	0.72	0.57	25.84	28.88	3775.44	5798.86
Tunisia	1995	9.34	7.86	82.42	73.79	1.41	5.11	0.66	0.72	6.18	12.52	5391.18	7647.42
Tunisia	2000	9.80	9.71	80.17	71.56	1.67	4.65	0.06	1.34	8.30	12.73	6438.05	8473.75
Tunisia	2005	11.09	10.13	79.25	68.60	2.26	2.53	0.48	3.05	6.93	15.69	10712.70	13027.22
United Arab Emirates	1965											0.00	0.00
United Arab Emirates	1970											0.00	0.00
United Arab Emirates	1975	2.85	10.09	35.13	33.03	12.39	15.90	0.00	2.19	49.63	38.79	6600.83	2611.10
United Arab Emirates	1980	4.59	7.50	26.93	33.64	14.21	14.36	0.00	1.68	54.27	42.82	22263.24	8076.54
United Arab Emirates	1985	9.22	10.45	9.25	30.16	4.63	11.18	0.14	1.82	76.76	46.39	15577.99	6361.43

Country	Year												
United Arab Emirates	1990	13.17	10.50	9.22	25.62	4.52	9.37	0.20	5.11	72.90	49.39	21093.49	11189.69
United Arab Emirates	1995	11.68	8.73	4.55	33.45	2.19	8.55	0.54	7.99	81.04	41.28	22192.63	20610.08
United Arab Emirates	2000	11.51	9.75	5.71	35.07	2.56	7.53	2.29	8.59	77.92	39.06	38872.40	26602.82
United Arab Emirates	2005	13.70	7.74	12.89	32.57	1.76	9.49	3.72	11.93	67.93	38.28	87405.64	98263.00
Yemen	1965											0.00	0.00
Yemen	1970											0.00	0.00
Yemen	1975											0.00	0.00
Yemen	1980											0.00	0.00
Yemen	1985											0.00	0.00
Yemen	1990	2.81	23.21	28.20	26.37	23.47	5.15	0.10	3.44	45.42	41.83	1702.30	2374.07
Yemen	1995	3.14	35.33	3.18	23.35	2.24	7.74	17.40	3.57	74.04	30.01	1978.48	1564.29
Yemen	2000	5.85	40.17	2.30	18.13	7.69	4.48	21.20	3.69	62.96	33.54	3473.55	2300.90
Yemen	2005	8.40	43.45	3.17	14.44	4.12	4.54	37.03	6.25	47.28	31.32	7354.94	4765.56
Djibouti	1965											0.00	0.00
Djibouti	1970											0.00	0.00
Djibouti	1975											0.00	0.00
Djibouti	1980	1.84	4.48	19.31	44.44	0.00	5.10	0.00	0.00	78.85	45.98	48.79	227.66
Djibouti	1985	3.48	23.64	4.56	48.30	0.52	1.69	0.00	1.50	91.44	24.88	38.78	300.13
Djibouti	1990	33.39	10.91	7.45	48.00	0.00	3.36	0.21	2.32	58.95	35.41	65.39	207.76
Djibouti	1995	13.31	10.12	8.84	33.11	0.00	2.47	0.13	2.52	77.72	51.77	104.88	431.35
Djibouti	2000	22.96	22.86	8.12	30.16	0.24	3.16	0.38	10.33	68.29	33.49	165.08	588.42
Djibouti	2005	6.55	28.29	2.83	12.31	0.33	4.54	0.40	11.15	89.89	43.71	300.19	1157.77
Iran	1965	1.72	3.50	39.10	33.84	6.60	18.66	0.00	0.00	52.58	44.00	1440.05	829.00
Iran	1970	0.81	2.02	28.59	30.17	2.98	21.56	0.00	0.00	67.63	46.25	2664.43	1512.24
Iran	1975	1.51	3.12	36.84	24.82	12.20	19.78	0.00	0.51	49.45	51.77	20052.25	10367.86
Iran	1980	5.63	7.19	22.65	35.52	3.12	0.22	0.38	0.40	68.21	56.67	15293.74	10539.20
Iran	1985	13.96	12.02	32.20	24.41	5.11	0.65	0.05	0.42	48.68	62.49	14938.05	11355.32

Table 2A.1 (continued)

Country	Year	MENA2 %		EU %		US %		China %		Other %		Total Value	
		Import	Export	Import	Export	Import	Export	Import	Export	Import	Export	Import	Export
Iran	1990	4.35	11.52	40.15	30.79	0.01	0.33	0.24	0.93	55.24	56.43	17908.46	18532.05
Iran	1995	8.42	6.82	38.18	40.96	0.00	3.88	1.26	1.90	52.14	46.43	17961.89	12249.44
Iran	2000	6.94	11.41	29.71	37.33	0.67	0.66	6.95	4.03	55.72	46.57	26079.87	14254.48
Iran	2005	12.07	14.83	27.39	39.90	0.35	0.24	13.45	8.52	46.74	36.51	51804.92	43393.87
Israel	1965	3.03	1.27	41.57	43.67	16.62	27.77	0.05	0.00	38.74	27.28	403.18	760.90
Israel	1970	3.32	0.48	39.89	42.78	22.09	24.16	0.00	0.00	34.69	32.58	719.81	1336.40
Israel	1975	3.57	0.28	41.68	43.01	19.16	28.78	0.00	0.03	35.59	27.90	1701.49	3471.52
Israel	1980	0.71	3.18	42.76	35.57	21.22	25.88	0.04	0.01	35.27	35.36	4609.68	5985.07
Israel	1985	0.77	0.19	34.69	43.37	40.54	24.57	0.00	0.00	24.01	31.87	5429.04	6943.08
Israel	1990	1.36	0.30	35.85	44.01	31.02	19.74	0.00	0.00	31.78	35.95	10964.29	13793.44
Israel	1995	1.10	1.15	36.07	56.61	33.95	20.32	0.70	0.52	28.18	21.41	17205.49	25596.53
Israel	2000	1.99	2.03	29.04	48.60	40.10	20.88	5.34	4.72	23.52	23.77	32167.16	31821.96
Israel	2005	2.47	3.48	26.71	44.13	39.80	15.77	8.01	8.27	23.00	28.35	43034.20	38302.36
Turkey	1965	7.25	8.88	42.15	29.61	17.13	28.66	0.44	0.00	33.02	32.85	525.25	565.60
Turkey	1970	6.64	6.42	39.69	29.88	11.20	19.36	0.13	0.01	42.33	44.34	660.60	888.50
Turkey	1975	19.25	18.11	33.31	30.28	9.68	9.01	0.10	0.47	37.66	42.13	1600.78	4723.61
Turkey	1980	22.05	39.20	31.24	23.17	5.80	5.86	0.06	0.00	40.84	31.76	3213.01	7547.95
Turkey	1985	40.04	32.63	27.04	25.29	8.57	10.11	0.53	0.57	23.82	31.40	7526.69	11242.34
Turkey	1990	17.97	17.00	32.92	28.34	8.10	10.10	0.37	1.94	40.64	42.62	14263.73	22590.24
Turkey	1995	14.36	10.82	56.97	47.42	9.12	10.47	0.68	1.52	18.87	29.77	21115.52	35557.02
Turkey	2000	10.97	10.21	59.49	50.55	11.74	7.42	0.88	2.84	16.92	28.98	27609.48	52720.49
Turkey	2005	16.65	10.05	53.45	39.37	7.44	4.66	1.00	6.06	21.46	39.86	75046.34	115340.58

3. Employment creation through inward FDI in the EMFTA and employment linkages within sectors

Sergio Alessandrini

3.1 INTRODUCTION

The main idea of this chapter is to investigate the relationship between inward Foreign Direct Investment (FDI), employment and productivity in three Mediterranean countries: Morocco, Tunisia and Egypt. In this context, one needs to consider the real contribution of the inflow of foreign capital, in particular the effects on domestic employment and labour productivity, since employment and job creation are central priorities for the region (FEMISE, 2010).

There are two channels for inward FDI to generate employment in the host country. First, foreign affiliates employ people in their domestic operations and this effect is maximized with greenfield investments. The new entry in the host market may have secondary effects, since it increases the number of competitors in the domestic industry and then it may reduce employment elsewhere in the economy, a sort of competition effect. Different effects occur in the case of acquisition or mergers with domestic firms, such as buying privatized firms. The immediate effects are ambiguous: these mergers may lower employment as an immediate effect of the rationalization in the use of labour and may reduce the number of competitors by taking out a local firm. In the medium term the post-merger effects may be positive when the competitive environment remains open and healthy, as it is when inward FDI flows are associated with the better export orientation.

Second, through backward and forward linkages, employment is created in enterprises that are suppliers, subcontractors or service providers. When measuring the effects, the evidence, as well as the literature, are somewhat ambiguous due to the difficulties in identifying the channels, the causality and the linkages between foreign affiliates and domestic firms. Mergers and acquisitions may have different outcomes when they reduce competition by absorbing the domestic firms. Greenfield investments, in contrast, are expected to be consistent with the employment objective, as the emphasis here is on the quantity of jobs created by inward FDI, while the quality of the jobs, their sectoral and geographic distribution, can be a matter of incentives provided by the national attraction laws.[1] For instance, the 1999 investment policy review of Egypt reported that the FDI projects have generated employment, particularly in the new industrial zones and free zones. In 2009 the employment benefits estimated by the Egyptian Industrial Development Authority (IDA) were 1 822 000 new jobs in 29 575 factories, with an average size of 62 employees.[2] In Tunisia, the Foreign Investment Promotion Agency (FIPA) indicated that there are 3102 foreign enterprises with a total of 324 730 jobs. On average, a foreign company has 105 employees. In Morocco the available statistics indicate that 2500 foreign firms or subsidiaries represent more than 20 per cent of total capital invested in the industrial sector, with a positive impact on employment.

The current chapter relates closely to the literature on inward FDI spillovers as well as that on transition/emerging economies. It also contributes to the literature in several ways. First, we include service sector firms in addition to manufacturing firms. Second, we use the input–output table to study the vertical spillover effects of FDI; that is, spillover effects of FDI in upstream and downstream industries in addition to spillovers to the firms in the same industry, or horizontal spillovers. Third, we explore the effects of mode of entry and ownership structure on productivity of foreign firms.

3.2   LITERATURE AND HYPOTHESIS DEVELOPMENT

Economic theory suggests that one of the important gains expected from FDI inflows is that it would bring in new skills and technologies and would generate productive linkages with the economy. We expect a positive correlation, since the presence of foreign affiliates in these three host countries can lead to technology transfer to domestic firms, that is, to spillovers of FDI to local enterprises (Aitken and Harrison 1999, p. 605). If foreign firms introduce new products and/or processes to their affiliates, domestic firms and other foreign enterprises *may benefit* from accelerated diffusion of new technologies. There are other kinds of spillover (such as transfer of managerial practices, marketing techniques or production methods and so on) that may occur through a number of channels (Gorodnichenko et al., 2007, p. 3) or negative spillovers when foreign affiliates crowd out domestic firms in the product and labour market.

FDI spillovers may be intra-industry (horizontal) or inter-industry (vertical) spillovers (Smarzynska, 2004). In this chapter we focus on the *vertical* spillovers' flow in the direction of suppliers (backward linkages) and customers (forward linkages) of the firms in consideration. The direction of these spillovers regarding domestic firms is an important factor to be considered.

The analysis of vertical spillovers is quite a new field since the contribution of new research by Smarzynska (2004). One result that is especially interesting for our analysis concerning the three Mediterranean countries is in her conclusion in support of vertical spillovers, since the empirical study shows that greater productivity benefits are associated with the domestic market rather than the export-oriented foreign companies, as was interpreted from the previously available empirical literature (Smarzynska, 2004, p. 625). Of course, this conclusion for a transition economy is based on Lithuanian data. However, for the developing countries the empirical results are mixed or even negative depending on regional characteristics or country-specific factors. For the case of oil-exporting Arab countries, Sadik and Bolbol (2001) fail to support the productivity spillover effects from foreign firms to local firms. The negative effects of FDI on productivity are significant for Tunisia and Egypt. The reasons suggested by the authors are the lack of absorptive physical and the weak human and institutional capacity, which both tap the benefits from foreign firms.[3]

Since we cannot assume automatic positive spillovers, the final impact depends on the interaction among firms and the impact on the domestic economy. We may expect that spillovers from forward linkages are more beneficial to the host economy than those associated with backward linkages, since forward linkages are more conducive to the transfer of technology and marketing know-how or less costly intermediate inputs produced by foreign affiliates in upstream sectors (Reuber et al., 1973; Ostry and Gestrin, 1993, Smarzynska, 2004). These relationships improve the efficiency in the host economy with a proportional and concomitant creation of employment.

In other words, the higher demand from the upstream sectors will lead to an increase in sales, and the demand for labour in the foreign affiliates is likely to increase. Therefore, the size of the effects may depend on the growth of the domestic economy (which is the main motivation for market-seeking investments) as well as the market share of the firm within the host economy. Both factors have positive effects on sales.

Several studies in the past years have investigated the effects of inward FDI on employment in the Mediterranean region using aggregate data. We review here the country-specific evidence and the findings in support of or contradicting the above hypothesis. For example, regressing aggregate data for the period 1974–2004, Nada Massoud (2008) showed that, in Egypt,

FDI *did not exert a positive influence on employment*. The author justified the results on the basis that FDI is not an aggregate phenomenon, suggesting that its different components, such as greenfield FDI and mergers and acquisitions, may have different effects. Therefore FDI should not be treated as a homogeneous group or simply an additive aggregate component of the national 'saving gap'. Controlling for investor motivations, the author's estimates confirm that greenfield FDIs have a positive effect on employment when they interact with the stock of human capital and exports. Otherwise, their effect on the demand for labour is insignificant or negative, as for mergers and acquisitions (M&As),[4] which is consistent with the crowding-out effect they had on domestic investments and which explains their overall negative effect on growth. When M&As interact with the level of human capital, the size of the technology gap, the financial development and the trade openness have both a direct effect and interactive insignificant effects on the demand for labour.

Very few studies have investigated the determinants of total factor productivity (TFP) in Egypt and the effects of foreign capital inflows. Kamaly (2008) regressed TFP growth with different economic variables such as capital stock, quality of human capital or imported capital goods or FDI. The results show that FDI indicators have a non-significant coefficient. The empirical evidence is fairly scarce and to our knowledge there are no previous studies based on firm or plant level in Egypt.

More definitive results on the effects of FDI inflows focusing on developing countries are presented by Lemi (2004) who found *negative spillover* effects on the host countries' productivity.[5] On the other hand, productivity is enhanced by foreign portfolio investment, availability of skilled manpower, capital intensity and the number of bilateral investment treaties signed by host countries. Only United States (US) manufacturing FDI increases value-added of host countries. The presence of FDI from all sources and the number of US FDI firms and US manufacturing FDI also increase exports of host countries to the rest of the world.

For Morocco, Haddad and Harrison (1993) used a comprehensive dataset at firm level in their pioneering study on productivity and FDI spillovers. The authors found that there are no spillover effects on domestic firms. There are some differences in performance and productivity between domestically and foreign-owned firms, but the weighted means of labour productivity of foreign firms did not differ from that of domestic firms. For all sectors the output for workers was 70 per cent of what was achieved by domestic firms of a similar size.[6]

More recently, Bouoiyour (2004) wrote several articles using the Moroccan Ministry of Trade and Industry database, with data for 18 sectors in the 1987–96 period, reaching completely different results. Four indicators were provided: labour productivity (LP) of foreign and domestic firms (total added value per worker); the average wage of the foreign and domestic firms; the export propensity as a ratio between export and value-added; and, finally, the technology gap. The sample allows a comparison of foreign and domestic firms at the sectoral level. The regressions show that there are statistically significant differences and the labour productivity of foreign firms was 1.7 times more productive than domestic firms (in the 1990s).

Although the author finds that inward FDI can impact the productivity level of Morocco *positively*, the relationship is more complex. The relationship is not linear with the gap in absorptive capacity and the technological level of the sector.

There may be positive spillovers on productivity, but they occur in low-tech sectors (Bouoiyour, 2003), while in high-tech sectors foreign presence decreases indigenous labour productivity, thereby confirming that foreign presence does not affect local productivity equally in all industries.

Ghali and Rezgui (2008) used data on 674 Tunisian manufacturing firms derived from the national survey on enterprises realized by the National Institute of Statistics (INS) available over the whole period of 1997–2001. The authors found that the contribution of FDI in terms of externalities (spillover effects) was positive but, in many cases, they were counterbalanced by the firms' internal technical inefficiency. For the textile and clothing sectors, the main recipient of foreign capital, low productivity was explained by negative internal technical efficiency growth. The results are very important as they imply that, while inward FDI could bring technological progress, this contribution would unfortunately be counterbalanced by firms' internal technical inefficiencies. Similar results have been found in Chaffai and Plane (2006) and Plane (2009) where the total factor productivity model was regressed with several variables, including FDI. The coefficients of FDI are positive and statistically significant only with a fixed effects model; they are not significant when introducing other TFP determinants such as local demand and the comparative advantage of external markets. The FDI contribution increased in the period 1990–2002. This means that FDI alone is not sufficient to enhance a firm's technical efficiency and that internal factors specific to the firm and particularly its internal organization should be further analysed.

Also, the rationale of foreign investment may produce different results. For the region, resource-seeking and local market targeted investment are common types of FDI, so the efficiency and the welfare benefits, if negative, may be of interest from the host country's viewpoint.

The literature has also identified the higher productivity of foreign affiliates and the associated spillovers on the host economy, by the assumption that foreign enterprises in general tend to be larger than their domestic counterparts (Blomström and Kokko, 1996; Caves, 1996) and operate with higher capital-to-labour ratios and higher average labour productivity levels since they may benefit from economies of scale and a more efficient allocation of resources.

3.3 INWARD FDI PATTERNS

In this chapter we consider Morocco and Tunisia where the export argument has been used and confirmed by the rapid development of off-shore companies and export-oriented sectors such as clothing and electronics. For Egypt we did not find a similar approach, excluding the oil sector, since a large number of foreign investments can be classified as market seeking or resource oriented.

Morocco and Tunisia also started FDI attraction policies long before Egypt and have very different track records of internationalization. These three countries have also adopted different privatization strategies. Tunisia, and later Morocco, have been much more FDI proactive and friendly in providing generous tax incentives and legal protection than Egypt. Comparing FDI inflows with domestic investment (Figure 3.1), we notice that Tunisia and Egypt have made considerable use of foreign capital to finance their domestic investments, particularly over the last decade. The ratio increased to 50 per cent from an average 10 per cent in the 1990s.

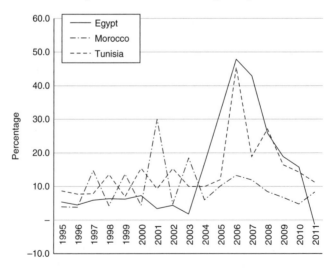

Figure 3.1 FDI inflows as a percentage of gross fixed capital formation

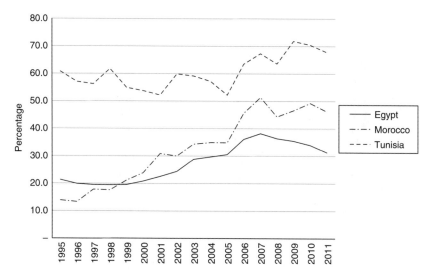

Figure 3.2   FDI inward stock as a percentage of gross domestic product

More recently, the ratio has returned to 10 per cent (or lower for Egypt), a level of financial integration that is still above the world average.

The second indicator is the ratio of total FDI stocks to GDP (Figure 3.2), which is an openness measure of the FDI regime and financial integration. We can see that FDIs have a stronger role in Tunisia and Morocco than in Egypt. Relative to economic size, Tunisia and Morocco are among the main destinations of FDI in the Mediterranean region, both in terms of recent FDI inflows and in terms of FDI stock. Egypt, which was among the first reformers, has shown a slower pattern and a critical decline as an FDI destination in more recent years.

Thus, based on these factual differences, one can argue that the effects of FDI on employment may differ between Egypt and Tunisia and Morocco, and studying the three countries can offer interesting results and policy implications.

3.4   DEFINITIONS AND DATA

3.4.1   Dataset

The dataset for the empirical investigation comprises the period 1995–2011 and combines information on foreign affiliates from different sources: reports from chambers of commerce, promotion agencies or registers

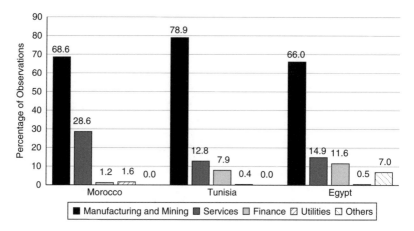

Notes: The figure shows the percentage of all firms in all available years in a given industry. Manufacturing and Mining refers to Manufacturing, Mining and Construction and corresponds to NACE Rev 1 sector classification: 11, 12, 13, 14, 15, 16, 17, 18, 19, 20, 21, 22, 23, 24, 25, 26, 27, 28, 29, 30, 31, 32, 33, 34, 35, 36, 37, 45; Services: 51, 52, 53, 55, 56, 58, 59, 60, 61, 62, 63, 64, 69, 70, 71, 72, 73, 74, 75, 77, 78, 79, 80, 81, 82, 85, 86, 87, 88, 90, 91, 92, 93, 94, 95, 96; Finance: 65, 66, 67; Utilities: 40, 41; Others, 1, 2, 5, 8 and unallocated.

Figure 3.3   Sectoral distribution of firms

or online information agencies (Zawya, Alacrastore etc.).[7] The retrieved information is organized at firm level to obtain the necessary variables. The advantage of combining information is in providing the researcher with a broader picture of the foreign affiliates' activities and character-istics, as well as offering basic quantitative and qualitative statistics that are currently missing. The DBMEDA data includes company sales and employment together with detailed information on location, sector, own-ership, type and year of investment, including information on the foreign owners.[8]

Figure 3.3 shows the average percentage of observations by sectoral categories. Manufacturing is the largest sector in the three countries, with more than 60 per cent of observations belonging to this sector. This sector is followed by the services sector with its diversified activities (12 to 28 per cent of observations in the three countries) and the highest foreign partici-pation in Morocco, while banking and finance represent 8 to 11 per cent in Tunisia and Egypt respectively.

Figure 3.4 shows that the ownership structure differs from country to country. The concentration of foreign affiliates with the highest level of control is in Morocco (48 per cent). Minority control, under 40 per cent, prevails in Morocco and Egypt (less than one fifth of the foreign firms of

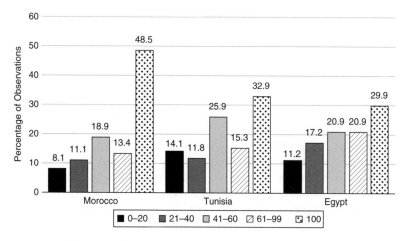

Figure 3.4   Ownership share of firms

the sample). The largest concentration on joint ventures (40–60 per cent of ownership) is in Tunisia, with one quarter of the foreign enterprises.

3.4.2   Variables

The financial variable used in the analysis is total sales in fiscal years 2008, 2009 and 2010, measured in US dollars. The nominal local currencies were converted into US dollars using the exchange rate at the end of each fiscal year.

In the analysis, productivity, as the dependent variable, is estimated as a ratio between sales and employment.[9] The productivity index is a proxy for the total factor productivity and is instrumental in measuring the improvements in pricing, marketing and other aspects of revenue generation that are crucial for corporate performance (Commander and Svejnar, 2007).[10] Although in the economic literature the productivity measurement is based on information about volume of outputs and inputs through a well-defined production function or through a value-added function, in only a few cases, usually for the listed companies, is there enough information available about the relevant variables. For our purposes we will interpret the productivity index in a rather unconventional way, consistent with the discussion in the introduction. The dependent variable will be related to the inward FDI spillovers and the other firm-specific characteristics if they affect, directly or indirectly, the sales and the employment of the foreign affiliates.

Among the explanatory variables the ownership of the foreign affiliate is defined and measured by the equity structure. DBMEDA contains information on owners, including country of residence, ownership stake, sector and type of investment. We adopted Dunning's (1995) approach of governance structure which distinguishes between hierarchical and cooperative or alliance modalities. Foreign subsidiaries were classified as fully-owned and joint-venture subsidiaries with majority or minority foreign equity. Acquisition was also included as a particular form of foreign participation and networking.

We assume that foreign firms enter the host countries as greenfield when they start new operational facilities from the ground up. Acquisitions are usually cross-border purchases of a local firm resulting in full control of the affiliate's local operations. Joint ventures are new entities or partial acquisition of local firms in which the foreign firms did not have full control of the affiliates' local operations. The three types of investment capture the extent of control a foreign company has over its affiliate's local operations and they will be used as control variables in the econometric specification.

The other independent variables are the spillovers as categorized by Hirschman (1958) as backward and forward linkages. FDI inflows have various types of impact on a domestic economy. One of the most important effects relates to 'vertical linkages', that is, the impact of FDI coming to a particular sector on inter-industry transactions. Vertical spillovers can be analysed through computing backward and forward linkages of sectors where the FDI is coming in.

Backward linkages refer to the impact of increases in the output of a downstream industry on its demand for inputs from upstream industries. For example, increased production of dairy products would boost demand for raw milk from local farmers, as in the case of Danone in Morocco and Tunisia. Forward linkages refer to increased production of an upstream industry due to requirements of downstream industries. Thus increased production of petroleum products would make their availability easy for downstream industries that use petroleum products as inputs.

The impact of both linkages is not uniform across downstream industries since their requirements of input from an upstream industry are not uniform. An industry may be strong in its backward linkage effects, forward linkage effects, both of these or neither of these.

One method to measure the spillover effects is to derive the parameters from the Input–Output Matrix (IOM) once adapted with the NACE Rev 1 sectors benefiting from FDI transactions. Considering the different level of disaggregation of the available IO tables for the three countries[11] and the need to have a larger sectoral and harmonized coverage of the input–output linkages and the corresponding transactions, we used the

Indian classification of 130 sectors (NCAER, 2009). From the transaction matrix we can derive two indicators using the Hirschman–Rasmussen Index method to compute backward and forward linkages. The backward linkage (BL) index refers to the demand–pull concept and is the ratio of the total demand of intermediate inputs over the total output of each sector, while the forward linkage (FL) index refers to the supply–push concept and is the proportion of intermediate supply of products on total output of each sector.

The linkage effects have been computed for all 130 IO sectors corresponding to the NACE classification of the foreign companies of the sample.

Sectors have then been identified under four different categories:

(a)   KS: key sectors with strong backward and forward linkages (BLj > 1 and FLi > 1);
(b)   BW: strong backward linkages (BLj > 1 and FLi < 1);
(c)   FW: strong forward linkages (BLj < 1 and FLi > 1); and
(d)   NK: non-key sectors with weak backward and forward linkages (BLj < 1 and FLi < 1).

3.4.3   Descriptive Statistics

A description of the foreign affiliates and the country of origin of the investors are listed in Table 3.1, which reveals a larger concentration in Morocco, followed by Tunisia, compared to Egypt, which is the largest economy of the region. This is partly due to the availability of registers of enterprises operating in Morocco and Tunisia, whereas in Egypt those administrative data collected by the promotion agencies or local authorities remain confidential and therefore unpublished or restricted in access by the general public.

Table 3.2 describes differences between employment sales and productivity levels of the firms in the three countries included in this study. Table 3A.1 in the Appendix provides more detailed descriptive statistics on all variables used in our analysis for the main sample and by country.

The average size of the foreign affiliates in Egypt is more than 1000 employees, double the size of those located in Morocco and Tunisia. The diversity in size is not reflected in the productivity index, that is, converging to a narrow range. However, we still observe higher values of productivity in foreign firms in Egypt than in Tunisia and Morocco. In 2010, the productivity index in Egypt is on average US$408 000, while in Morocco the same figure amounted to US$381 000, that is, a difference of less than 10 per cent. The productivity index in Tunisia falls between the two.

Table 3.1   Number of foreign enterprises in the sample

	Morocco	Tunisia	Egypt	Total sample	Morocco (%)	Tunisia (%)	Egypt (%)
Arab countries	16	27	67	110	3.4	10.5	33.8
United States	26	17	29	72	5.5	6.6	14.6
European Union 15	243	204	71	518	51.5	79.1	35.9
Others	187	10	31	228	39.6	3.9	15.7
Total foreign affiliates	**472**	**258**	**198**	**928**	**100.0**	**100.0**	**100.0**

The ranking of the foreign affiliates according to the origin of the investor (Table 3.2) shows that Arab-controlled firms have the highest average level of employment, followed by European and North American firms. Arab-controlled affiliates also have the highest level of sales and consequently the highest level of productivity index. American affiliates in the sample are smaller than European ones, on average, but they have larger sales per unit.

From Table 3A.1 we notice that the highest productivity index is to be found in Arab-controlled affiliates: US$476 000 in 2010. North American and EU15 firms are lower, US$390 000 and US$429 000 respectively.

The mode of entry has important implications for the operational behaviour and the integration abilities of the foreign affiliates. We notice that the acquisitions are directed to large firms in both employment and sales. Instead, according to common wisdom, greenfield investments are comparatively smaller than joint ventures, which are proposed as an efficient solution for managing and mitigating coordination problems and for governing relationships and transactional costs.

The differences in productivity indices in the three host countries are also large across the sectors. Table 3A.1 indicates that the productivity index in the service sector and in banking and finance surpasses the level of manufacturing: in 2010 the productivity of services was US$710 000 against US$298 000 in manufacturing. This is partly due to the larger value of sales compared to the employment created.

Among the three types of investment, greenfield projects have the smallest size in terms of employment and sales, while acquisition projects have the highest level of size and sales. In terms of productivity, joint ventures have the highest level compared to greenfield and acquisition projects.

As far the spillover direction is concerned, the distribution of the four categories is presented in Table 3.3. The largest number of foreign affiliates

Table 3.2   Descriptive statistics

	Obs.	Mean	Median	Std. Dev.
Overall				
empl	890	606.395	200.000	1314.580
sale10	850	125.492	26.200	409.489
sale09	519	229.023	61.650	629.014
prod10	802	0.389	0.097	1.043
prod09	466	0.634	0.230	1.391
Morocco				
empl	461	500.436	160.000	1059.291
sale10	435	102.343	21.940	347.266
sale09	244	185.871	56.720	459.538
prod10	135	0.381	0.114	0.931
prod09	233	0.555	0.237	1.134
Tunisia				
empl	254	488.161	200.000	974.784
sale10	246	71.419	18.135	148.321
sale09	135	189.895	48.200	590.010
prod10	242	0.394	0.097	1.307
prod09	123	0.747	0.202	1.923
Egypt				
empl	175	1057.131	455.000	2055.903
sale10	169	263.788	63.930	692.000
sale09	140	341.959	101.215	867.238
prod10	145	0.408	0.092	0.843
prod09	110	0.673	0.271	1.162

Table 3.3   Number of enterprises and characteristics of spillovers

	Morocco	Tunisia	Egypt	Morocco (%)	Tunisia (%)	Egypt (%)
KS: Key sectors	75	41	31	16.4	16.1	19.3
BW: Backward linkages	249	164	91	54.6	64.6	56.5
FW: Forward linkages	88	43	32	19.3	16.9	19.9
NK: Non-key sectors	44	6	7	9.6	2.4	4.3
Total	**456**	**254**	**161**			

operates in sectors classified with strong backward linkages in all three host countries.

3.5   MODELLING THE SPILLOVER EFFECTS

The literature shows that vertical spillovers are more likely to be positive than horizontal spillovers. We tested the positive sign hypothesis for backward and forward spillovers under various specifications. The independent variables are constructed from input–output tables at the industry level, as specified earlier, due to the lack of direct firm-specific measures of the three countries.

We estimate the following baseline regression with pooled data for the three countries:

$$\text{lprod10} = \alpha_1 \text{backward} + \alpha_2 \text{forward} + \alpha_3 \text{source} + \alpha_4 \text{sector} + \alpha_5 \text{mode}$$

where

lprod10 is the logarithm of the productivity index; *backward* and *forward* for backward and forward linkages, the two industry-specific variables.

The dummy variables identify other control variables as origin of the foreign investor, the sector of activity and the mode of entry.

We perform the analyses by using four different levels of aggregation according to the host country, the sector, the mode of entry, and the source of investment. Based on the different theoretical approaches and their predictions, we try to derive hypotheses for the effect of spillovers on firm performance as measured by the productivity index.

Based on our definition of the dependent variable it is clear that there are two forces driving the effect in opposite directions. On the one hand, the interdependence with domestic firms can benefit the foreign affiliate with a more diverse spectrum of possibilities to externalize some phases of the production process, creating alliances and relationships and enlarging the dimension of the firm, which in turn fosters employment.

We may think also about the growth of spatial clusters of economic activities that offer external or agglomerative economies to firms located within the cluster, as in the case of the Egyptian industrial cities or in Morocco (Casablanca and Tangier) and Tunisia (the coastal regions from Tunis to Sfax).

We would expect the spillovers, in particular the backward ones, to generate more inter-firm transactions and then more employment in manufacturing sectors and more firms and growth. We would also expect that the sales/employment ratio, which we defined as productivity, will be lower because of the workforce diversification. The empirical evidence is the higher average values of the foreign affiliates in the service sector dealing with wholesale and distribution activities compared to the average productivity in the manufacturing sector.

On the other hand, the vertical spillovers may also increase the sales of the foreign affiliates because of higher demand from the upstream sectors. We may think of the interdependence of the construction sector with tourism activities or the distribution and services in the telecommunication sector or in the refining and distribution of petroleum products. Foreign affiliates can respond with diversification and the introduction of more products or services in order to increase their sales. We would expect that these policies are more likely to materialize in the service sector with well-organized structures and practices, such as the distribution of imported products, with a minor effect on local employment and lower productivity.

The general criteria that we apply in drawing conclusions with regard to the effect of FDI on productivity is that, to reach a conclusion on a relation (whether positive or negative), all coefficients of the variable have to be statistically significant with at least a 90 per cent degree of confidence and also all coefficients have to be of the same direction (all positive or negative).

If some of the coefficients of the same variable in the same regression vary across the models between positive and negative, or if some or even one of the coefficients of the same variable are not statistically significant, then we do not rely on the results of the regression in drawing a robust conclusion and we assume that the relation is ambiguous.

3.6　RESULTS

The results of the overall specification are presented in Table 3.4, column 1, whereas results using more disaggregated categories are presented in the other columns identified by country. The columns show the effects of the spillovers on the productivity index. The coefficient of backward linkages is negative for all host countries, whereas the forward linkages are significantly positive for Morocco and Tunisia with the exception of Egypt.

To make sure that the coefficients attached to the spillovers do not reflect effects coming from the sector composition or other firm characteristics, we add sector and firm ownership dummies to the most full model specification. Adding those controls changes the magnitude of the spillover effects but leaves their sign unchanged. Non-significant coefficients are not presented.

Table 3.4   Regression results of the estimated model: by host country

	Overall		Morocco					Tunisia	
BL	−2.217***	−2.267***				−2.634***	−2.723***	−2.233***	
	(0.063)	(0.082)				(0.756)	(0.130)	(0.115)	
FL	0.108***	0.169***	0.108***	0.181**	0.091	0.834***	−0.506***	0.572	0.100
	(0.034)	(0.038)	(0.044)	(0.073)	(0.115)	(0.182)	(0.157)	(0.069)	(0.081)
BL*ue15			−1.796***						−2.274***
			(0.094)						(0.128)
BL*noam				−1.890***					
				(0.240)					
BL*arab					−1.848***				
					(0.444)				
manuf						−0.182			
						(0.896)			
BL*FL							1.069***		
							(0.240)		
R2 adj	0.6720	0.6885	0.6622	0.6994	0.5525	0.7281	0.7023	0.6908	0.6964
F	812.22	454.18	222.55	32.41	10.26	284.91	323.37	271.27	221.16
	0.0000	0.0000	0.0000	0.0000	0.0021	0.0000	0.0000	0.0000	0.0000
n obs	792	410	226	27	15	318	410	242	192

Notes:
The dependent variable in all estimations is the productivity index, defined as total sales in 2010/employment.
Estimated standard errors are shown in parentheses.
Significance levels: t-statistics at 1% confidence (***), 5% confidence (**) or 10% confidence (*).

The two variables identifying the vertical spillovers are statistically valid and largely confirmed by the F-statistics reported in the notes below Table 3.4. We find again a negative effect of backward linkages and a positive effect of forward linkages.

More specifically, an increase in backward linkages implies a reduction of the productivity index, that is, a faster growth in domestic employment than in sales. The coefficient of the forward linkages is significantly positive in the overall specification but it turns out to be negative when introducing interaction terms or insignificant in the more disaggregated level for host countries, as in the case of Egypt. The results are consistent with prior work on foreign direct investment, where empirical evidence was found for intra-industry and backward spillovers (Smarzynska, 2004; Blalock, 2001; Kugler, 2006).[12] This finding may also explain the particular characteristic of inward FDI to developing countries, which mostly targets downstream industries.

From the source of investors, the North American affiliates have the highest effect on productivity in Tunisia, while for European firms the coefficients are statistically significant but lower, in particular in Egypt. In

	Tunisia					Egypt				
		−3.013***	−2.631***	−1.800***					−2.846*	−1.717***
		(1.048)	(0.193)	(0.189)					(1.591)	(0.258)
−0.528**	0.162	0.438**	−0.595**	−0.239***	−0.293*	0.724	−0.277*	−0.303	−0.0973	
(0.227)	(0.140)	(0.205)	(0.263)	(0.128)	(0.174)	(0.579)	(0.174)	(0.300)	(0.325)	
					−1.254***					
					(0.304)					
−1.419***						−2.981***				
(0.440)						(0.556)				
	−2.711***						−1.858***			
	(0.352)						(0.280)			
		.618						1.337		
		(1.327)						(1.848)		
			0.999***							−.206
			(0.390)							(0.432)
0.6692	0.769	0.7198	0.6978	0.6127	0.4972	0.6845	0.7283	0.5940	0.6105	
17.18	42.60	177.41	187.23	111.72	21.75	29.21	58.63	60.49	74.14	
0.0000	0.0000	0.0000	0.0000	0.0000	0.0000	0.0000	0.0000	0.0000	0.0000	
16	25	206	242	140	46	26	43	122	140	

the case of Morocco we find less diversity in the values of the coefficients, which might be explained by the smaller size of the foreign affiliates and better competitive conditions for operation.

In the next steps we test the different hypotheses considering the sectors (Table 3.5) and the mode of entry of the foreign investors (Table 3.6). We start with the investigation of whether the productivity index can be influenced by the activity of the sector. For instance, more integrated activities as in the manufacturing sector or in firms with higher capacity to decentralize operations might have a greater effect on local employment. Furthermore, there might be complementarities among different activities and operations through knowledge transfers which may generate intra-firm spillover effects.

The test of the hypothesis is presented in Table 3.5 with the interaction of the contribution of European firms. Again we find a negative and significant coefficient for the backward linkages effects and a positive effect of forward linkages. Surprisingly we did not find large differences in the values, in particular between manufacturing and service sectors. More diversified instead are the positive coefficient for the forward linkages, with the higher value for utilities and the lowest for services. For the banking sectors we find a negative value, but the coefficient is not statistically significant. This suggests that the effects on productivity are more sensitive to the country environment than the sectoral specificities.

As regards the mode of entry (Table 3.6), we notice a difference in the

Table 3.5   Regression results of the estimated model: by sector

	Overall	Manufacturing		Services		Banking		Utilities	
BL	-2.217***	-2.468***		-2.372***		-2.659***		-2.122***	
	(0.063)	(0.109)		(0.262)		(1.127)		(0.346)	
FL	0.109***	0.449***	0.379***	0.113***	0.114**	-0.059	-0.460***	0.845***	0.898***
	(0.033)	(0.121)	(0.150)	(0.043)	(0.051)	(0.217)	(0.105)	(0.142)	(0.174)
BL*ue15			-2.178***		-2.362***		-1.240**		-2.146***
			(0.133)		(0.294)		(0.498)		(0.372)
R2 adj	0.6720	0.6977	0.6756	0.4928	0.5206	0.6741	0.9614	0.8522	0.8502
F	812.22	745.16	389.35	54.93	41.72	29.95	125.59	21.19	18.03
	0.0000	0.0000	0.0000	0.0000	0.0000	0.0000	0.0000	0.0036	0.0100
n obs	792	645	373	111	75	28	10	7	6

Notes:
The dependent variable in all estimations is the productivity index, defined as total sales in 2010/employment.
Estimated standard errors are shown in parentheses.
Significance levels: t-statistics at 1% confidence (***), 5% confidence (**) or 10% confidence (*).

Table 3.6 Regression results of the estimated model: by mode of entry

	Overall		Acquisition				Greenfield			Joint venture			
BL	-2.217*** (0.063)	-1.796*** (0.127)				-2.416*** (0.886)				-2.156*** (0.124)			
FL	0.109*** (0.033)	0.122* (0.073)	0.028 (0.082)	0.297* (0.161)	1.955*** (0.271)	0.116*** (0.048)	0.088 (0.065)	0.024 (0.131)	1.990*** (0.180)	0.098* (0.059)	0.0735 (0.065)	-0.037 (0.119)	1.169*** (0.226)
BL*ue15			-1.515*** (0.140)				-2.259*** (0.109)				-1.672*** (0.156)		
BL*arab				-2.562*** (0.305)				-1.943*** (0.366)				-2.345*** (0.290)	
BL*FL					-3.210*** (0.343)				-3.395*** (0.224)				-2.157*** (0.281)
R2 adj	0.6720	0.6592	0.6455	0.7542	0.4867	0.7040	0.7023	0.6222	0.4657	0.6436	0.5623	0.7912	0.3354
F	812.22	133.48	85.68	43.96	488.46	65.95	291.15	19.12	179.70	202.39	72.30	59.72	57.28
	0.0000	0.0000	0.0000	0.0000	0.0000	0.0000	0.0000	0.0000	0.0000	0.0000	0.0000	0.0000	0.0000
n obs	792	137	93	28	137	410	246	22	410	223	111	31	223

Notes:
The dependent variable in all estimations is the productivity index, defined as total sales in 2010/employment.
Estimated standard errors are shown in parentheses.
Significance levels: t-statistics at 1% confidence (***), 5% confidence (**) or 10% confidence (*).

effects on productivity index, with the largest impact deriving from greenfield investment, as evidenced by the empirical literature in recent years, while the lowest coefficients are for acquisitions. This may suggest that competitive conditions have a positive impact on productivity. The results reported in Table 3.6 indicate that the productivity index of the foreign firms is higher if they have full control over the affiliates' operations, as in the case of greenfield investments.[13] We suggested above that this might reflect the foreign firms' preference for full control before committing significant resources for growth in a foreign subsidiary in the host countries. The statistical evidence is particularly significant for the European and the Arab investors. By definition, greenfield investments also create new employment, so limiting the ability of foreign enterprises to operate wholly owned subsidiaries in these countries may be counterproductive.

Table 3.7 displays the results of the estimation for the origin of investors. Overall, we confirm the above results on the significant coefficient for the backward linkages originating from all major groups of investors. When comparing the magnitude of the coefficients, investments originating from Arab countries and North America have greater effects than the coefficient associated with the European investors. We also find that European investors have positive and significant forward linkages.

3.7   CONCLUSION

Using a comprehensive dataset of foreign subsidiaries in three southern Mediterranean countries, this chapter investigated the effect of the vertical spillovers on the productivity index, defined as sales/employment.

We provide a number of findings that may concretely address the direction of the Euro–Mediterranean partnership towards employment goals.

Using the coefficients of the input–output table at the maximum differentiation (130 sectors), we define the multipliers for the backward and the forward linkages. Controlling for the firm-specific characteristics (source of investor, sector), we find stronger and significant effects from the backward linkages on the productivity index as an indirect measure of employment.

In contrast, diversity in the country of origin of the firms brings mixed results – with strong effects of European investors and greenfield projects in Tunisia, American investors in Egypt and Arab investors through acquisitions in the overall region after controlling for the interactions. Minor differentiations have been found in Morocco.

Thus our empirical analysis clearly provides evidence of the positive contribution of foreign capital.

Table 3.7 *Regression results of the estimated model: by origin of investor*

	Overall	ue15		noam		arab	
BL	-2.217***	-1.977***	-2.282***	-2156199	-2.852***	-2.212***	-2.593***
	(0.063)	(0.077)	(0.135)	(0.215)	(0.4995)	(0.188)	(0.188)
FL	0.109***	0.086**	-0.390**	0.1086461	-0.958	0.041	-0.476
	(0.033)	(0.041)	(0.178)	(0.096)	(0.697)	(0.079)	(0.079)
BL*FL			0.744***		1.727		0.859
			(0.271)		(1.119)		(0.663)
R2 adj	0.6720	0.6506	0.6555	0.6364	0.6438	0.7088	0.7112
F	812.22	433.06	295.30	61.39	42.57	102.00	69.13
	0.0000	0.0000	0.0000	0.0000	0.0000	0.0000	0.0000
n obs	792	464	464	69	69	83	83

Notes:
The dependent variable is the ratio sale/employment.
t-values are not reported; instead we used stars to show the significance of the t-statistics at 1% confidence (***), 5% confidence (**) or 10% confidence (*).

Further research is required in order to better understand how foreign subsidiaries interact with domestic firms in host countries, especially when the motivations are the consolidation in the host market instead of being export or re-export oriented. More detailed firm data are required for the definition and estimation of the production function and the value-added contribution.

The short- and long-term strategic orientations of investors also have important implications on the effects of productivity and employment. The created spillovers, or more generally the externalities, do not benefit all sectors equally. The effects are specific and localized; they are technically driven by the interdependence and the transactions among firms. In part they depend on the absorptive capacity of the domestic firms, but this is only part of the picture of economic interdependence.

Therefore it seems preferable to design the attraction policies and incentives to more targeted strategies geared towards industries or clusters of firms that are likely to generate positive externalities and to foster technology transfers.

NOTES

1. While policies that level the playing field for foreign firms operating inside the host country are prerequisites for capital inflow seeking higher rate of returns, the policies that subsidize foreign investors through lower tax rates and tolerant environmental requirements can only be justified if positive externalities on domestic firms are created with the inflow of FDI (Moran, 2007).
2. According to GAFI, up to 1997 the approved projects have generated 592 000 new jobs, one third of them in the eight new industrial cities in the desert and one third in upper Egypt. In 1997 the average size of the projects in the new cities was 172 jobs for projects with an average cost of LE 149 290 (US$44 063) per job. In the industrial zone the size of the projects is smaller, with an average cost of LE 27 174 (US$8021). Most recent figures from the IDA estimate 1 822 000 new jobs created by 29 576 factories, with an average cost of LE 191 040 (US$33 224).
3. Resource-oriented FDI, and in particular those in the oil sector, are expected to have a more limited favourable impact on growth due to restricted linkages with the rest of the economy and lower technology transfer. See also the recent contribution of Herrera et al. (2010).
4. When using aggregate data we miss an important distinction in the transmission channel effects. In fact, the effects on employment can be both direct and indirect. Greenfield investments generate new employment and this is a direct effect; however, FDI also creates jobs through forward and backward linkages with domestic firms, and that is the indirect effect on employment in the host country.
5. The flows of FDI are disaggregated at industry level during the period 1989–98. In the sample of 26 countries, mainly Asian and Latin American, data are available only for Egypt and Morocco.
6. See Haddad and Harrison (1993, Table 2, p. 58).
7. http://www.kerix.net/index; http://www.u-web2.com/sites/accueilulysoft/Lists/Annuaire_ Ulysoft/, Annuaire des Entreprises Marocaines; http://www.tunisieindustrie.nat.tn/fr/

Portal de l'Industrie Tunisienne of the Agence de Promotion de l'Industrie et de l'Innovation of the Ministry of Industry; http://www.securities.com/Public/company-profile/EG/ and the websites of the companies which have made available their balance sheets and financial information; http://investing.businessweek.com/research/stocks/; http://www.wvb.com/corporations/list/index/company and http://www.gulfbase.com/ http://www.africanmanager.com/site_eng/ important databases containing listed companies in the Mediterranean and Gulf region; http://maroc1000.net/Ordre-alphabtique; http://www.les500.com/ for the Moroccan enterprises; http://www.alacrastore.com/; http://www.zawya.com/.

8. The database contains a total of 972 firms over the period 1980–2012. The initial number of enterprises in the panel was more than 5000; over 75 per cent of firms were excluded for lack of data on revenues and employment, while having a rich set of information related to the investor origin, the year of investment, the type of investment and the sector of activity.

9. The sales/employment ratio has been used by Gorodnichenko et al. (2007) as a measure of revenue efficiency to assess the extent and nature of spillovers in 27 emerging economies.

10. 'The reason we use this broader measure is that the performance of different types of firms may vary for a number of reasons, including differences in their efficiency of generating output from inputs, ability to charge high prices due to diverse product quality or marketing, intangible assets and the cost of capital, location in highly competitive industries, efficiency of vertical integration, and extent of outsourcing' (Commander and Svejnar, 2007, p. 9).

11. We use the most detailed IO table of India with 137 sectors, since the most recent IO table for Egypt for the year 2008–2009 prepared by CAPMAS has only ten supply sectors and 27 sectors for uses (http://www.capmas.gov.eg/pages_ar.aspx?pageid=1475). Similar problems have been found for Tunisia and Morocco. The Tunisian IO table has 18 sectors, while the Moroccan table has 32 sectors. There exists one input–output table (IOT) for Morocco for 1990 which includes 133 industry sectors (Bussolo and Roland-Holst, 1993).

12. These studies could not find any evidence for the existence of forward spillover effects, while reporting significant productivity-enhancing backward spillovers to local upstream firms. However, Belderbos and Van Roy (2011) find negative signs for backward and forward spillovers depending on the international trade relations of the firms, in particular the empirical analysis shows that the exporters have low backward linkages and importers have low forward linkages. Firms with an international profile are likely to be less dependent on the domestic economy and consequently may benefit less from local knowledge spillovers, while exposure to international markets may instead lead to international knowledge spillovers. Therefore, further analysis restricting attention to firms that do not engage in import or export activities does show a positive and significant effect of forward spillovers. This suggests that the mixed findings in prior studies on forward spillovers may be due to the failure to take into account alternative ways to productivity growth through input sourcing on international markets.

13. Similar conclusions on the ability of greenfield investments to increase employment are in Bhaumik et al. (2004).

REFERENCES

Aitken, B.J. and A.E. Harrison (1999), 'Do domestic firms benefit from direct foreign investment? Evidence from Venezuela', *American Economic Review*, **89**(3), 605–18.
Belderbos, R. and V. Van Roy (2011), 'Productivity spillovers from foreign affiliates

and domestic firm internationalization: firm-level evidence for Belgium', Katholieke Universiteit Leuven, UNU-MERIT and Universiteit Maastricht, paper presented at the DIME Final Conference, 6–8 April, Maastricht.

Bhaumik, S.K., S. Estrin and K. Meyer (2004), 'Determinants of employment growth at MNEs: evidence from Egypt, India, South Africa and Vietnam', IZA Discussion Paper no. 1272, August.

Blalock, G. (2001), 'Technology from foreign direct investment: strategic transfer through supply chains', mimeo, University of California, Berkeley.

Bouoiyour, J. (2004), 'Foreign direct investment in Morocco', in S. Perrin and F. Sachwald (eds), *Foreign Direct Investment in Developing Countries: Leveraging the Role of Multinationals*, Agence Française de Développement and Institut Français des Relations Internationales, pp. 149–67.

Bouoiyour, J. (2003), 'Productivity and spillovers diffusion in Morocco: is there a difference between high tech and low tech sectors?', WP-CATT, University of Pau.

Bussolo, M. and D. Roland-Holst (1993), 'A detailed input–output table for Morocco 1990', OECD Development Centre, Working Paper no. 90, November 1993.

Caves, R.E. (1996), *Multinational Enterprise and Economic Analysis*, Cambridge: Cambridge University Press.

Blomström, M. and A. Kokko (1996), 'The impact of foreign direct investment on host countries: a review of the empirical evidence', Policy Research Working Paper no. 1745, Washington, DC: World Bank.

Chaffai, M. and P. Plane (2006), 'Total Factor Productivity within the Tunisian manufacturing sectors and international convergence with OECD countries', working paper in Etudes et Documents series, E.2006.22, CERDI, Auvergne.

Commander, S. and J. Svejnar (2007), 'Do institutions, ownership, exporting and competition explain firm performance? Evidence from 26 transition countries', IZA DP no. 2637, February, Bonn, Germany.

Dunning, J.H. (1995), 'Reappraising the eclectic paradigm in an age of alliance capitalism', *Journal of International Business Studies*, **26**(3), 461–91.

FEMISE (2010), 'The Euro–Mediterranean Partnership at the Crossroads', FEMISE Report on Euro–Mediterranean Partnership, Marseille.

Ghali, S. and S. Rezgui (2008), 'FDI contribution to technical efficiency in the Tunisian manufacturing sector', ERF Working Paper no. 421, August.

Gorodnichenko, Y., J. Svejnar and K. Terrell (2007), 'When does FDI have positive spillovers? Evidence from 17 emerging market economies', IZA DP no. 3079, September, Bonn.

Haddad, M. and A. Harrison (1993), 'Are there positive spillovers from direct foreign investment? Evidence from panel data for Morocco', *Journal of Development Economics*, **42**(1), 51–74.

Herrera, S., H. Selim, H. Youssef and C. Zaki (2010), 'Egypt beyond the crisis: medium-term challenges for sustained growth', World Bank, Policy Research Working Paper no. 5451, October, p. 11.

Hirschman, A. (1958), *The Strategy of Economic Development*, New Haven, CT: Yale University Press.

Kamaly, A. (2008), 'Modeling total factor productivity in developing countries: the case of Egypt', The American University in Cairo, unpublished.

Kugler, M. (2006), 'Spillovers from foreign direct investment: within or between industries?', *Journal of Development Economics*, **80**, 444–77.

Lemi, A. (2004), 'Foreign direct investment, host country productivity and export:

the case of US and Japanese multinational affiliates', *Journal of Economic Development*, **29**(1), 163–87.

Massoud, N. (2008), 'Assessing the employment effect of FDI inflows to Egypt: does the mode of entry matter?', paper presented at the International Conference on 'The Unemployment Crisis in the Arab Countries', 17–18 March, Cairo.

Moran, T. (2007), 'How to investigate the impact of foreign direct investment on development, and use the results to guide policy', in M.S. Collins (ed.), *Brookings Trade Forum 2007: Foreign Direct Investment*, Washington, DC: Brookings Institution, pp. 1–60.

National Council of Applied Economic Research (2009), *FDI in India and its Growth Linkages*, August, New Delhi, National Council of Applied Economic Research.

Ostry, S. and M. Gestrin (1993), 'Foreign direct investment, technology transfer and innovation-network model', *Journal of Transnational Corporations*, **2**(3), 7–30.

Plane, P. (2009), 'Compétitivité prix et efficacité productive dans les secteurs manufacturiers des pays d'Afrique du Nord et du Moyen Orient – Rapport de Synthèse', Research FEM31-19R, January.

Reuber, G., H. Crookell, M. Emerson and G. Callais-Homonno (1993), *Private Foreign Investment in Development*, Oxford: Clarendon Press.

Sadik, A. and A. Bolbol (2001), 'Capital flows, FDI, and technology spillovers: evidence from Arab countries', *World Development*, **29**(12), 2111–25.

Smarzynska, B. (2004), 'Does foreign direct investment increase the productivity of domestic firms? In search of spillovers through backward linkages', *American Economic Review*, **94**(3), 605–27.

UNCTAD (1999), 'Investment policy review Egypt', New York and Geneva: United Nations.

APPENDIX

Table 3A.1   Descriptive statistics

cod_host	Empl. (unit)	sale10 (million US$)	sale09 (million US$)	prod10 (million US$)	prod09 (million US$)
Total					
Mean	606.7326	125.4926	229.0226	0.3899	0.6341
Median	200.0000	26.2000	61.6474	0.0979	0.2308
Sd	1315.0530	409.4891	629.0146	1.0438	1.3913
Arab					
Mean	874.2083	193.5574	264.3809	0.4762	0.6402
Median	409.5000	45.0500	60.9000	0.0960	0.1320
Sd	1342.3490	549.0136	602.8663	1.9031	2.4015
NoAm					
Mean	662.9583	105.2608	160.5731	0.3901	0.5244
Median	197.5000	37.2600	68.3000	0.1463	0.2655
Sd	1230.4080	239.5193	299.8460	0.7454	0.7782
EU15					
Mean	675.1098	145.9580	250.6123	0.4292	0.6382
Median	217.0000	28.7950	61.8400	0.1238	0.2293
Sd	1509.3400	463.6372	715.7089	0.9919	1.2289
Acquisition					
Mean	1021.7050	321.5507	474.8198	0.5459	0.7496
Median	419.0000	78.8900	104.6000	0.1610	0.2569
Sd	1625.4090	764.1442	995.9841	1.6808	2.0979
Greenfield					
Mean	440.2417	56.9891	108.5229	0.2966	0.5343
Median	160.0000	16.4400	40.2000	0.0847	0.2273
Sd	779.2141	201.6593	280.6342	0.6651	0.8753
Joint venture					
Mean	666.7197	124.5928	221.6166	0.4372	0.6658
Median	180.0000	30.3100	72.2500	0.0985	0.2119
Sd	1704.5900	324.1775	597.6199	1.0849	1.3802
Bank and finance					
Mean	1100.465	185.1117	290.3394	0.7779	0.8162
Median	760.0000	93.2000	125.8700	0.1075	0.1539
Sd	1234.8640	395.6381	489.3597	3.1887	3.0376
Manufacturing					
Mean	536.4787	102.5876	185.1773	0.2982	0.4592
Median	200.0000	20.8900	56.8950	0.0865	0.2029
Sd	1193.647	399.1316	567.6976	0.6678	0.7667

Table 3A.1   (continued)

cod_host	Empl. (unit)	sale10 (million US$)	sale09 (million US$)	prod10 (million US$)	prod09 (million US$)
Services					
Mean	652.314	217.8297	314.1953	0.7099	0.9504
Median	138.0000	42.5450	63.8500	0.3338	0.4348
Sd	1710.2880	463.2033	806.6346	1.1784	1.4425
Utilities					
Mean	1140.75004	278.0778	306.2029	2.3631	2.6631
Median	658.5000	254.5000	203.6500	0.1999	1.3410
Sd	1265.3720	230.9721	272.9802	4.1929	4.3067

4. International trade, female labor and entrepreneurship in MENA countries

Silvio Contessi, Francesca de Nicola and Li Li

4.1 INTRODUCTION

The relationship between trade and gender has recently emerged as an important theme in the international economics and development literature. The United Nations' Millennium Development Goal No. 3 is to promote gender equality and empower women, a broad goal that can cover many areas of economic and non-economic activity. The entire World Development Report 2012 (WDR) (World Bank, 2011) is devoted to the study of gender issues, and its Chapter 5 focuses specifically on the relationship between trade and gender, highlighting the main conceptual issues and presenting several interesting research avenues. In fact, this explicit effort is reinforcing research on gender at both the macroeconomic and microeconomic levels.

At the macroeconomic level, the evidence suggests that female labor participation decisions have important aggregate consequences and are correlated with certain forms of technological change that may affect women differently from men, as women tend to have a comparative disadvantage in brawn-intensive activity independent of the fact that the distribution of 'brain' skills and abilities is the same for men and women. At the microeconomic level, there is a better understanding of some of the mechanisms that 'empower' women, for example, within the household in both advanced economies and in a development context. In this chapter, we attempt to analyze the relationship between international trade and gender – defined here as both female labor participation and female ownership and entrepreneurship – in the Mediterranean and North African (MENA) countries. This region is interesting in a cross-country perspective because international comparisons of *de jure* indicators suggest that MENA countries are characterized by more marked gender discrimination in female labor participation and entrepreneurial activity than most other regions of the world.

To this end, we adopt a factor-endowment perspective and construct measures of female labor use (or intensity) at the country/industry pair level and match them to manufacturing trade data to determine the female labor content of exports. Next, we identify country/industry pairs characterized by comparative advantage in female labor for five countries for which aggregated data are available. We then compare our classification of country/industry pairs based on comparative advantage in aggregate data with a similar classification based on firm-level data from the World Bank Enterprise Surveys (WBESs). We find that the two sets of data track each other quite well, which allows us (and potentially other researchers using the same procedure) to exploit the firm-level data for other MENA countries for which aggregate data are not available.

Finally, we study whether exposure to trade in comparative advantage country/industry pairs empowers women by increasing the probability of female entrepreneurship and ownership in firms belonging to country/industry pairs with comparative advantage. We find some support for the (theory-free) hypothesis that comparative advantage empowers female entrepreneurs in country/industry pairs with comparative advantage.

The chapter is structured as follows. The next section provides an overview of female labor market and entrepreneurship in MENA countries. We then discuss the relevant literatures and detail the data used in the empirical analysis detailed in the following sections. Finally, we provide our conclusions.

4.2   AN OVERVIEW OF FEMALE LABOR MARKETS AND ENTREPRENEURSHIP IN MENA COUNTRIES

In addition to anecdotal evidence, MENA countries stand out in international comparisons of *de jure* indicators as being characterized by more marked gender discrimination in female labor participation and entrepreneurial activity than other countries. This position is clearly represented in Figure 4.1, which shows a summary measure of female discrimination by groups of countries based on the 2010 Women, Business and the Law (WBL) dataset of the World Bank.[1]

The WBL is a cross-country dataset reporting information on whether women experience differential legal treatment in various activities connected to business activity. We use this information and plot the number of differential treatments by both aggregate geographic regions and individual countries. The top panel of Figure 4.1 reports the statistics by geographic regions; the number of countries in each region is listed in parentheses. In

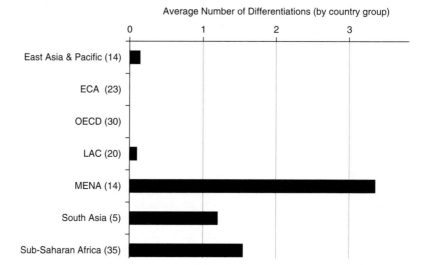

Average Number of Differentiations (by country group)

Notes:
OECD: Organization for Economic Co-operation and Development.
The MENA countries are Algeria, Arab Republic of Egypt, Islamic Jordan, Kuwait, Lebanon, Morocco, Oman, Saudi Arabia, Syrian Arab Republic, Tunisia, United Arab Emirates, West Bank, Gaza and Yemen.
LAC countries are Argentina, Bolivia, Brazil, Chile, Colombia, Costa Rica, Dominican Republic, Ecuador, El Salvador, Guatemala, Honduras, Jamaica, Mexico, Nicaragua, Panama, Paraguay, Peru, Puerto Rico, Uruguay and Venezuela.
ECA countries are Albania, Armenia, Azerbaijan, Belarus, Bosnia, and Herzegovina, Bulgaria, Croatia, Georgia, Kazakhstan, Kosovo, Kyrgyz Republic, Latvia, Lithuania, Macedonia, FYR, Moldova, Montenegro, Romania, Russian Federation, Serbia, Tajikistan, Turkey, Ukraine and Uzbekistan.

Source: 2010 Women, Business and the Law dataset of the World Bank.

Figure 4.1   De jure *differentiations (by country group and country)*

particular, the top graph is constructed using a subset of questions that focus specifically on entrepreneurship and business.[2] Each question in the WBL highlights whether women in business face restrictions in a specific activity (for example, starting a business) relative to men. For each group of countries, each bar in the graphs represents the average count of differential treatment instances. Similar to sub-Saharan Africa and South Asia, the MENA countries clearly stand out for the high number of reported *de jure* discrimination episodes against women. The bottom panel focuses only on the MENA region and indicates that gender discrimination is particularly severe in Jordan, Syria and Yemen.

The graphs underscore the importance of *de jure* discrimination in the

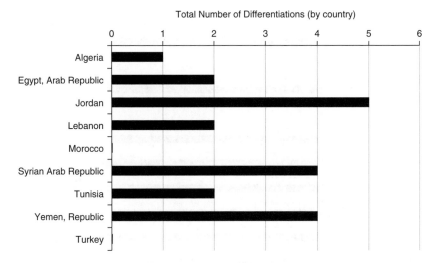

Figure 4.1   (continued)

MENA region and suggest that female labor participation and entrepreneurship may be negatively affected. However, they do not address whether *de jure* obstacles translate directly into *de facto* discrimination and whether this is then reflected in women's labor and/or entrepreneurship decisions. Figure 4.2 uses data from the World Bank's World Development Indicators for 2011 to plot male and female labor participation for the world and the MENA region at both regional and country levels. The figure shows that while male labor force participation in the MENA countries is aligned with the world level, female labor force participation is substantially lower in the MENA area. There is some heterogeneity within the MENA group: Turkey and – to a lesser extent – Morocco, Egypt and Yemen stand out for the high incidence of female workers in the manufacturing sector. Conversely, Lebanon and Jordan show a more skewed distribution that more closely correlates with the *de jure* measures of discrimination in the WBL data. Even within the rough picture provided by aggregate data, substantial heterogeneity exists both within the group of countries and within individual countries.

A somewhat comparable neighboring region consists of the 27 transition economies in Eastern Europe and Central Asia (ECA). Figure 4.3 considers the firm-level dispersion of the use of female labor and plots the frequency of female workers as shares of total workers in surveyed firms in the MENA and ECA regions in firm-level data collected from WBESs, as described in the next section. The histograms clearly indicate a more lopsided distribution of this measure in the MENA countries, with a large

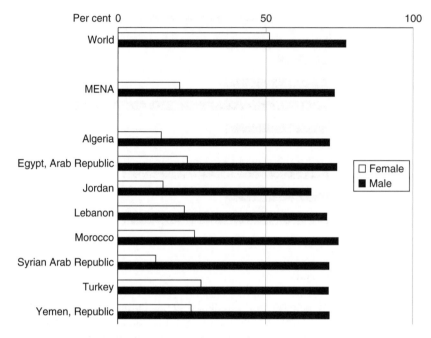

Note: The participation rate is the percentage of working male and female population 15 years of age or older in 2010.

Source: World Development Indicators 2011.

Figure 4.2   Labor participation rate in 2010 (by gender)

mass at 0 to 4 per cent. By comparison, firms in the ECA region show a more uniform distribution that is closer to similar plots for advanced economies. Figure 4.4 breaks down this histogram by country and further suggests cross-country heterogeneity in female labor as an input in each country's firms. The distributions in Morocco and Turkey are closer to those in the ECA region, while the histograms for other countries show approximately a negative exponential distribution, which is extremely lop-sided in the case of Yemen.

Finally, Figure 4.5 uses the same data source to consider *de facto* indicators of female entrepreneurship participation, particularly the incidence of female ownership and female management. While Lebanon and Turkey show measures of the incidence of female owners comparable to the world in general, Algeria, Jordan, Morocco, Syria and Yemen contribute to the low incidence in the MENA region overall. In contrast, the incidence of female managers in top management is higher than in the rest of the world

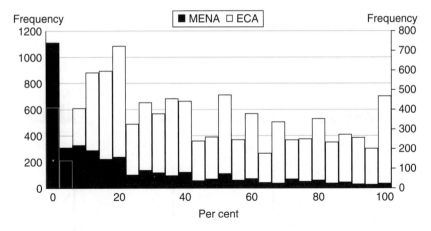

Note: BEEPS: Business Environment and Enterprise Performance Survey. BEEPS data refer to the 2007 fiscal year; MENA data refer to countries' fiscal years as specified in Table 4.1.

Source: World Bank Enterprise surveys and Business and Enterprise Performance Survey.

Figure 4.3 Frequency of female workers as a share of total workers in surveyed firms in the MENA region and in the BEEPs

for most countries in the MENA group for which data are available – that is, Egypt, Lebanon and Syria – but extremely low in Yemen.

4.3 RELATED LITERATURE

This chapter contributes to an emerging body of literature that highlights the role of gender differences in microeconomic data and macroeconomic models. In quantitative macroeconomic and labor economics, the availability of data on the composition of occupations has generated a small segment of the literature centered on the concept of 'brain-based technological change' (BBTC). Male and female labor are not perfect substitutes because individuals are endowed with similar brain abilities (mental labor) but different brawn abilities (physical labor) that favor men (Galor and Weil, 1996). As long as brawn skills have a positive marginal return, men enjoy a favorable gender wage gap. However, when technological change is biased in favor of brain-intensive activity, women can specialize according to their comparative advantages. The related increase in female labor demand then pushes wages up and contributes to reducing the wage gap with men, as observed in the data (see Rendall, 2010 and Keller, 2012).

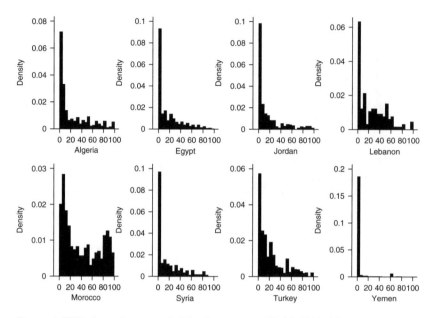

Notes: MENA data refer to contries' fiscal years as specified in Table 4.1.

Source: WBES.

Figure 4.4   Density of female workers as a share of total workers in surveyed firms (by MENA country)

While this theoretical argument holds in the data for the US economy, the evidence from international data is less clear. Cross-country comparisons show a consistent picture for richer but not poorer countries (Oostendorp, 2009). In the former, the wage gap tends to decrease with increasing trade and foreign direct investment (FDI) as well as economic development. In the latter, trade and FDI do not appear to reduce the occupational gender wage gap. These findings are consistent with the possibility that BBTC may have a smaller impact in poorer countries, and may be related to differential access to education for women in emerging and developing countries. However, Aguayo-Tellez et al. (2010) reach a different conclusion in their study of the impact in Mexico of liberalization measures resulting from the North American Free Trade Agreement. Women's relative wages increased, and both between- and within-industry shifts favored female workers since tariff reductions expanded sectors that were initially female-intensive. Women also gained intra-household bargaining power as documented by the change in expenditure toward goods associated with female preferences (for example, clothing and education).

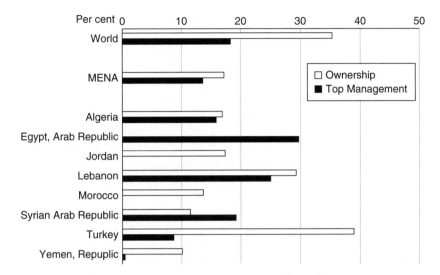

Note: 'Ownership' is the percentage of firms with some female participation in ownership. 'Top Management' is the percentage of firms with a female top manager.

Source: UNIDO.

Figure 4.5   Incidence of female ownership and top management (within-country average, various years)

Do et al. (2012) offer a different perspective that reconciles these findings. Improvement in trade openness changes the opportunity cost of women staying out of the formal labor market and therefore the trade-off between work and fertility, a point also made by Rees and Riezman (2012). In particular, Do et al. (2012) develop a specific factor model of trade in which male and female labor are combined with capital in two manufacturing sectors. As trade increases the demand for female labor in country/ industry pairs with comparative advantage with intensive use of female labor, it also induces increases in female labor wages which, in turn, affect fertility decisions. Their model is supported by empirical evidence in a large cross-section of countries.[3] Sauré and Zoabi (2009) study similar relationships but focus on the role of capital accumulation on labor by gender. These authors argue that when globalization improves work opportunities for women, female labor participation may drop if international specialization promotes sectors that use female labor intensively. This effect arises because expansions of the former sectors come along with contractions of others that induce male workers to move to the expanding sectors, driving female workers out of formal employment. Thus, a country that is exporting female labor content may be actually substituting male labor for female.

Finally, there is a sizeable amount of literature on female labor participation and job mobility, which includes Gayle et al. (2012); this paper is important for our analysis of entrepreneurship and management because it focuses on job progression and selection, particularly the reasons why fewer women than men become executive managers, earn less over their careers, hold more junior positions, and exit the occupation at a faster rate. The authors find that, controlling for executive rank and background, women earn higher compensation than men, experience more income uncertainty, and are promoted more quickly but also that these differences are related to the difficulties of surviving in the organization. Amongst survivors, being female increases the chance of becoming CEO because survival is rewarded with promotion and higher compensation.

Because extensive coverage of the literature is beyond the scope of this chapter, we refer interested readers to the WDR 2012 (World Bank, 2011), which summarizes the debate on the relationship between gender inequality and development. The portions of the report most relevant to our chapter are Chapter 5 (on gender differences in employment) and Chapter 6 (on the relationship between globalization and gender inequality). The data in these chapters support the arguments that (1) developing countries are experiencing reductions in male/female wage gaps; and (2) part of these reductions may be related to a country's openness. We contribute to this debate by providing further evidence on the degree of gender labor participation in the MENA region and linking it to international trade.

4.4   DATA

We maintain a flexible definition of the MENA countries because of differences in the availability of data across countries and thus combine multiple data sources. The largest group of countries (Algeria, Egypt, Jordan, Lebanon, Morocco, Turkey, Syria and Yemen) is constrained by the availability of individual WBESs. In addition, we use the United Nations Industrial Development Organization (UNIDO) Industrial Statistics databases (UNIDO INDSTAT2) and the United Nations Commodity Trade Statistics (UN COMTRADE) as data sources.[4]

The WBESs collect firm-level data from a selected number of countries to provide a representative picture of the population of firms in the countries' economies. From the available data, we select country/year pairs for the years between 2006 and 2009 to maintain a cross-country perspective that is as broad as possible (Table 4.1). Table 4.2 shows the distribution of

Table 4.1 Summary information on the WBES

Country	Survey year	Fiscal year	No. of obs.	% of total MENA8	Population (millions)	% of total MENA8
Algeria	2007	2006	423	10.51	36	12.84
Egypt	2008	2007	1156	28.73	82.5	29.43
Jordan	2006	2006	352	8.75	6.2	2.21
Lebanon	2009	2008	140	3.48	4.3	1.53
Morocco	2006	2005	466	11.58	32.3	11.52
Syria	2009	2008	349	8.68	20.8	7.42
Turkey	2008	2007	896	22.27	73.4	26.19
Yemen	2009	2009	241	5.99	24.8	8.85
TOTAL MENA8			4023	100	280.3	100

Source: WBES.

Table 4.2 *Distribution of firms (by industry and MENA country)*

Sector	Country						
	Algeria	Egypt	Jordan	Morocco	Turkey	Yemen	Total
Textiles	12.47	16.91	2.85	11.60	19.15		17.77
Garments	12.21		24.50	22.98	16.00	10.04	15.25
Food	31.43		26.50	26.26	13.29	29.28	14.16
Metals and machinery	28.05	19.89	6.27	0.66	18.48	16.13	18.2
Electronics	2.34	12.01	1.99	0.44	1.39	0.09	1.67
Chemicals and pharmaceuticals	8.05	7.62	10.26	20.79	4.87	3.30	5.15
Nonmetallic and plastics	0.00	11.66	9.12	0.00	11.38	25.60	11.86
Other manufacturing	5.45	31.90	18.52	17.29	15.45	15.57	15.93
Total	100	100	100	100	100	100	100

Notes: MENA data refer to individual countries fiscal years as specified in Table 4.1. Figures are in percentages.

Source: WBES.

firms by country and by industry. Each survey questionnaire is constructed to capture the economic and institutional environment in addition to the main business constraints faced by firms within the country. This information is captured by quantitative and qualitative indicators used in the questionnaire to measure, for example, the level of the firm's sales, the amount of exports, FDI intensity and qualitative perceptions about the business environment. We use all available information regarding the gender dimension of the firm's activity. In addition to standard firm demographic information, the datasets include information on whether any of the owners, top managers or largest shareholders of the firm is a woman and the total percentage of women employees in the firm.

The UNIDO INDSTAT2 dataset contains industry-level data organized by country, year and industry and collects information for a large cross-section of countries. We focus on the countries in the MENA region during the period the WBESs were collected (Table 4.1). The UNIDO INDSTAT2 dataset contains seven indicators: number of establishments, employment, wages and salaries, output, value-added, gross fixed capital formation and number of female employees. We focus on the total employment (number of employees) and the female labor composition of the workforce by industry (number of female employees). The dataset adopts the International Standard Industrial Classification (ISIC) code system, which classifies industries broadly along product lines (such as food, textiles, iron and steel). The ISIC code covers all areas of economic activity but data availability constrains us to the manufacturing sector. We use a fairly aggregate level of industry classification at the 2-digit level of ISIC Revision 3.[5]

The information from UNIDO INDSTAT2 is matched with that from UN COMTRADE, which details annual international trade statistics data by commodities and partner countries. Data availability from the UNIDO INDSTAT2 and UN COMTRADE databases reduces the set of matchable MENA countries to Algeria, Egypt, Jordan, Morocco and Turkey.

4.5   THE FEMALE LABOR CONTENT OF EXPORTS IN AGGREGATE DATA

Our first step is to construct a country-level measure of the female labor content of exports following the work of Do et al. (2012), which is based on Almeida and Wolfenzon's (2005) approach to measuring the external finance content in production and exports. The Do et al. (2012) measure is based on a model in which a country's comparative advantage contains both a Ricardian component (due to total factor productivity differences across countries) and a factor proportions component (due to different country-level endowments of male and female workers related to differences in labor participation).

We follow this approach and compute a sector-level measure of female labor intensity (FLI_{cs}) that is the share of the female labor force at the country-industry level:

$$FLI_{cs} = \frac{FL_{cs}}{TL_{cs}},$$

where FLI_{cs} corresponds to the number of female employees in country c and sector s and TL_{cs} represents the number of total workers in country c and sector s as reported in the UNIDO INDSTAT2 database.[6] We then match each sector with the UN COMTRADE data and compute the female labor content in export production as follows:

$$FLNX_{cs} = \frac{X_{cs}}{X_c} FLI_{cs},$$

where $\frac{X_{cs}}{X_c}$ is the share of industry s in total manufacturing exports to the rest of the world by country c. Therefore, $FLNX_{cs}$ gives a measure of the female labor content of exports from each country/sector pair. Similarly, a country-level measure summarizes the manufacturing-wide content of female labor of exports:

$$FLNX_c = \sum_{s=1}^{s} \frac{X_{cs}}{X_c} FLI_{cs}.$$

Conceptually, the $FLNX_c$ measure captures the female labor content of exports, but it also reveals the comparative advantage of individual countries in certain industries. The model developed by Do et al. (2012) delivers the Heckscher–Ohlin-style prediction that countries with relatively abundant female labor – as measured by female labor force participation – should be observed as exporting relatively larger shares of the goods that make intense use of female labor. Do et al. (2012) use cross-sectional country data and find support for this theoretical prediction. Countries with a higher female labor force participation show larger export shares in sectors that use female labor intensively, after controlling for country and industry fixed effects. Here, we take a less formal approach to verify whether this fact is confirmed in our sample of countries and years. Figure 4.6 plots a scatter diagram with the product of each country's female labor participation (*FLP*) times the female share of total labor for each country/industry pair (*FL*) on the *x*-axis and the level of export from country/industry *cs* as

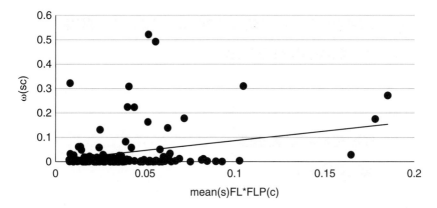

Note: Each dot represents a country/industry pair measure. The horizontal axis measures the interaction between female labor participation at the country level and female labor content of exports at the industry level. The vertical axis measures the share of exports in the country/industry pair *sc* in total exports from country *c*.

Figure 4.6   Relationship between comparative advantage in female labor and industry export shares

a share of total country *c* exports ($\omega_{cs} = \frac{X_{cs}}{X_c}$) on the *y*-axis.[7] The solid line indicates the linear interpolation of the scatter dots and shows the positive relationship predicted by the theory. Consistent with the findings of Do et al. (2012), the solid line in Figure 4.6 shows a positive relationship between, broadly speaking, female labor participation and exports.

Now a new question arises: which industries in each country have a comparative advantage in female labor? To answer this question, we pool countries and consider the cross-section of sectors and compute the measure $FLNX_c$ at the country level (Figure 4.7). The ranking of industries is determined by pooling all the MENA countries for which data are available in the UNIDO INDSTAT 2 database. Figure 4.8 indicates which sectors are female (male) labor-intensive on average; that is, they display a higher-than-average share of female (male) labor of the total labor used by industry.[8]

The ranking of industries according to FLI_S and the ranking of countries according to the $FLNX_c$ measures also help us to define in which industries individual countries have a comparative advantage in female labor relative to the MENA group overall. Morocco and Jordan have a comparative advantage in female labor-intensive industries, while Egypt and Turkey have a comparative advantage in male labor-intensive industries. We also consider Algeria as having a comparative advantage in male labor-intensive industries, although the UNIDO data were available only for 1996; therefore, this country's measures should be considered with a grain of salt.

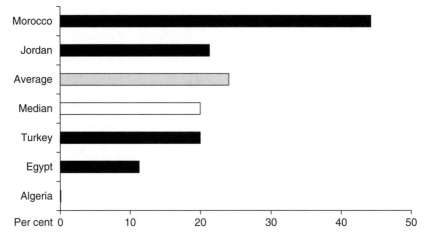

Note: Algeria is not included in the measure of the average and median value.

Source: Comtrade, UNIDO and authors' calculations.

Figure 4.7   Female labor content of exports

4.6   USING FIRM-LEVEL DATA TO IDENTIFY COMPARATIVE ADVANTAGE IN COUNTRY/INDUSTRY PAIRS

In previous sections, comparative advantage at the country level was defined on the basis of the factor content of trade, particularly focusing on female and male labor as inputs. We continue to assume that these are the only two factors of production and abstract from the measurement of capital, given the available data. Our next step is to link our analysis to the firm-level implications of recent theories of comparative advantage in international trade theory that introduce firm heterogeneity in more standard factors. Typical Heckscher–Ohlin models imply within-industry homogeneity in factor intensity. 'New trade theory' approaches with firm heterogeneity usually model firms as using only labor as a production factor, therefore abstracting from factor intensities. However, the evidence shows that factor intensities vary greatly within industries. For example, Leonardi (2007) documents (1) the wide capital-to-labor ratio dispersion within US industries using Compustat reported firms, and (2) its upward trend over time, and relates the dispersion to the increase in residual wage inequality. In Figure 4.9 we use our firm-level data to show the within-

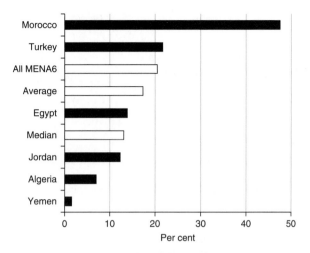

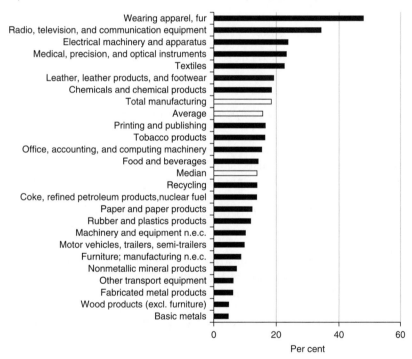

Source: UNIDO.

Figure 4.8   Female workers as a share of total workers by industry
(pooling countries) and MENA country (pooling industries)

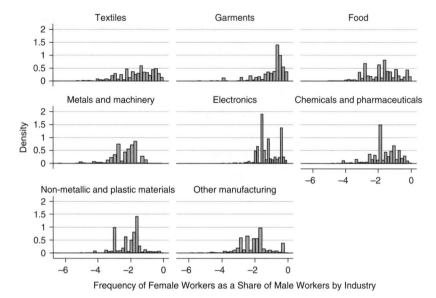

Frequency of Female Workers as a Share of Male Workers by Industry

Note: Factor intensity is the log of the female-to-male labor ratio.

Source: UNIDO.

Figure 4.9   Within-industry dispersion of factor intensity measures

industry dispersion in the female-to-male labor ratio across MENA countries and note a vast dispersion both within and between sectors. The results hold true when the graphs for each country are plotted separately (not shown).[9]

Consider the following two definitions consistent with Crozet and Trionfetti (2012):

1. *Female labor-intensive* industries are defined as those in which the female-to-male labor ratio of the industry is larger than the female-to-male labor ratio for the region.
2. *Female labor-abundant countries* are defined as those in which the female-to-male labor ratio of the country is larger than the female-to-male labor ratio for the region as a whole.

Making these two definitions operational with firm-level data can be challenging because there are multiple options to measure the female-to-male labor ratio within a country/industry pair. The two most intuitive choices are within-country and within-industry averages and median female-to-male labor ratios. However, the within-country/industry distributions of firm size are very skewed, which tends to distance the average from the median and, most importantly, identify country/industry pairs with comparative advantage, at odds with the procedure used in the previous sections based on aggregate data. Therefore, we rely on a third option and compute country/industry pair measures of female-to-male labor by first summing workers by gender within a country/industry group and then measuring the ratio. We denote measures constructed using micro data with lower case letters, as opposed to the capital letters used for aggregate data:

$$fmlr_{cs} = \frac{\sum_{i \in cs} fl_{ics}}{\sum_{i \in cs} ml_{ics}}.$$

We have country/industry pairs for 8 sectors × 5 countries and corresponding measures of the female-to-male labor ratio $fmlr_{cs}$. We then sum the firm-level female employment and male employment within a country across industries $fmlr_s$ and across countries in the same industry $fmlr_c$. By summing female and male workers across sectors and countries we obtain $fmlr$. A sector is female labor-intensive if $fmlr_s > fmlr$, while a country is female labor-abundant if $fmlr_c > fmlr$.

These definitions identify the country/industry pairs with comparative advantage in either female or male labor (Table 4.3). The table reports the $fmlr$ measures in the top box and identifies the country/industry pairs with comparative advantage in female labor based on: (1) firm-level data in the middle box (identified by a dummy variable called DV-CA micro); and (2) aggregate data and the *FLNX* measure developed by Do et al. (2012). The table shows that the partition of countries using micro and aggregate data delivers the same classifications of countries in female labor-abundant (FL-AB) and male labor-abundant (ML-AB) industries except for the chemicals and pharmaceutical industry. It should be noticed that this industry measure of *FLI* is particularly close to the total manufacturing measure (Figure 4.8) based on aggregate data, which suggests that the mismatch between classification may be influenced by small differences between the firm-level data and aggregate data.

More generally, our match shows that the firm-level surveys could be used to define comparative advantage country/industry pairs even when the aggregate data are not available, a result that we plan to exploit in future research. In this chapter, we use this methodology to add another country for which we have firm-level data to our set of countries for the remainder of the analysis.

Table 4.3   Determination of country/industry pairs: comparative advantage industries using firm-level data

Sector/Country	Turkey	Egypt	Morocco	Jordan	Algeria	Yemen	fmlr(s)	
Textiles	0.39	0.21	1.71	0.72	0.57		0.38	FL-INT
Garments	1.02		2.96	0.94	0.72	0.10	1.05	FL-INT
Food	0.25		0.41	0.08	0.20	0.07	0.24	ML-INT
Metals and machinery	0.11	0.08	0.06	0.03	0.09	0.01	0.10	ML-INT
Electronics	0.19	0.79	1.11	0.07	0.19	0.00	0.36	FL-INT
Chemicals and pharmaceuticals	0.19	0.45	0.56	0.17	0.09	0.53	0.28	ML-INT
Nonmetallic and plastic materials	0.14	0.20		0.02		0.03	0.14	ML-INT
Other manufacturing	0.06	0.27	0.42	0.11	0.11	0.04	0.10	ML-INT
fmlr(c)	0.303	0.256	1.070	0.431	0.199	0.068	0.305	
	ML-AB	ML-AB	FL-AB	FL-AB	ML-AB	ML-AB		

DV-CA micro

Sector/Country	Turkey	Egypt	Morocco	Jordan	Algeria	Yemen
Textiles	0	0	1	1	0	0
Garments	0		1	1	0	1
Food	1		0	0	1	1
Metals and machinery	1	1	0	0	1	1
Electronics	0	0	1	1	0	0
Chemicals and pharmaceuticals	1	1	0	0	1	0
Nonmetallic and plastic materials	1	1		0		1
Other manufacturing	1	1	0	0	1	1

DV-CA macro

Sector/Country	Turkey	Egypt	Morocco	Jordan	Algeria	Yemen
Textile	0	0	1	1		
Garment	0	0	1	1		
Food	1	1	0	0		
Metals and Machinery	1	1	0	0		
Electronics	0	0	1	1		
Chemicals and pharmaceuticals	0	0	1	1		
Nonmetallic and plastic products	1	1	0	0		
Other manufacturing	1	1	0	0		
	ML-AB	ML-AB	FL-AB	FL-AB	ML-AB	ML-AB

Note: These three tables compare the determination of country/industry pairs with comparative advantage (identified as '1') using aggregate and firm-level data. FL-AB and ML-AB identify a country that is abundant in either female labor or male labor relative to the group of countries. FL-INT and ML-INT identify industries intensive in the use of either female or male labor relative to the manufacturing sector as a whole.

Source: UNIDO and WEBS.

125

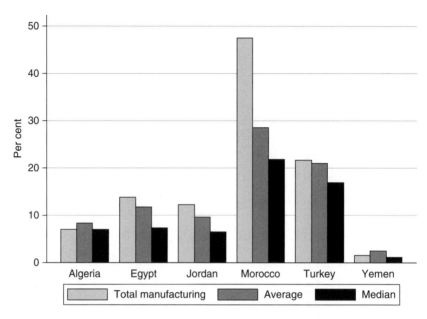

Source: UNIDO.

Figure 4.10   Female workers as a share of total workers (by country)

Before we use these classifications of country/industry pairs in our firm-level analysis, in Box 4.1 we discuss some evidence on hiring practices related to the gender of workers and managers based on the Jordan WBES for 2006.

4.7   FEMALE ENTREPRENEURSHIP

We investigate the main factors that hinder a firm's operation and growth in order to better grasp the business environment faced by firms. WBES respondents identify 'the biggest obstacle for the operation and growth of [the] establishment' from an extensive country-specific list of possible constraints to business.[10] Figure 4.16 plots the survey answers according to whether the firm has any female managers. Interestingly, access to capital is the most frequent issue raised by firms regardless of the gender composition of the managerial board. Political instability, high tax rates and illegal or unfair competition from the informal sectors (such as smuggling or dumping) are also cited by both types of firms. However, there is more heterogeneity in the relative importance of these issues across firm types.

BOX 4.1   HIRING PRACTICES RELATED TO THE GENDER OF WORKERS AND MANAGERS IN JORDAN

According to our classification of countries based on the aggregate data, Jordan is abundant in male labor relative to other countries in the MENA group (Figure 4.10). The classification also reveals a relatively high number of legal differentiations affecting female workers and entrepreneurs (Figure 4.1), low female labor participation rate (Figure 4.2) and a low incidence of female ownership among entrepreneurs. These findings are highly consistent with the firm-level data from the WBESs.

Several indicators suggest that firms' hiring preferences are biased in favor of male workers. Here we exploit a unique section of the Jordanian WBES that further details the respondents' explanations for such bias. They were directly asked whether they prefer to hire male or female workers; the number of firms that preferred to hire men as production workers is about 4.4 times larger than those that preferred to hire women. This measure is in line with the country-level data showing that the participation rate of male workers is about 4.3 times larger than that of female workers (Figure 4.2). More interestingly, this bias varies among exporters and non-exporters (Figure 4.11) and establishments with and without female ownership (Figure 4.12). Figures 4.11 and 4.12 show that exporters and establishments with female ownership have a higher tendency to hire women and a higher percentage of reporting managers indifferent about gender preferences in recruitment.

In addition, the surveyed firms reported the reasons they prefer male or female workers; the major reasons tend to be similar. The survey also lists the three most important reasons respondents prefer firms to hire men (or alternatively women) after answering the question on their gender-based recruiting preferences. Figures 4.13 and 4.14 plot the percentage of answers to the 'the most important reason' question. The top-rated reason is 'productivity'. Somewhat surprisingly, the second most important reason is listed as 'other – specify' which, once deconstructed, consists essentially of answers that can be grouped together as 'nature of the job/business' followed by 'flexibility' and 'lower rates of absenteeism'. The fact that productivity ranks high for both male and

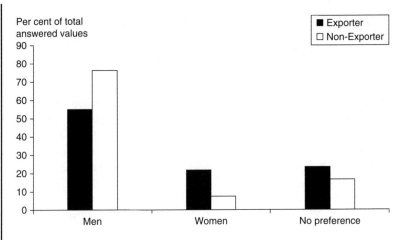

Source: WBES.

*Figure 4.11   Preference for hiring females/males as production
             workers in manufacturing sectors*

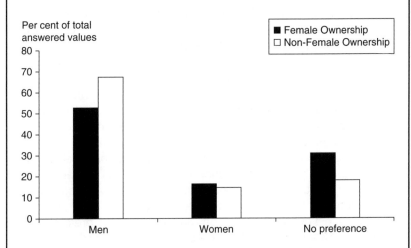

Source: WBES.

*Figure 4.12   Preference for hiring females/males as production
             workers in manufacturing sectors*

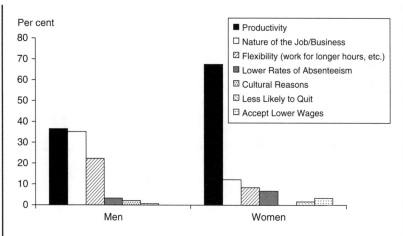

Source: WBES.

Figure 4.13 The most important reason for hiring men/women

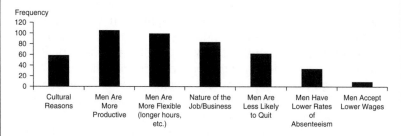

Source: WBES.

Figure 4.14 Reasons for preferring to hire men (pooling reasons)

female workers supports the sector-specific technological bias in favor of either male or female workers.

'Cultural reasons' play a less important role in influencing the hiring process compared with other factors as this is listed as the third most important reason to hire men as production workers. When we pool the entire set of the three most important reasons, 'cultural reasons' ranked fifth among the major reasons (Figure 4.14), accounting for 13 per cent of total responses. Among the cultural reasons, 'Men have to support families' accounts for 76 per cent of the responses after pooling the three

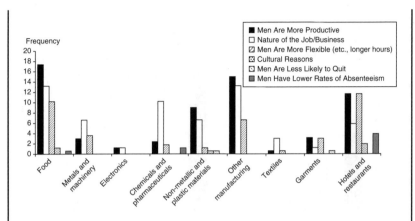

Source: WBES.

Figure 4.15   The most important reason for the establishments hiring men

most important reasons. This finding is highly consistent with the answers to the binary gender differentiation question 'Can a married woman be "head of a household" or "head of a family" in the same way as a man?' in the WBL data. Finally, the survey supports the view that technology and industries may be brawn-labor biased (Figure 4.15) even if there is some discrimination because of cultural values. First, 'nature of the job/business', which usually means that the type of the job requires physical effort, ranked third after pooling the reasons (Figure 4.14) and second in the 'the most important reason' category (Figure 4.13) for firms that prefer to hire men as production workers. Second, as Figure 4.15 shows, 'nature of job/business' is one of the leading factors in male labor-intensive industries (such as food, metals and machinery, non-metallic and plastic materials, and other manufacturing) in which female-to-total-labor ratios are below average in a male-abundant country like Jordan. Therefore, the low female participation rates may be partially explained by the higher demand for brawn labor than brain labor in these industries.

Firms with women in management place more importance on political instability and less on the competition from the informal sector or the high tax rate.

Because the WBESs provide a representative sample of firms within but

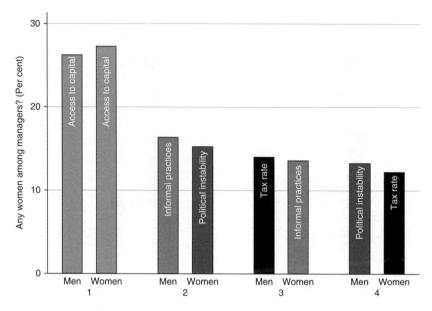

Note: The figure shows the four most frequently mentioned constraints by firms that have women or men as managers.

Source: WBES.

Figure 4.16   *'What is the biggest obstacle for the operation and growth of your establishment?' (responses by gender)*

not necessarily across countries (see Table 4.1 for a cross-country comparison of the representativeness of our data), in Figure 4.17 we plot the two most frequent answers by gender and country to uncover the possible presence of country-specific differences masked by the aggregates. The main constraint to business is common among male- and female-managed firms in all MENA countries except Syria, where women suffer more because of competition from the informal sector, and to a larger extent, Yemen, where the country's complicated taxation policies are the main barrier to female labor. The second most important constraint typically differs across countries and gender composition of a firm's managerial board. Algeria and Lebanon are the only exceptions where access to capital and electricity is always difficult. Within-country responses uncover more heterogeneity between male- and female-managed firms.

We test this descriptive evidence to gain further insights. In particular, respondents to the WBESs not only identified the two most important constraints to business, but they also ranked all possible business constraints in

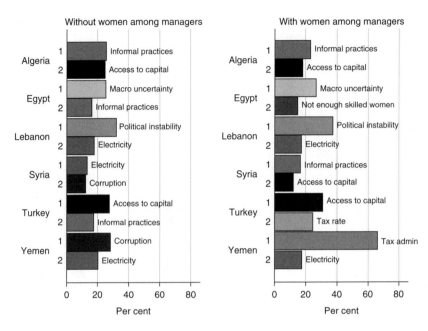

Note: The figure shows the two most frequently mentioned constraints by country and firms that have women/men as managers.

Source: WBES.

Figure 4.17   *'What is the biggest obstacle for the operation and growth of your establishment?' (responses by country and respondent gender)*

order of importance. In particular, they were asked to determine whether each constraint was 'not an obstacle' or a 'minor, moderate, severe or very severe obstacle'. We used the answers to these qualitative questions to construct an index ranging from 0 to 4 to indicate the importance of each business constraint.[11] We use these answers and add firm-level controls (such as the firm age, labor productivity and size) to determine whether there are significant systematic differences across gender (Tables 4.4 and 4.5). Firms with female managers appear to have fewer telecommunication problems but face greater macroeconomic uncertainty (that is, uncertainty about inflation and exchange rate fluctuations) and have more problems in obtaining access to financing, for instance because of insufficient collateral; the latter result is likely to be related to the fact that firms run by female managers tend to be smaller. While macroeconomic uncertainty harms exporters as expected, access to capital is more problematic for

Table 4.4 'Do business constraints have a differential impact on firms managed by women?'

Controls	Constraints				
	Macro uncertainty	Tax rate	Corruption	Informal practices	Not enough skilled women
Women manager? Yes = 1	0.19** (0.07)	0.01 (0.15)	−0.01 (0.20)	−0.15 (0.27)	−0.15 (0.28)
Exporter? Yes = 1	0.21** (0.09)	0.19 (0.14)	0.19 (0.20)	0.02 (0.16)	0.1 (0.14)
No.	1192	2145	2124	2277	2334

	Electricity	Tax administration	Access to capital	Labor regulations	Business licensing
Women manager? Yes = 1	0.07 (0.20)	−0.21 (0.27)	0.27* (0.15)	0.13 (0.26)	−0.05 (0.15)
Exporter? Yes = 1	−0.14 (0.18)	0.29** (0.15)	−0.33** (0.15)	0.18 (0.15)	0.12 (0.20)
No.	2303	2140	1851	2314	2131

	Customs regulations	Legal system	Transportation	Telecommunications	Crime
Women manager? Yes = 1	−0.19 (0.20)	−0.13 (0.28)	−0.07 (0.08)	−0.22** (0.09)	0.16 (0.20)
Exporter? Yes = 1	0.57*** (0.19)	0.29 (0.20)	−0.14 (0.17)	0.05 (0.10)	−0.01 (0.17)
No.	1870	1980	1657	1161	2251

Notes:
Ordered probit, marginal effect. The regressions include the following variables (not displayed): dummy for exporter, age of the firm, total employment (log), total sales (log) and labor productivity (log).
Robust standard errors are reported in parentheses.
*, ** and *** indicate significance at the 10 per cent, 5 per cent and 1 per cent levels.

Source: UNIDO and WBES.

Table 4.5 'Do business constraints have a differential impact on firms owned by women?'

Controls	Constraints				
	Macro uncertainty	Tax rate	Corruption	Informal practices	Not enough skilled women
Women owner? Yes = 1	0.01	—	0.18	-0.08	0
	(0.14)	—	(0.14)	(0.16)	(0.13)
Exporter? Yes = 1	0.06	—	0.22	0.03	0.11
	(0.11)	—	(0.19)	(0.16)	(0.15)
No.	605	—	1564	1700	1776

	Electricity	Tax administration	Access to capital	Labor regulations	Business licensing
Women owner? Yes = 1	-0.27*	—	0.25**	0.04	-0.32**
	(0.14)	—	(0.12)	(0.15)	(0.14)
Exporter? Yes = 1	-0.17	—	-0.31**	0.20	0.14
	(0.18)	—	(0.15)	(0.15)	(0.20)
No.	1772	—	1682	1760	1579

	Customs regulations	Legal system	Transportation	Telecommunications	Crime
Women owner? Yes = 1	-0.16	0.01	0.11	-0.19	-0.01
	(0.16)	(0.15)	(0.36)	(0.15)	(0.16)
Exporter? Yes = 1	0.60***	0.28	-0.24	0.14	-0.01
	(0.20)	(0.20)	(0.25)	(0.11)	(0.17)
No.	1581	1104	772	614	1694

Notes:
Ordered probit, marginal effect. The regressions include the following variables (not displayed): dummy for exporter, age of the firm, total employment (log), total sales (log) and labor productivity (log).
Robust standard errors are reported in parentheses.
*, ** and *** indicate significance at the 10 per cent, 5 per cent and 1 per cent levels.

Source: UNIDO and WBES.

Table 4.6   Does trade empower female managers or owners?

	Women owner? Yes=1		Women manager? Yes=1	
Firm-level female labor	0.21*		0.10**	
share	(0.12)		(0.04)	
Female labor-intensive		0.04		−0.03
sector		(0.06)		(0.03)
Log(Employment)	−0.61	−0.62	−0.33	−0.38
	(0.63)	(0.62)	(0.26)	(0.25)
Age	0	0	0	0
	(0.00)	(0.00)	(0.00)	(0.00)
Log(MPL)	−0.67	−0.69	−0.33	−0.40*
	(0.61)	(0.60)	(0.25)	(0.24)
Log(Sales)	0.65	0.68	0.31	0.38
	(0.61)	(0.60)	(0.25)	(0.24)
Mean dep. var.	0.37	0.37	0.08	0.07
N	2185	1921	2336	2076

Notes:
Probit, marginal effect.
Robust standard errors are reported in parentheses.
*, ** and *** indicate significance at the 10 per cent, 5 per cent and 1 per cent levels.

Source: UNIDO and WBES.

non-exporters, consistent with the idea that there is a selection into export. Access to capital remains more difficult for enterprises owned by women rather than men. Macroeconomic conditions lose their relevance but obtaining business licensing becomes harder for women and electricity gains importance for male owners.

    Finally, we investigate whether trade plays a role in empowering women. Specifically, we analyse: (1) whether women are more likely to be business owners or managers of a company (Table 4.6); and (2) whether the fact that the sector in which they work may or may not have comparative advantage in their country affects the likelihood of women being business owners (Table 4.7). We find evidence that suggests women are likely to climb professional ladders in sectors where their presence is stronger, a fact that is consistent with the evidence analyzed in Gayle et al. (2012). In our analysis, this empowerment through employment narrative is motivated by the positive and significant correlation (the point estimate is 0.21 with a corresponding *p*-value of 0.0000) between the average share of female employment and the average share of female-owned firms by sector and country that results after controlling for other observable characteristics of the firm (Table 4.6). Female owners are more likely to be observed

Table 4.7   Trade or de jure *constraints: what empower female owners?*

| | Female owners? Yes=1 | | | |
	FL-AB Countries (Morocco and Jordan)			
Index of *de jure* constraints	−0.09*	−0.12**	0	−0.05
	(0.05)	(0.06)	(0.04)	(0.05)
Female–male labor ratio	0.05***	−0.05		
	(0.02)	(0.06)		
Index of *de jure* constraints × Female–male labor ratio		0.10*		
		(0.06)		
Female labor-intensive			0.05*	−0.04
			(0.03)	(0.05)
De jure constraints × Female labor-intensive				0.13**
				(0.06)
Log(Employment)	0.34**	0.33**	0.30**	0.31**
	(0.17)	(0.16)	(0.15)	(0.15)
Age	0	0	0	0
	(0.00)	(0.00)	(0.00)	(0.00)
Log(MPL)	0.33**	0.32*	0.28*	0.29*
	(0.17)	(0.16)	(0.15)	(0.15)
Log(Sales)	−0.33**	−0.32**	−0.28**	−0.29*
	(0.16)	(0.16)	(0.14)	(0.15)
Mean dep. var.	0.14	0.14	0.14	0.14
N	775	775	775	775

Notes:
Probit, marginal effect.
Robust standard errors are reported in parentheses.
*, ** and *** indicate significance at the 10 per cent, 5 per cent and 1 per cent levels.
MPL refers to marginal product of labor.

Source: UNIDO and WBES.

in industries with a higher presence of female workers or in female labor-intensive industries (with a larger-than-the-median share of female workers). These results, however, are not economically or statistically significant. Conversely, we find that women are significantly more likely to be managers of firms with lower labor productivity.

Table 4.7 also accounts for the role of the *de jure* constraints analyzed in a previous section. We construct an index between 0 and 1 where 1 (0) corresponds to the maximum (minimum) number of *de jure* constraints faced by women in a given country. As expected, women are more likely to become business owners in female-labor-abundant countries when they face fewer *de jure* constraints and operate in industries with a higher concentration of female workers. The negative effect of *de jure* constraints is reduced by being employed in a female labor-intensive sector.

4.8 CONCLUSION

This chapter contributes to the small but growing body of literature on the relationship between female labor participation and openness to globalization. We focus on two aspects of this relationship: the analysis of comparative advantage in female labor using both aggregate and firm-level data and the role of trade openness in favoring female entrepreneurship and ownership.

We focus specifically on MENA countries because they represent a somewhat extreme case in international comparisons of *de jure* obstacles to female employment and entrepreneurship, in addition to having low female labor participation and low entrepreneurship and ownership rates. We use a novel approach to match the classification of country/industry pairs with comparative advantage based on aggregate data with a corresponding definition in firm-level data from the WBESs. Our approach suggests a fruitful avenue for research if aggregate data are not available and researchers are interested in identifying country/industry pairs with and without comparative advantage in certain factors that may be available in micro data (for example, high- and low-skill labor). We provide informal evidence of a link between a country's specialization and its measures of female labor participation consistent with theories of brain-based technological bias and comparative advantage.

Finally, we use the classification of countries and industries as being or not being characterized by comparative advantage to test a form of female empowerment through export orientation – that is, we test whether it is more likely to observe women entrepreneurs in industries characterized by comparative advantage in female labor in countries where female labor is relatively abundant. We find that women are more likely to be business owners in female-labor-abundant countries when they face fewer *de jure* constraints and operate in industries with a higher concentration of female workers. In terms of magnitude, the negative effect of *de jure* constraints is dwarfed by being employed in a female labor-intensive sector.

We leave it to future research to embed our results in a model of international trade with a specific role for female labor and to extend the cross-section of countries beyond the MENA region.

NOTES

1. These data are available at http://wbl.worldbank.org/.
2. The survey questions reflected in these graphs are as follows: (1) Can a married woman apply for a passport in the same way as a man? (2) Can a married woman travel outside the country in the same way as a man? (3) Can a married woman travel outside her home in the same way as a man? (4) Can a married woman get a job or pursue a trade or profession in the same way as a man? (5) Can a married woman sign a contract in the same way as a man? (6) Can a married woman register a business in the same way as a man? (7) Can a married woman be 'head of household' or 'head of family' in the same way as a man? (8) Can a married woman confer citizenship on her children in the same way as a man? (9) Can a married woman open a bank account in the same way as a man? (10) Can a married woman choose where to live in the same way as a man? Similar questions are available for unmarried women but are not shown here.
3. In section 6, we detail the differences between Do et al.'s (2012) methodology and ours.
4. The databases are available at www.enterprisesurveys.org (WBES), http://data.un.org/ (UNIDO INDSTAT2), and http://tpis6.ita.doc.gov/cgi-bin/wtpis/prod/tpis.cgi (UN COMTRADE).
5. Industry classification changes to some extent across countries, although it is fairly consistent for the five MENA countries available.
6. Data at the industry level are available and comparable for Egypt, Jordan, Morocco, Turkey and, with some limitations, for Algeria.
7. The interaction between FLP and FL provides a measure of comparative advantage. Analogous indicators are used in Romalis (2004) and Do et al. (2012).
8. The female labor-intensive industries are chemicals and chemical products; leather, leather products and footwear; textiles; medical, precision and optical instruments; electrical machinery and apparatus; radio, television, and communication equipment; and wearing apparel, fur. The male labor-intensive sectors are basic metals; wood products (excluding furniture); fabricated metal products; other transport equipment; nonmetallic mineral products; furniture-manufacturing not elsewhere classified; motor vehicles, trailers, semi-trailers; machinery and equipment not elsewhere classified; rubber and plastics products; paper and paper products; coke, refined petroleum products, nuclear fuel; recycling; food and beverages; office, accounting and computing machinery; tobacco products; and printing and publishing.
9. There is little research explaining this within-industry dispersion of factor intensities in a trade context. At least two factors of production and heterogeneous productivity must be postulated to generate within-industry dispersion of factor intensity. In an open economy, Bernard et al. (2007), Harrigan and Reshef (2011) and Burstein and Vogel (2012) model heterogeneous firms that use multiple inputs in the production function, thereby moving beyond the standard Melitz (2003) approach. Both papers focus on two inputs – high- and low-skilled – and discuss the relationship between factor intensity and trade. Bernard et al. (2007) show that standard Heckscher–Ohlin results carry over to a framework with heterogeneous total factor productivity. Burstein and Vogel (2012) identify how heterogeneous firms' decisions shape the factor content of trade and the changes in relative factor prices and between-sector factor allocations as a response to trade liberalization. However, neither of these papers applies the theory to the data. Crozet and Trionfetti (2012) also develop a two-factor model of trade with heterogeneous firms in which the marginal product of individual factors (capital and labor) is heterogeneous and, therefore, unlike the Bernard et al. (2007) model, the two-factor model translates in Hicks-biased technology. This heterogeneity can generate a within-industry dispersion that is then measured in firm-level data from the Amadeus dataset.
10. Problematic access to capital, competition from the informal sector, high tax rates, political instability, the lack of skilled or educated workers, access to electricity, and corruption account for almost 90 per cent of all problems reported. The remaining 10 per cent of problems include difficulty in registering the firm and obtaining licenses,

labor regulations, access to land, customs regulations, macroeconomic instability, tax administration, transportation, economic uncertainty, difficulties in dealing with the legal system, conflict resolution and crime.

11. Recent research shows that qualitative self-reported measures are representative of objective conditions of the firms. For example, Hallward-Driemeier and Aterido (2009) show that subjective measures are significantly correlated with objective measures of problematic access to electricity, skills shortage and other variables.

REFERENCES

Aguayo-Tellez, E., J. Airola and C. Juhn (2010), 'Did trade liberalization help women? The case of Mexico in the 1990s', Working Paper no. 16195, National Bureau of Economic Research.

Almeida, H. and D. Wolfenzon (2005), 'The effect of external finance on the equilibrium allocation of capital', *Journal of Financial Economics*, **75**(2005), 133–64.

Bernard, A.B., J.B. Jensen, S.J. Redding and P.K. Schott (2007), 'Firms in international trade', *Journal of Economic Perspectives*, **21**(3), 105–30.

Burstein, A. and J. Vogel (2012), 'International trade, technology, and the skill premium', Working Paper no. 16459, National Bureau of Economic Research.

Crozet, M. and F. Trionfetti (2012),'Firm-level comparative advantage', working paper, Paris School of Economics.

Do, Q.T., A.A. Levchenko and C. Raddatz (2012), 'Comparative advantage, international trade, and fertility', Discussion Paper no. 624, University of Michigan: Research Seminar in International Economics.

Galor, O. and D.N. Weil (1996), 'The gender gap, fertility, and growth', *American Economic Review*, **86**(3), 374–87.

Gayle, George-Levi, Limor Golan and Robert A. Miller (2012), 'Gender differences in executive compensation and job mobility', *Journal of Labor Economics*, **30**(4), 829–72.

Hallward-Driemeier, M. and R. Aterido (2009), 'Comparing apples with ... apples: how to make (more) sense of subjective rankings of constraints to business', Working Paper no. 5054, World Bank Policy Research.

Harrigan, J. and A. Reshef (2011), 'Skill biased heterogeneous firms, trade liberalization, and the skill premium', Working Paper no. 1760, National Bureau of Economic Research.

Keller, E. (2012), 'Experience and the gender wage gap across occupation', University of Iowa manuscript.

Leonardi, M. (2007), 'Firm heterogeneity in capital–labour ratios and wage inequality', *Economic Journal*, **117**(518), 375–98.

Melitz, M.J. (2003), 'The impact on trade on intra-industry reallocations and aggregate industry productivity', *Econometrica*, **71**(6), 1695–725.

Oostendorp, R.H. (2009), 'Globalization and the gender wage gap', *World Bank Economic Review*, **23**(1), 141–61.

Rees, R. and R.G. Riezman (2012), 'Globalization, gender and growth', *Review of Income and Wealth*, **58**(1), 107–17.

Rendall, M. (2010), 'Brain versus brawn: the realization of women's comparative advantage', Working Paper no. econwp077, University of Zurich.

Romalis, J. (2004), 'Factor proportions and the structure of commodity trade', *American Economic Review*, **94**(1), 67–97.

Sauré, P. and H. Zoabi (2009), 'Effects of trade on female labor force participation', unpublished manuscript, Swiss National Bank.

World Bank (2011), *World Development Report 2012: Gender Equality and Development*, Washington, DC: World Bank.

5. Climate change challenges and policies for the MENA countries

Ali H. Bayar and Hoda Youssef

5.1 MENA REGION AND CLIMATE CHANGE

Introduction

The potential impact of global climate change poses serious challenges for the MENA region, its economies, societies and its people.

Hotter and drier conditions would extend the area prone to desertification. The impacts of climate change will be also felt in the region's water resource system, especially with regard to reductions in water availability. Consequently, food security would also be threatened by falls in production and world price rises. The consequences on human health are hence obvious: reductions in food security can increase the risks of malnutrition and hunger, and the combination of heat and pollution would lead to an upsurge in illness, especially among urban populations. Finally, the region's economies would be adversely affected not only by the direct impacts of climate change, but also through the cost of adaptive measures. Table 5.1 provides, for some of the Mediterranean countries, an order of magnitude of the cost of environmental degradation as a percentage of GDP induced by the health impacts of urban air pollution and waterborne illnesses, the economic cost of water resources and soil/land degradation, impacts related to waste management, and the cost of coastal zone degradation.

A common trend in the Mediterranean countries shown in Table 5.1 is that the most significant impact and losses are induced by health impacts of severe air pollution associated with lack of safe water and sanitation. Productivity losses associated with soil degradation amount to a significant percentage of GDP in countries where agricultural share of GDP is substantial.

Climate change may also have significant implications for global and regional travel patterns and destination choices. For many Mediterranean countries, tourism is one of the most significant economic sectors, creating foreign exchange earnings, job opportunities, infrastructure investments,

*Table 5.1   Annual cost of environmental degradation (mean estimate), last
year available, percentage of GDP*

	Algeria	Egypt	Jordan	Lebanon	Morocco	Tunisia	Syria
	1999	2002	2000	2000	2000	1999	2001
Air	0.9%	2.1%	0.8%	1.0%	1.0%	0.6%	1.3%
Soil	1.2%	1.2%	0.6%	0.6%	0.5%	0.5%	1.0%
Water	0.8%	1.0%	1.2%	1.1%	1.2%	0.6%	0.9%
Coastal Zones	0.6%	0.3%	–	0.7%	0.5%	0.3%	0.1%
Waste	0.1%	0.2%	0.2%	0.1%	0.5%	0.1%	0.1%
Sub-total	**3.6%**	**4.8%**	**2.8%**	**3.4%**	**3.7%**	**2.1%**	**3.4%**
Global environment	1.2%	0.6%	1.0%	0.5%	0.9%	0.6%	1.3%
Total	**4.8%**	**5.4%**	**3.8%**	**3.9%**	**4.6%**	**2.7%**	**4.7%**

Source: The Mediterranean Environmental Technical Assistance Program (METAP).

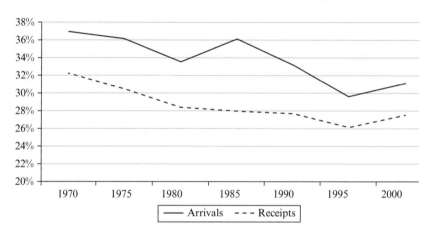

Source: United Nations Environment Programme (UNEP) (http://ede.grid.unep.ch/).

*Figure 5.1   Tourist arrivals to Mediterranean countries, percentage of
world total*

as well as being a source of substantial tax revenues for governments
(Figure 5.1). Climate change is a serious threat for these countries because
it can lower the attractiveness of some destinations. Alternative destinations such as European countries are likely to attract more tourists as the
weather gets warmer. Consequently, an increase in average temperatures

may cause a dramatic decrease in the tourism revenues for Mediterranean countries.

Another geographic sub-region of the MENA region is covered by the countries of the Gulf Cooperation Council (GCC),[1] a region that is characterized by its dry, harsh climate and limited natural resources of water, soil and vegetation, and where rainfall is erratic and droughts are frequent. Levels of water scarcity in this region are among the highest in the world. Although there are no specific estimations of the costs of environmental degradation for the region, conducted studies underline that erosion and loss of productivity have been aggravated by climatic factors, population growth and urbanization. The availability of freshwater resources is probably the most important environmental challenge facing all the GCC countries. The health effects attributable to poor air quality cause significant economic losses, especially in large cities.

5.2 THE CONTRIBUTION OF THE MENA REGION TO CLIMATE CHANGE

MENA Countries as Consumers: Energy Consumption by Source and by Sector

The significance of the energy-rich countries in the MENA region as major suppliers of world energy is well established. In 2006, four countries in the region, namely Saudi Arabia, Iran, Kuwait and UAE, produced about 25 per cent of the world's crude oil and in 2005 they exported around 31 per cent of the world's oil exports. Saudi Arabia's share, alone, was 12.9 per cent and 17 per cent respectively of the world's production and exports.[2] With a quarter of the world's proven oil reserves and some of the lowest production costs, it is also likely to remain the world's largest net oil exporter for the foreseeable future. Other countries in the region have large proven reserves of both oil and natural gas. UAE holds the fifth largest proven oil reserves in the Middle East and the fifth largest proven natural gas reserves in the world, while Qatar contains the third largest natural gas reserves and the largest non-associated gas field in the world. Qatar is also emerging as a major exporter of liquefied natural gas.[3]

However, the significance of the region as a user of energy and, consequently, as a contributor to carbon emissions and climate change is not well studied. Oil- and gas-rich countries of the MENA region have among the highest per capita energy consumption. Figure 5.2 shows the total energy consumption per capita, which measures the amount of primary energy consumed, on average, by each person living in the country for

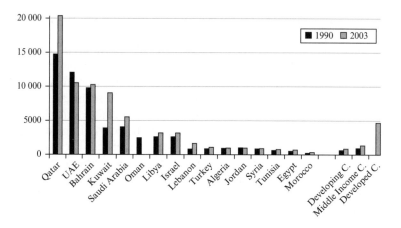

Source: World Resources Institute and International Energy Agency (IEA) Statistics
Division (2006a, 2006b).

*Figure 5.2   Total energy consumption per capita (kilograms of oil
              equivalent (kgoe) per person)*

the year indicated. All primary sources of energy, including coal and coal
products, oil and petroleum products, natural gas, nuclear, hydroelectric,
and so on, are included, and data are reported in kilograms of oil equivalent (kgoe) per person. Figure 5.3 shows the evolution of per capita energy
consumption between 1990 and 2003.

It appears from Figures 5.2 and 5.3 that there are large discrepancies
within the MENA region in per capita energy use. The energy consumption in the GCC countries is much higher than in the Mediterranean countries. They also have witnessed the highest rates of growth of per capita
consumption. This is mainly due to the hot climate, which necessitates
considerable air conditioning, in addition to other factors such as heavy
price subsidies, which lead to inefficient use.

Conversely, the consumption in the Mediterranean countries is in most
cases far below the level in developed countries. Despite the rapid growth
of per capita energy consumption in GCC countries especially, domestic
energy consumption still absorbs only a moderate portion of the region's
overall energy production, as the share of oil exports in MENA[4] production was 77 per cent in 2003. Table 5.2 represents the distribution of final
energy consumption (fossil fuels and electricity) by source and sector in the
Arab countries.[5]

In 2004 (see Figure 5.4), the industrial sector has the biggest share of oil
consumption in the Arab countries, with a share of 51 per cent, followed

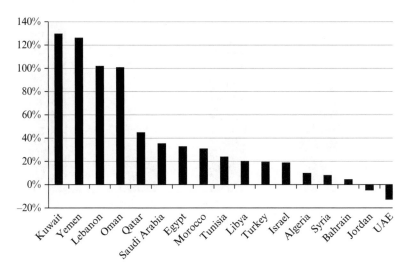

Source: World Resources Institute and author's calculation.

Figure 5.3 *Growth of per capita energy consumption: percentage change 1990–2003*

Table 5.2 *Final energy consumption in Arab countries by source and sector, 2004 (in %)*

	Transport sector	Industrial sector	Other sectors*	Total energy
Oil	20.8	32.1	10	62.9
Natural gas	20.7	0	1.9	22.6
Electricity	3	0	11.1	14.1
Coal	0.4	0	0	0.4
Total energy	44.9	32.1	23	100

Note: * Household, commercial and agriculture sectors.

Source: OAPEC (2006).

by the transport sector with about a third (33 per cent). The other sectors combined (household, commercial, and agricultural) consume around 16 per cent of petroleum. As for natural gas, the transport sector is the main consumer in the Arab countries, accounting for 91.6 per cent of final natural gas consumption.

The industrial sector is the main consumer of energy in the Arab countries, with a 44.9 per cent share of total final consumption, and with

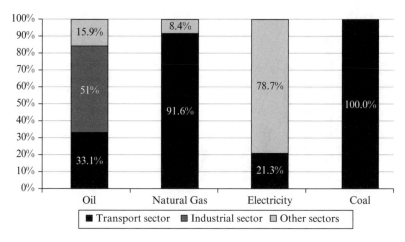

Source: OAPEC (2006).

Figure 5.4   Distribution of final energy consumption by source, 2004, in %

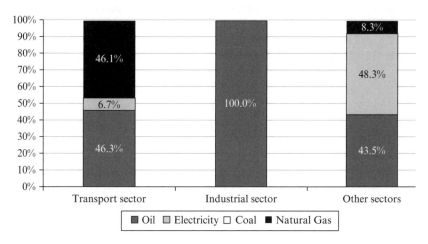

Source: OAPEC (2006).

Figure 5.5   Distribution of final energy consumption by sector, 2004, in %

petroleum and natural gas playing the major role in this sector. The industrial sector is completely reliant on oil in its consumption. As for the other sectors, including the household sector, they rely primarily on electricity to meet their energy needs (Figure 5.5).

Table 5.3   MENA energy-related CO$_2$ emissions (million tonnes), 2003

	Middle East*	North Africa	MENA
Power sector	383	98	481
Industry	232	54	286
Transport	239	66	305
Other**	248	77	325
Total	**1102**	**298**	**1397**

Note: * Includes Iran and Iraq; ** includes other transformation, residential and services and non-energy use.

Source: IEA (2005).

CO$_2$ Emissions: A Sectoral Approach

The MENA region is not just a victim of climate change; it also contributes to its causes. Abundant and cheap oil and gas supplies in MENA countries have led to a concentration of energy-intensive industries. The structure of the economies and energy consumption pattern, especially in oil- and gas-rich countries, has significant implications in terms of carbon emissions. Table 5.3 shows the energy-related carbon dioxide emissions from the MENA region.

Examining per capita emission trends is used to nullify the effect of population growth, since population growth – either through higher birth rates or immigration – can be a significant driver of GHG emissions growth. Figure 5.6 represents per capita carbon dioxide emissions (CO$_2$) for each of the region countries.

Among the GCC countries, three countries (respectively Qatar, UAE and Kuwait) are ranked by the World Resources Institute[6] as the world's top polluters with relevance to GHG emissions per capita in 2000, with Saudi Arabia ranked number 15 among the top polluters. Figure 5.7 reflects the per capita GHG emissions of these countries, as compared to developing countries, OECD countries as well as to the world average.

Figure 5.8 represents the carbon dioxide emissions by economic sector in recent years in MENA, in comparison with the EU and selected countries known as big polluters. It appears that carbon dioxide emissions from the MENA countries taken together are in most sectors less than those emitted by the other countries, except for the refining activities.

Figure 5.9 represents the CO$_2$ emissions by economic sector in each of the MENA countries. It appears that Saudi Arabia is the top producer of

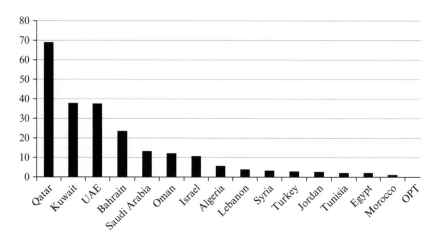

Source: UN statistics division.

*Figure 5.6   Carbon dioxide emissions (CO₂), metric tons of CO₂ per
             capita, 2004*

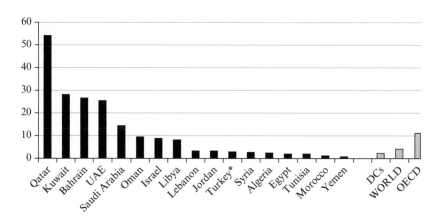

Note: * 2004 figures.

Source: Enerdata (http://www.enerdata.net/enerdatauk/knowledge/subscriptions/
database/).

*Figure 5.7   GHG emissions from fuel combustion per capita (tco2/hab),
             2005*

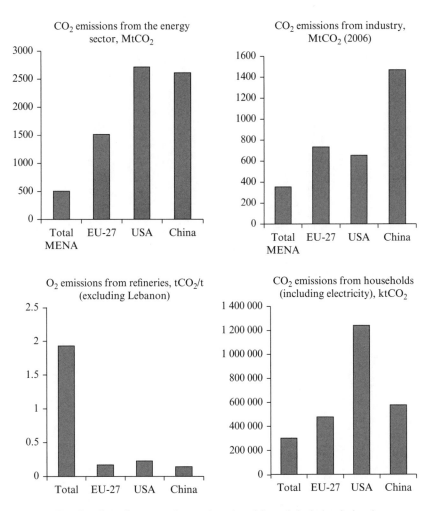

Source: Enerdata (http://www.enerdata.net/enerdatauk/knowledge/subscriptions/database/).

Figure 5.8   Carbon dioxide emissions by economic sector in selected countries/regions, 2005

CO_2 from all of the represented sectors (the energy sector, industry, refining and the residential sector). In second place comes Egypt for CO_2 emissions from the energy sector, Turkey for emissions from industry and the residential sector, and Kuwait for the refining sector.

Figure 5.10 shows the total contribution of economic sectors in the

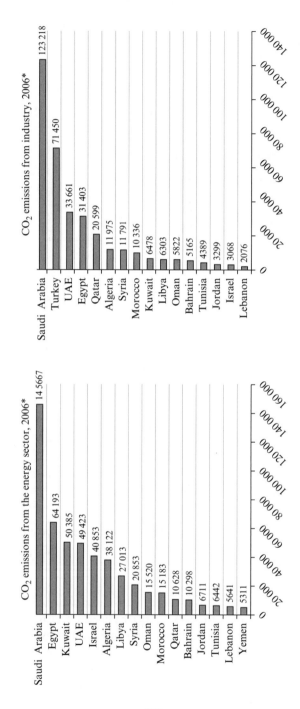

CO₂ emissions from the energy sector, 2006*

Country	Value
Saudi Arabia	145 667
Egypt	64 193
Kuwait	50 385
UAE	49 423
Israel	40 853
Algeria	38 122
Libya	27 013
Syria	20 853
Oman	15 520
Morocco	15 183
Qatar	10 628
Bahrain	10 298
Jordan	6711
Tunisia	6442
Lebanon	5641
Yemen	5311

CO₂ emissions from industry, 2006*

Country	Value
Saudi Arabia	123 218
Turkey	71 450
UAE	33 661
Egypt	31 403
Qatar	20 599
Algeria	11 975
Syria	11 791
Morocco	10 336
Kuwait	6478
Libya	6303
Oman	5822
Bahrain	5165
Tunisia	4389
Jordan	3299
Israel	3068
Lebanon	2076

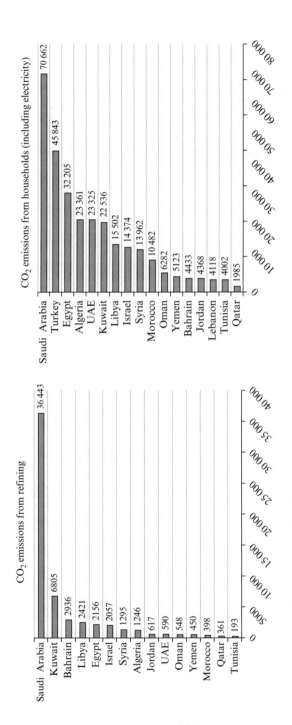

CO_2 emissions from refining

CO_2 emissions from households (including electricity)

Saudi Arabia	36 443
Kuwait	6805
Bahrain	2936
Libya	2421
Egypt	2156
Israel	2057
Syria	1295
Algeria	1246
Jordan	617
UAE	590
Oman	548
Yemen	450
Morocco	398
Qatar	361
Tunisia	193

Saudi Arabia	70 662
Turkey	45 843
Egypt	32 205
Algeria	23 361
UAE	23 325
Kuwait	22 536
Libya	15 502
Israel	14 374
Syria	13 962
Morocco	10 482
Oman	6282
Yemen	5123
Bahrain	4433
Jordan	4368
Lebanon	4118
Tunisia	4002
Qatar	1985

Note: Data for Jordan, Syria, Bahrain and Yemen are for 2005.

Source: Enerdata (http://www.enerdata.net/enerdatauk/knowledge/subscriptions/database/).

Figure 5.9 Carbon dioxide emissions by economic sector in individual MENA countries, ktCO₂, 2005

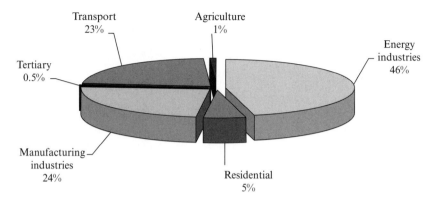

Note: * Excluding Iran and Iraq.

Source: Enerdata (http://www.enerdata.net/enerdatauk/knowledge/subscriptions/
database/) and author calculations.

Figure 5.10   CO₂ emissions from combustion in MENA countries, by
sector, 2005*

emission of carbon dioxide in the MENA countries in 2005. It appears
that the bulk of emissions come from energy industries, followed by the
manufacturing industries and the transport sector. The weak share of
both the tertiary and agriculture sectors may be attributed to the non-
availability of data.

Regarding the energy sector, oil consumption is responsible for most of
the CO_2 emissions in Saudi Arabia, Egypt, Kuwait, Libya, Syria, Jordan,
Lebanon and Yemen. In Tunisia, Bahrain, Qatar, Oman, Algeria and
the UAE, gas consumption is responsible for most of the CO_2 emissions.
Morocco and Israel are the only countries where coal consumption
is responsible for the bulk of CO_2 emissions (see Figure 5.11).

The MENA region's rapidly expanding population (Table 5.4) is
expected to continue to drive up gas emissions. In addition, the region's
macroeconomic progress will determine the pace of domestic energy
demand growth: steady economic growth and heavy subsidies are expected
to increase the contribution of the region to the problem of GHG emissions, especially if they continue to rely almost exclusively on oil and
natural gas to meet their energy needs.

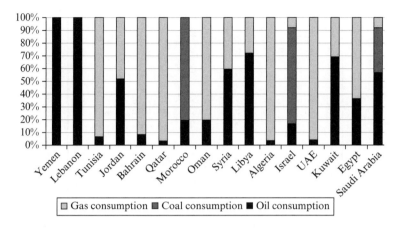

Source: Enerdata (http://www.enerdata.net/enerdatauk/knowledge/subscriptions/database/).

Figure 5.11 *CO$_2$ emissions from the energy sector due to oil, coal and gas consumption*

5.3 ENVIRONMENTAL PERFORMANCE IN MENA

The Environmental Performance Index (EPI), designed to mirror the priorities expressed by policy makers, most notably the environmental dimension of the United Nations' Millennium Development Goals, is a method of quantifying and analyzing the environmental performance of countries based on various policy indicators. A report published by the Center for Environmental Law & Policy at Yale University and the Center for International Earth Science Information Network (CIESIN) at Columbia University in collaboration with the World Economic Forum comes up with a list of countries ranked by the EPI. Figure 5.12 represents the MENA countries' scores compared to EU countries and other developing countries. It clearly shows that the region is far behind in terms of environmental performance.

Figure 5.13 shows that, except for Egypt and Tunisia, all the MENA countries have witnessed degradation in their ranking among the 149 countries listed in the report. For instance, Israel, the best performer in the region, is ranked at 49 in 2008 and has dropped four places compared to its rank in 2006 (45). The UAE is ranked at 112 in 2008, with a net degradation compared to its rank in 2006 (47). On the other hand, Tunisia and Egypt have achieved a better performance, with their ranking improving from 82 to 59 and from 85 to 71 respectively.

Table 5.4   MENA countries population prospects (000)

	2010	2015	2020	2025	2030	2035	2040	2045	2050
Algeria	35423	38088	40630	42882	44726	46255	47570	48721	49610
Egypt	79357	86219	92578	98513	104070	109238	113895	117921	121219
Israel	7272	7797	8269	8722	9160	9575	9946	10262	10527
Jordan	6453	6923	7469	8029	8554	9029	9445	9813	10121
Lebanon	4227	4431	4616	4784	4925	5037	5123	5184	5221
Morocco	32381	34330	36200	37865	39259	40397	41314	42052	42583
OPT	4409	5090	5806	6553	7320	8085	8837	9566	10265
Tunisia	10664	11204	11712	12170	12529	12797	12992	13121	13178
Turkey	77703	82111	86070	89557	92468	94887	96787	98145	98946
Syria	21428	23510	25573	27519	29294	30921	32403	33754	34887
Kuwait	3051	3378	3690	3988	4273	4547	4807	5039	5240
Oman	2767	3051	3339	3614	3865	4088	4291	4476	4639
Qatar	885	966	1040	1102	1161	1215	1263	1303	1333
Saudi Arabia	26416	29265	32089	34797	37314	39591	41594	43394	45030
United Arab Emirates	4732	5263	5774	6268	6753	7232	7698	8134	8521
Yemen	24475	28288	32390	36567	40768	45036	49393	53765	58009

Source: Population Division of the Department of Economic and Social Affairs of the United Nations Secretariat, World Population Prospects (2006 Revision).

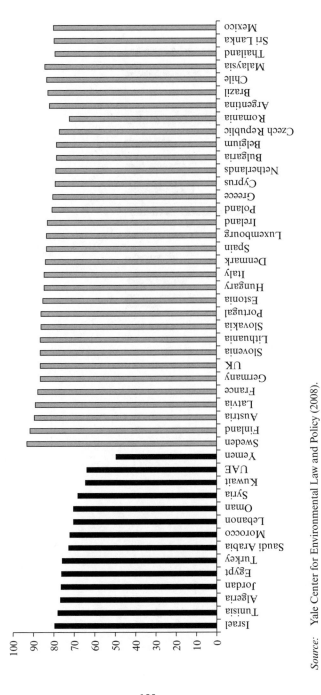

Source: Yale Center for Environmental Law and Policy (2008).

Figure 5.12   EPI in MENA, EU and selected developing countries, 2008

Country	Rank 2006	Rank 2008
UAE	47	112
Lebanon	36	90
Oman	60	91
Turkey	49	72
Saudi Arabia	59	78
Yemen	122	141
Morocco	68	82
Jordan	64	70
Israel	45.0	49
Syria	97	99
Tunisia	82	59
Egypt	85	71

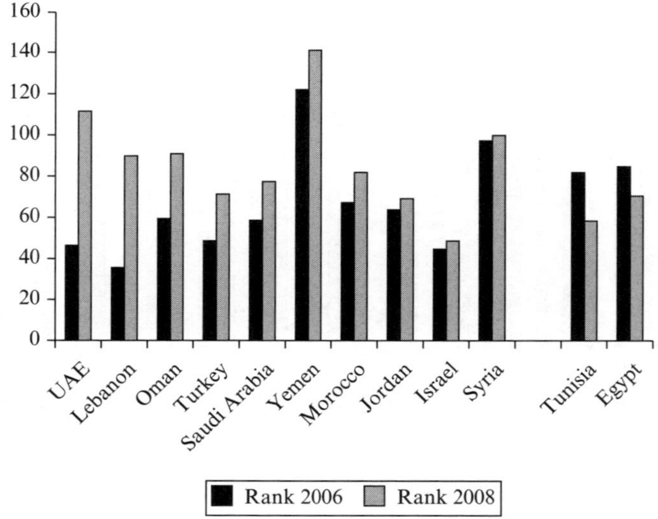

Source: Yale Center for Environmental Law and Policy (2008).

Figure 5.13   MENA countries' EPI ranking, 2006 and 2008

5.4 ECONOMIC IMPACT OF EU POLICIES ON MENA COUNTRIES

Implications for Mediterranean Partners (MPs) and GCC Countries

Concerns in the MPs come from the impact of environmental measures and standards on the penetration of their products into the EU markets. As trade partners of the European countries, the MPs must satisfy the European environmental standards in order to be able to export their products. Ecological criteria of the products include their environmental impacts, defined on the basis of life cycle, which means that the complete life cycle of a product or service is taken into consideration, starting with the extraction of raw materials, progressing through production, distribution and use and ending with disposal.

These concerns are more pronounced in the case of pollution-intensive industries given the growing international pressures on developing countries in general to set up measures to protect the environment and prevent climate change, which may lead to an increase in production costs and reduction in exports.

For some of the MPs that are resource-rich (Algeria, Libya and to a lesser extent Syria) and hence that are relying on revenues from oil exports, there are concerns about the possible implications of the EU environmental policies on oil demand and, consequently, on their oil exports. The possible implications are analyzed in more detail in the next point.

The introduction of Kyoto-type constraints (and possible post-Kyoto targets) is expected to impact the EU energy system and, consequently, its demand for energy. Given the great reliance of the GCC countries' economies on fossil fuel production and exports, what are the repercussions for these countries of the announced action to combat rising consumption of fossil fuels and related greenhouse-gas emissions?

Reducing reliance on oil suppliers was underlined by EU policy makers as one driver for moving towards a low-carbon economy. In the oil-producing countries, concerns are growing about the impact of climate change and environmental EU policies on their national economies.

The possible fall in oil and gas demand in the EU consuming countries may not only lead to a reduction in the region's production and exports, but it can also drive prices down.

Although the above-described scenario is unlikely to happen in the short or medium term, the implications for the GCC (and other resource-rich MENA) countries of a future decrease in fossil fuel demand are obvious. The GCC economies are mainly dependent on oil production and exports and, despite the efforts undertaken in recent years to reduce the

Table 5.5   Share of oil in total exports of MENA oil-producing countries, 2005

	Bahrain	Kuwait	UAE	Qatar	Saudi Arabia	Oman	Algeria*	Libya	Syria
Oil exports (% of total exports)	80	95	38	5	90	71	73	97	59

Source: National Central Banks; * Office of Statistics.

dependence on the oil sector through the development of manufacturing and services sectors, the contribution of oil exports in GCC economies remains quite high. The lower call on MENA oil and gas, combined with lower international prices, can result in a reduction in oil and gas export revenues. Table 5.5 reflects the degree of dependence of the GCC countries and resource-rich MENA countries through the share of oil in their total exports.

Another concern is related to the rate of investment in developing crude oil production capacity in the MENA region, especially with increasing attention being given to investment in renewable sources. Without sizeable investments, a shortfall in production capacity can emerge, with serious long-run implications for both producers and consumers within the region's countries. As shown in Figure 5.2, resource-rich MENA countries have above the average per capita energy consumption compared to both developing and developed countries.

This is in large part explained by abundant, cheap, subsidized energy supply in these countries. Hence, a drop in future infrastructure investments in fossil fuel production, with possible implications in terms of higher energy prices, carries short-term security risks for these countries, especially with regard to meeting the increasing demands of economic and population growth.

Addressing Environmental Policies' Implications

Predictions about the approaching end of the fossil fuel era combined with concerns about climate change induced by GHG emissions, the growing economic interdependence and the increasingly globalized energy market have brought attention to the issue of MENA countries' economic structure and the energy consumption pattern, especially in the resource-rich countries of the region. In spite of the considerable differences in the situation in each individual country within the region, there are, however, a number of common elements with regard to the energy sector: inefficient use of energy supply, high energy intensity in energy use, increasing environmental problems and a rapidly increasing burden on government finances. In addition, these countries are facing challenges regarding how to finance the rapidly growing demand for energy, given their population growth, rapid urbanization, and economic growth, which are putting pressure on existing infrastructure and causing relatively high demand for new investments in the energy sector. According to the World Bank, over the next 30 years the total investment needs in energy in the region are estimated at about 3 per cent of the region's total projected GDP over the period, which is three times higher than the world's average.[7] Further, the rapidly increasing domestic energy requirements in these economies can seriously curtail their capacity to export to other consuming countries in the future. Finally, climate change resulting from high energy consumption and induced gas emissions will definitely aggravate the region's vulnerability to climate conditions and natural disasters, which include, among others, higher temperatures, drought and food shortage.

Acknowledging the above-mentioned threats to the social and economic development of their economies, the MENA region countries are increasingly realizing the necessity of taking serious steps to tackle the climate change problem. The necessary measures are twofold. First, they have to address the repercussions of the international (including the EU) environmental and energy policies resulting from the commitment of international actors to various environmental agreements and treaties. Second, they have to promote the efficient and sustainable use of energy resources within their own economies in order to meet the challenges they are facing with regard to climate conditions, economic development and growing populations.

Economic Diversification

Meeting in Abu Dhabi within the framework of the Environment and Energy Exhibition and Conference 2003, the Arab ministers responsible for the environment and for energy affairs urged the industrialized countries to help Arab countries, whose economies are mainly based on the production and sale of oil and gas, regarding all the economic and social damages they may suffer as a consequence of the commitments of industrialized countries in the various environmental agreements and treaties.[8] Consumer countries should not only focus in their energy policies on energy efficiency, security of supply and climate change issues but rather on finding mechanisms to reconcile their interests with those of the producer countries to achieve mutually beneficial outcomes.

Nevertheless, MENA countries dependent on the revenues of commodity exports should aggressively pursue policies to diversify their economies. The GCC states in particular need to expand their economic activity to fit their endowment of human capital rather than simply relying on their natural resource endowment.

Figure 5.14 is a representation of how oil-producing countries in MENA (especially the two GCC states, Saudi Arabia and UAE, and to a lesser extent Algeria) are highly dependent on their oil exports for their GDP. When oil prices go up, both the value of exports and GDP increase; the opposite happens when prices go down. The fluctuations in export earnings induced by fluctuations in oil prices can trigger exchange rate volatility, which can create uncertainty that is harmful not only to non-oil exports but also to foreign and domestic investment. According to the Dutch disease theory, large revenues from natural resources, in this case oil exports, can result in overvaluation of national currency which, in turn, makes the manufacturing sector less competitive and reduces the export potential of other sectors.

In order to address their dependency on oil revenues, as well as the non-renewable characteristic of oil and gas resources, which means that their current consumption forfeits their future use, the GCC countries must ensure that the present depletion of these non-renewable resources increases long-term welfare. This can be done by increasing investments in capital, infrastructure and human capital through education, and by moderating the consumption of these rents in the short term.

But the shift from a natural resource management economy to an economy that is increasingly reliant on industrial production and services provision requires reforms in more than just the economic sphere. For example, it requires reforms in the education system to support the development of skills appropriate to sustainable social and economic development. Labor markets also need to be reformed to absorb these newly trained citizens and to reduce the reliance on imported labor.

Economic diversification is probably more advanced in smaller areas of the Gulf region such as Dubai and Qatar. Dubai is becoming a regional financial hub and has been heavily promoting itself as a tourist destination, while Qatar has invested billions of dollars to improve its education system.

Adjusted net savings, also known as genuine savings, is a sustainability indicator calculated by the World Bank to measure the true rate of savings in an economy after taking into account investments in human capital, depletion of natural resources and damage caused by pollution. In addition to serving as an indicator of sustainability, adjusted net savings is

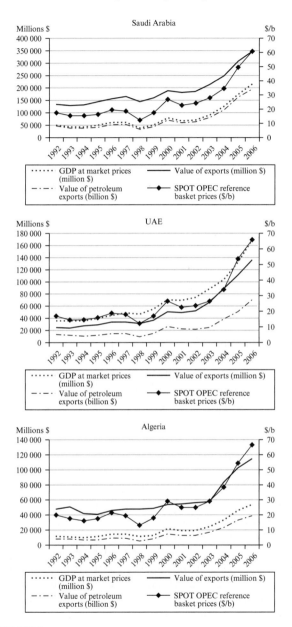

Source: OPEC (2006).

*Figure 5.14   Evolution of GDP, exports, oil exports and oil prices in Saudi
                Arabia, UAE and Algeria, 1993–2004*

Table 5.6   Adjusted net savings, 2004

Country	ANS (% of GNI)
Bahrain	−9.87
Kuwait	−10.53
Oman	−40.56
Saudi Arabia	−11.1
Algeria	3.65
Egypt	1.6
Turkey	9.44
Israel	1.62
Jordan	13.48
Lebanon	−9.33
Morocco	22.26
Syria	−28.42
Tunisia	12.11

Source: World Bank (2004a).

a policy indicator that highlights the fiscal aspects of environment and resource management. Negative adjusted net savings rates imply that total wealth is in decline and that adopted policies can be interpreted as policies that could lead potentially to long-term unsustainability. Table 5.6 represents the results for some of the MENA countries. It can be seen that almost all resource-rich countries (except Algeria) have negative net savings.

Promoting the Efficient and Sustainable Use of Energy Resources

In order to promote the efficient and sustainable use of energy resources, MENA countries should consider adopting appropriate pricing policies in the oil and gas and electricity sectors.

As mentioned earlier, inefficient use of energy is partially due to the existent subsidies in energy prices. Such subsidies are usually very costly from an economic and environmental perspective. On one hand they place a heavy burden on government finances and weaken the potential for economies to grow. On the other hand they often lead to a wasteful energy consumption pattern in transportation, commercial and residential sectors, in addition to a concentration on energy-intensive industries. As for their social justification, they are ill targeted and rarely end up helping the poor people that need them most.

In addition to the introduction of appropriate pricing policies and other incentives, governments in the MENA region countries should assist in improving energy efficiency and reduction of energy intensity by facilitating the introduction of energy-efficient equipment, the establishment of energy services companies and the development of appropriate financing mechanisms.

Renewable Energy

Countries in the MENA region, both the oil importers and the oil producers, must meet the challenge of reducing their emissions of greenhouse gases and invest in developing more efficient and clean fuels. One of the strong arguments in favor of investing in renewable sources of energy is that the MENA countries have a great potential in this field, with high levels of solar, wind, biomass and hydro (in some countries) resources abundant in the region.

The use of these renewable energy resources will not only contribute to the protection of the environment, but it can also contribute to diversifying the energy mix and increasing energy accessibility. Solar and wind power, in particular, are identified as very promising areas given the abundant resources that the MENA countries can exploit.

The renewable energy field can also represent an opportunity for a new relationship with the EU, besides the traditional relationship currently existing in the field of conventional energy production and trade. This relationship could, for example, be generated by the synergies of a renewable energy cooperation between the abundant solar energy resources in MENA and the developed solar technologies available in Europe. The export of clean and affordable power from the excellent solar fields in MENA to the huge power markets in Europe would support global climate stabilization, technological and economic development in MENA, and could establish an economic and political partnership for sustainability between the two regions, Europe and MENA.

During the past decades, most renewable energy resources were not considered as an element of the national energy plan. In spite of the high potential of renewable energy resources available in the region, small portions of these resources are exploited at present, as renewables (excluding biomass and hydropower) represented in 2007 less than 0.1 per cent of the total energy supply and less than 0.3 per cent of the electric power capacity. Biomass used in rural villages of MENA countries represents the main renewable energy source in these areas. In urban areas, solar water heating accounts for less than 0.01 per cent of the total energy supply. For electricity generation, the renewable energy resources share is only 7.32 per cent of the total electricity capacity.[9]

Table 5.7   Renewable energy applications in selected MENA countries, 2003

Country	Share of renewable energy
Algeria	0.3% of total energy supply
Egypt	11% of total energy supply
Morocco	25% of total energy supply
Tunisia	12% of total energy supply
Jordan	0.68% of total energy supply
Lebanon	7.36% of total energy supply
Syria	40.91% of total energy supply

Source: UNEP (http://ede.grid.unep.ch/).

Table 5.7 shows the situation for renewable energy applications in some of the MENA countries in 2003. As for the other countries not reported in the table, the national renewable energy activities are almost limited to R&D activities of the academic community, in addition to a few projects that are implemented with the support of regional and international organizations.

The figures presented in Table 5.7 show that the utilization of renewable energy in MENA countries is almost negligible as 2003 figures show. Figures for Egypt, Morocco and Tunisia may seem high, but if we exclude hydro and biomass, other renewables represent 0.1 per cent for Egypt and Morocco and 1 per cent for Tunisia of total energy supply.

The adoption of renewable energy alternatives in the region still faces several barriers and constraints, the most important being the financial and economic ones. The cost of renewable energy technologies remains high when compared to the subsidized low fuel prices, which explains the lack of willingness and/or ability to invest in renewable energy technology. Large hydrocarbon resources and discoveries in recent years continue to strategically shift the government's attention away from developing the renewable energy sector and markets, except large hydropower, which has extensively been exploited in the region. On the technical side, technology transfer remains insufficient. Technical implementation and maintenance hinder renewable energy technology market development, and the capacity-building programs are still limited. Besides, there is a great need to increase awareness among both consumers and decision makers of the potential and benefits of renewable energy technology utilization.

5.5 OPPORTUNITIES FOR THE MENA REGION

The Kyoto Protocol Flexible Mechanisms

The Kyoto Protocol to the United Nations Framework Convention on Climate Change envisages three market-based 'flexible mechanisms' to enable industrialized countries to meet their emission targets. In addition to the Joint Implementation (JI) mechanism that gives industrialized countries (called Annex 1 countries[10]) the possibility to finance emission-saving projects in other developed countries, and the Emissions Trading (ET) mechanism that enables industrialized countries to buy and sell emission credits among themselves, the Clean Development Mechanism (CDM)[11] is the only market mechanism in the Kyoto Protocol that is open to the participation of developing countries. The objective of the CDM is to assist industrialized countries in achieving compliance with their emissions reductions commitments under the Kyoto Protocol, while opening a way of sustainable growth to developing countries by promoting environmentally friendly investment from industrialized country governments and businesses, and helping them to contribute to the stabilization of the GHG concentration in the atmosphere. One important characteristic of the CDM is that the emission credits are added to the overall emissions budget of Annex B countries,[12] meaning that they receive credit in the form of 'Certified Emission Reductions', or CERs, which they may count against their national reduction targets.

From the developing-country perspective, the CDM is interesting as it can attract foreign investment through projects that assist in the shift to a less carbon-intensive economy. It also encourages the participation of both private and public sectors and provides a tool of technology transfer. However, there are two preconditions for a country to be able to host CDM projects: a political commitment to the Kyoto Protocol in some clear manner (ratification, acceptance, accession or approval) and an institutional acknowledgment of the CDM option in the form of establishment of a Designated National Authority (DNA)[13] and/or other local capacity to handle CDM activity. Table 5.8 presents the ratification date of each of the MENA countries of the Climate Change Convention and of the Kyoto Protocol, as well as the (non)establishment of a DNA. All the MENA countries are listed in the Non-Annex 1 to the UNFCC except Turkey, which is listed in Annex 1 but not listed in Annex B to the Kyoto Protocol (no quantified emissions limitation or mitigation commitments). Therefore, Turkey is not a party to the Kyoto Protocol. It appears from the table that, except Turkey, which is not a party to the Kyoto Protocol, all of the MENA countries have ratified the Kyoto Protocol and most of them have the necessary

Table 5.8   Climate change convention and Kyoto Protocol ratification date of MENA countries

Country	Climate Change Convention Date of ratification	Kyoto Protocol Date of ratification	DNA
Algeria	June 1993	February 2005	Yes
Bahrain	December 1994	January 2005	Yes
Egypt	December 1994	January 2005	Yes
Israel	June 1996	March 2004	Yes
Jordan	November 1993	January 2003	Yes
Kuwait	December 1994	March 2005	Yes
Lebanon	December 1994	November 2006	Yes
Libya	June 1994	August 2006	No
Morocco	June 1992	January 2002	Yes
Oman	February 1995	January 2005	No
Qatar	April 1996	January 2005	Yes
Saudi Arabia	December 1994	January 2005	No
Tunisia	July 1993	January 2003	Yes
Turkey	February 2004	Not ratified	No
Syria	January 1996	January 2006	Yes
UAE	December 1995	January 2005	Yes
Yemen	February 1996	September 2004	Yes

Source: UNFCCC (2008).

conditions required to host CDM projects, with the exception of Libya, Oman, Saudi Arabia and Turkey, which have not established a DNA.

Despite the eligibility of most of the MENA countries to host CDM projects and the great potential to promote sustainable development and increase foreign investment flows, especially for renewable energy projects, the region's share in CDM activity is very low.

Figure 5.15 shows the distribution of the total number of CDM projects in the pipeline by region, as well as the share of each region of the total 2012k CERs, which is the amount of CERs expected to be accumulated by the end of the first commitment period in 2012.

Appendix Table 5A.1 presents an analysis of all CDM projects in the pipeline by country/region and status in the project cycle, including expected annual amount of CERs. Up to March 2008, there have been 948 projects registered under the CDM Executive Board (UNEP Risø, 2008). The projects are unevenly distributed across regions and countries, as shown in Figure 5.15. Projects are concentrated in Asia and Latin America; Africa and the Middle East have been poorly represented so far. The MENA region hosts only 20 projects as of March 2008, which

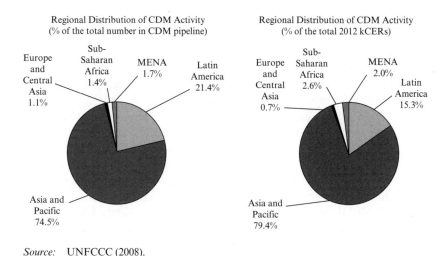

Regional Distribution of CDM Activity
(% of the total number in CDM pipeline)

Europe and Central Asia 1.1%
Sub-Saharan Africa 1.4%
MENA 1.7%
Latin America 21.4%
Asia and Pacific 74.5%

Regional Distribution of CDM Activity
(% of the total 2012 kCERs)

Europe and Central Asia 0.7%
Sub-Saharan Africa 2.6%
MENA 2.0%
Latin America 15.3%
Asia and Pacific 79.4%

Source: UNFCCC (2008).

Figure 5.15 Regional distribution of CDM activity, as of March 2008

represents only 2 per cent of the total number of CDM projects. Moreover, when incorporating into the analysis projects under validation and those which have already requested registration (CDM pipeline), it appears that this inequitable distribution is unlikely to change, at least during the first commitment period, as the MENA countries will continue to host a very small number of projects and will see their market share reduced by 0.4 per cent to the level of only 1.7 per cent of the total number of CDM projects. This is indeed a very small share, especially when compared with other regions and countries. For instance, India and China, taken together, will host around 62 per cent of the total number of CDM projects in the world.

The CDM is an opportunity to support sustainable development in the Southern and Eastern Mediterranean region, and to help European countries achieve their Kyoto targets in accordance with the objectives of the European Union, the Mediterranean countries and the Kyoto commitments. In this regard, there are several regional cooperation strategies from which the Mediterranean countries should benefit. Examples of these initiatives include:

• The Mediterranean Renewable Energy Program (MEDREP),[14] a sub-regional Mediterranean partnership and an Initiative of the Italian Ministry for Environment and Territory which aims at developing a sustainable renewable energy market system in the greater Mediterranean Region, removing project, policy and trade barriers, and linking capabilities and markets between developed and developing countries throughout the region.

• The MEDENER Network,[15] an actor in energy collaboration between the EU and the MENA region, working towards the development of a common approach to energy issues and the exchange of information and experience among its members.

• The Mediterranean Strategy for Sustainable Development (MSSD),[16] an initiative of the Mediterranean countries and the European Community and a framework strategy with the purposes of adapting international commitments to regional conditions, guiding national sustainable development strategies and initiating a partnership between countries at different levels of development.

• CDMEDI project (promoting and financing Clean Development Mechanism renewable energy projects in the Mediterranean region),[17] funded by DG Research under the EU's Fifth Framework Programme for Research and Technological Development.

As for the GCC region, the EU can support the improvement of the region's energy efficiency, and promote the development of the renewable energy sector (RES) in these countries that can take advantage of the unexploited renewable energy sources potential, with particular reference to solar and wind power, and gain additional revenues from the sale of CERs. In this regard, the region offers massive business potential for regional and international companies involved in the power generation and renewable energy industries. Hence, the development of CDM projects in the GCC region would have mutual benefits for both the EU and the GCC countries.

CDM projects, especially in the field of renewable energy sources, can make a significant contribution to improving environmental protection and to guaranteeing continuing oil supplies in conditions of stability and security. The associated technology transfer can also strengthen the security of supply by improving access to resources and by contributing to the diversity of fuel availability. The GCC region can even become a leading producer and exporter of solar energy in the form of electricity. Finally, the development of CDM projects would provide support to exhaustible energy (hydrocarbon resources) which can be used more wisely.[18]

The MENA region is really endowed with a high potential for energy resources other than the conventional ones. However, their full potential and advantages are currently hindered in the region due to the existence of many barriers, the most important of which being the institutional barriers and the price of fossil fuels, which is often subsidized. Hence, they do not always reflect their full cost, not to mention the 'externalities' associated with the use of such resources, such as additional health and environmental costs, which are not taken into consideration.

But in order to carry out CDM projects smoothly, the necessary institutions have to be built in the host countries as well as in the developed countries. Due to restricted financial resources and/or organizational deficiencies, the institutional network in MENA countries – as in many Non-Annex I countries – is still incomplete or entirely missing. A lot of capacity building is needed to enable the region to benefit from the opportunities the CDM offers, especially considering the complexity of CDM's modalities and procedures.

The Post-Kyoto Negotiations

Under the Kyoto Protocol, the commitments of industrialized countries average 5.2 per cent. These reductions are considered as a first – albeit vital – step to address the climate change problem.

Discussions on how to proceed beyond Kyoto's first period have been ongoing as part of the UNFCCC process. The second and third commitment periods of the Kyoto Protocol, with a time horizon of 2018 to 2022, aim to impose substantial reduction targets on its signatory states.

Post-Kyoto negotiations took place at the meeting of the G8+5[19] Climate Change Dialogue in February 2007. A non-binding agreement was reached to cooperate on tackling global warming, and the group called for a global system applying to both industrialized nations and developing countries to be in place by 2009 to supersede the Kyoto Protocol, the first phase of which expired in 2012. Although the talks were informal and did not represent official government policy, they provided a good indication of current thinking post-Kyoto. In December 2007, The United Nations Climate Change Conference took place in Bali, Indonesia, during which negotiations on a successor to the Kyoto Protocol dominated.

For a post-2012 climate agreement to succeed, it should address both mitigation and adaptation, which should be seen as part of sustainable development. Key issues surrounding a post-2012 international climate pact should include technical transfers, capacity building and helping developing countries adapt to climate change. Developing countries, including the MENA countries, need more help and funding for new technologies and to build a modern infrastructure so they can better control carbon emissions without slowing their expanding economies. These countries also stress the fundamental importance of the principle of 'common, but differentiated responsibilities and respective capabilities'.[20] The pact should also include vulnerability assessments, enhancing resilience to climate impacts, access to information and best practices, building human and institutional capacity, and making public and private investments in developing countries less susceptible to climate change.[21]

Sustainable Development and Environmental Initiatives in the Region

MENA countries are increasingly aware that climate change has negative repercussions on the development of the region and that the protection of the environment is essential in order to achieve sustainable development. Hence, they have started to link environmental protection to political and economic policies, and many initiatives have taken place in the Arab world.

In 1991, the Council of Arab Ministers Responsible for the Environment (CAMRE) adopted the Arab Declaration on Environment and Development and Future Prospects and agreed on principles and directives for the protection and improvement of the environment in the region.

It established the Joint Committee on Environment and Development in the Arab Region (JCEDAR) to enhance cooperation and coordination among Arab regional and national organizations.

More recently, many declarations have been issued following regional forums:

- The Declaration of the First Conference on the Environment from an Islamic Perspective (2000) emphasized the shared responsibility of states to prevent the exhaustion of natural resources and to decrease environmental pollution.
- The Abu Dhabi Declaration on Environment and Energy (2003) called for supporting Arab countries to mobilize sufficient resources to meet their demands so as to be able to adjust to the negative effects which may be caused by climate changes. This is to be done by putting in place national strategies to face those effects squarely, helping countries in the region to change their energy production and consumption habits, activating the efforts of scientific research institutions at the Arab and international levels, encouraging initiatives on clean energy and producing and encouraging the use of unleaded petrol.

  The declaration also urged industrialized countries to meet their commitments signed in the various environmental agreements and treaties and to compensate Arab countries, whose economies are mainly based on the production and sale of oil and gas, for all the economic and social damages those countries may suffer.
- The Arab Initiative for Sustainable Development (2002) called upon the international community to support the efforts of Arab countries to cope with the deterioration of the quality of the air in many Arab

BOX 5.1   THE SUSTAINABILITY MANAGEMENT
          REPORT: AN INITIATIVE OF THE
          ENVIRONMENT AGENCY OF
          ABU DHABI (EAD)

In May 2008, the Environment Agency of Abu Dhabi (EAD) released its Sustainability Report, which represents an important step towards an increased awareness in the Arab world of the climate change problem, and of the necessity to give special attention to environment protection.

With the impressive and dramatic economic development that the Emirate of Abu Dhabi is undergoing, it has become clear that this economic value has to be coupled with environment protection, regulation, and natural resources conservation. The report explains the EAD management approach to environmental performance, including issues related to energy consumption, climate change and greenhouse gas emissions.

By issuing such a report, the EAD aimed to set a practical example for business and the community, and to create optimal value for all key stakeholders in an ecologically sustainable manner. Hence, it can be considered as a tool to influence business and society, raise awareness, support research, and to enforce minimum standards in order to improve environmental performance. One of the outcomes of this initiative is the 'Sustainability Excellence Group', comprising Abu Dhabi's leading private companies and Abu Dhabi's government departments, who have expressed their commitment to sustainability management

This Sustainability Management Report is another effort which comes after other types of reports previously produced by EAD, including EAD Annual Reports, as well as Abu Dhabi's first 'State of the Environment' (SOE) report, which provided facts and information about the forces and changes that affect the state of the environment in Abu Dhabi, in addition to topics such as environmental management, future scenarios, and recommendations on what can be done to improve the state of the environment in the Emirate.

cities, including programs of control of air emissions, and to support the promotion of cleaner and safer production mechanisms and a cleaner and more efficient utilization of oil and natural gas. (See also Box 5.1, The Sustainability Management Report.)

- The Arab Declaration to the World Summit on Sustainable Development (2002) recognized that achieving sustainable development requires the development of economic and environmental policies that take into account the conservation and development of non-renewable energy, rationalize energy use, and mitigate the negative impacts on the environment and human health.
- The Arab Ministerial Declaration on Climate Change (2007), adopted by the Council of Arab Ministers Responsible for the Environment in its nineteenth session at the headquarters of the Secretariat of the League of the Arab States, constitutes the base for future action through the inclusion of policies to deal with climate change issues in all sectors within national and regional policies for sustainable development.

In the field of renewable energy, many conferences – known as the Middle East / North Africa Renewable Energy Conferences (MENAREC) – have been held annually in the MENA countries.[22] Following MENAREC4 in 2007, the Damascus Declaration has been issued on the role of renewable energy and energy efficiency for future EU–MENA cooperation. The declaration underlined the rapidly growing energy demand while acknowledging the concern of the MENA countries about climate change and its related adverse impact. It also recognized the need to diversify energy resources, and underscored the considerable potential of renewable energy on achieving sustainable development.

Despite these achievements, efforts towards cooperation among MENA countries need to be strengthened and coordinated. Although there has been a growth in declarations on environmental protection, with many involving the formulation of agreements stating the general goals of the parties, not all have imposed a mechanism that obliges them to achieve the goals.

5.6   CONCLUSION

There is no doubt that the availability of energy is crucial to the satisfaction of human needs and to the achievement of sustainable development. However, the way in which energy is produced, distributed and used affects the social, economic and environmental dimensions of any development efforts. The international community is increasingly realizing the necessity of relying on cleaner and more efficient energy systems, which means a gradual move away from conventional and polluting sources of energy. In this context, oil-producing countries are as much concerned about security of demand as consuming countries are about security of energy supply.

The implications of environmental and energy policies for the MENA region are evident, as both the consumer and producer countries are likely to face serious challenges in the medium to long term. Therefore, the aim should be to improve market transparency by developing more effective ways of exchanging information and by cooperating on policies to enhance the efficiency of the oil and gas sector in the resource-rich countries. The Joint Oil Data Initiative (JODI)[23] is a good starting point in this respect as it collects and releases monthly oil statistics, in addition to raising political awareness of all oil market players of the need for more transparency in oil market data. As for the non-oil producers, more steps should be undertaken towards the promotion of alternative sources of energy, which will allow for energy source diversification and imports reduction, defer production for energy exporters, while helping to stabilize the climate change problem.

NOTES

1. Bahrain, Kuwait, Oman, Qatar, Saudi Arabia and the United Arab Emirates.
2. IEA (2007).
3. IEA, Country Analysis Briefs, Middle East.
4. Including Iran, Iraq and Yemen.
5. Including Iraq.
6. Baumert, Herzog and Pershing (2005, chapter 4).
7. The World Bank (2004b).
8. Abu Dhabi Declaration on Energy and Environment, 2003.
9. UNEP (2007).
10. Annex I countries agree to reduce their emissions to target levels below their 1990 emissions levels. If they cannot do so, they must buy emission credits or invest in conservation. By default, the other countries are referred to as Non-Annex I countries. Annex II countries, which have to provide financial resources for the developing countries, are a sub-group of the Annex I countries consisting of the OECD members. Developing countries have no immediate restrictions under the UNFCC.
11. Article 12 of the Kyoto Protocol.
12. Annex B in the Kyoto Protocol include countries that have agreed to a target for their greenhouse gas emissions, including all the Annex I countries (as amended in 1998) except Turkey and Belarus.
13. A requirement of the Marrakesh Accords (2001), a set of agreements reached at the Conference of the Parties 7 (COP7) meeting in 2001 on the rules of meeting the targets set out in the Kyoto Protocol. The mandatory role of the DNA is the approval of CDM project activities. The DNA defines criteria for sustainable development as well as the sectoral and technological priorities.
14. http://uneprisoe.org/MedREP.
15. http://www.medener.net.
16. http://www.medstrategy.org.
17. http://www.ome.org/cdmedi.
18. European Commission (2005).

19. The G8 includes Canada, France, Germany, Italy, Japan, Russia, the United Kingdom and the United States, and the five emerging economies are Brazil, China, India, Mexico and South Africa.
20. OPEC Statement, 2007.
21. Global Leadership for Climate Action (2007).
22. MENAREC1 in Sanaa, Yemen (2004), MENAREC2 in Amman, Jordan (2005), MENAREC3 in Cairo, Egypt (2006), MENAREC4 in Damascus, Syria (2007) and MENAREC5, planned in Morocco (2009).
23. For more information about JODI and its World Database, see the organization website: http://www.jodidata.org.

REFERENCES

Baumert, K.A., T. Herzog and J. Pershing (2005), *Navigating the Numbers: Greenhouse Gas Data and International Climate Policy*, Washington, DC: World Resources Institute.
European Commission (2005), 'EUROGULF: An EU–GCC dialogue for energy stability and sustainability', research report presented at the EUROGULF Conference in Kuwait, 2–3 April.
Global Leadership for Climate Action (2007), 'Framework for a post-2012 agreement on climate change', available at: www.unfoundation.org.
IEA Statistics Division (2006a), 'Energy balances of OECD countries', Paris: International Energy Agency.
IEA Statistics Division (2006b), 'Energy balances of Non-OECD countries', Paris: International Energy Agency.
International Energy Agency (IEA) (2005), 'World Energy Outlook 2005: Middle East and North Africa insights', Paris: International Energy Agency.
International Energy Agency (IEA) (2007), 'Key world energy statistics', Paris: International Energy Agency.
Organization of Arab Petroleum Exporting Countries (OAPEC) (2006), 'Annual report, 2006', Kuwait: OAPEC.
Organization of the Petroleum Exporting Countries (OPEC) (2006), 'Annual Statistical Bulletin, 2006', OPEC.
Organization of the Petroleum Exporting Countries (OPEC) (2007), 'Statement to the United Nations Climate Change Conference', Bali, 11–14 December.
United Nations Environment Programme (UNEP) (2007), 'Current status of renewable energies in the Middle East–North African region', Nairobi: UNEP.
UNEP Risø (2008), UNEP Risø Centre, available at: http://cdmpipeline.org/.
UNFCCC (2008), Kyoto Protocol Status of Ratification, March.
World Bank (2004a), 'Adjusted net saving statistics, 2004', available at: http://web.worldbank.org.
World Bank (2004b), 'Energy in MENA', Sector Brief, September 2004, available at: http://web.worldbank.org.
Yale Center for Environmental Law and Policy (2008), '2008 Environmental Performance Index', New Haven, CT: Yale Center for Environmental Law and Policy, available at: http://sedac.ciesin.columbia.edu/es/epi/.

APPENDIX

Table 5A.1   Host region/country for CDM projects by status, as of March 2008

	At validation		Request registration		Registered		Total		
	Number	kCERs	Number	kCERs	Number	kCERs	Number	Percentage	kCERs
Latin America	**303**	**24711**	**27**	**2003**	**330**	**36796**	**660**	**21.40%**	**63510**
Argentina	12	869	1	37	10	3786	23	1%	4692
Bolivia	4	444	0	0	2	224	6	0%	668
Brazil	125	8710	12	955	125	16994	262	9%	26659
Chile	23	2487	2	282	22	3934	47	2%	6703
Colombia	13	2354	0	0	10	958	23	1%	3312
Costa Rica	0	0	1	42	5	252	6	0%	294
Cuba	3	351	0	0	1	342	4	0%	693
Dominican Republic	2	342	0	0	1	124	3	0%	466
Ecuador	8	478	1	3	10	449	19	1%	930
El Salvador	1	7	0	0	5	475	6	0%	482
Guatemala	10	892	0	0	5	277	15	0%	1169
Guyana	1	45	0	0	0	0	1	0%	45
Honduras	7	277	2	51	12	224	21	1%	551
Jamaica	1	232	0	0	1	53	2	0%	284
Mexico	75	4803	6	389	101	7007	182	6%	12199
Nicaragua	1	44	0	0	3	456	4	0%	500
Panama	3	531	0	0	5	119	8	0%	650
Paraguay	3	74	0	0	0	0	3	0%	74
Peru	10	1733	2	244	10	909	22	1%	2886
Uruguay	1	41	0	0	2	212	3	0%	252

Table 5A.1 (continued)

	At validation		Request registration		Registered		Total		
	Number	kCERs	Number	kCERs	Number	kCERs	Number	Percentage	kCERs
Asia & Pacific	**1607**	**197530**	**116**	**22448**	**572**	**144839**	**2295**	**74.5%**	**364816**
Bangladesh	2	65	0	0	2	170	4	0%	235
Bhutan	2	3809	0	0	1	1	3	0%	3810
Cambodia	2	73	0	0	1	52	3	0%	125
China	839	140357	56	18700	161	92933	1056	34%	251990
Fiji	0	0	0	0	1	25	1	0%	25
India	498	30448	45	2751	316	29397	859	28%	62595
Indonesia	45	4557	3	456	12	2060	60	2%	7073
Lao PDR	0	0	0	0	1	3	1	0%	3
Malaysia	79	9119	2	101	26	2431	107	3%	11650
Mongolia	1	181	0	0	3	70	4	0%	251
Nepal	1	33	0	0	2	94	3	0%	127
Pakistan	6	1821	0	0	1	1050	7	0%	2871
Papua New Guinea	0	0	0	0	1	279	1	0%	279
Philippines	50	2141	2	35	16	482	68	2%	2658
Singapore	1	16	0	0	0	0	1	0%	16
South Korea	23	1449	4	275	17	14357	44	1%	16081
Sri Lanka	9	259	0	0	4	116	13	0%	375
Thailand	34	2195	4	130	5	639	43	1%	2964
Vietnam	15	1007	0	0	2	681	17	1%	1688

	23	2983	1	200	10	387	34	1.10%	3571
Europe and Central Asia									
Armenia	3	150	0	0	4	195	7	0%	345
Azerbaijan	3	785	0	0	0	0	3	0%	785
Cyprus	4	73	0	0	2	73	6	0%	146
Georgia	1	234	0	0	1	73	2	0%	307
Kyrgyzstan	1	73	0	0	0	0	1	0%	73
Macedonia	0	0	1	200	0	0	1	0%	200
Malta	1	20	0	0	0	0	1	0%	20
Moldova	2	309	0	0	3	47	5	0%	357
Tajikistan	1	51	0	0	0	0	1	0%	51
Uzbekistan	7	1287	0	0	0	0	7	0%	1287
Sub-Sahara Africa	25	7184	1	130	16	4261	42	1.40%	11574
Congo	1	443	0	0	0	0	1	0%	43
Equatorial Guinea	0	0	0	0	0	0	0	0%	0
Ivory Coast	2	1027	0	0	0	0	2	0%	1027
Kenya	4	469	1	130	0	0	5	0%	599
Mali	1	160	0	0	0	0	1	0%	160
Mauritius	1	298	0	0	0	0	1	0%	298
Mozambique	1	46	0	0	0	0	1	0%	46
Nigeria	1	2532	0	0	1	1497	2	0%	4029
Senegal	1	131	0	0	0	0	1	0%	131
South Africa	10	1701	0	0	13	2525	23	1%	4226
Tanzania	1	318	0	0	1	202	2	0%	520
Uganda	2	60	0	0	1	36	3	0%	96

Table 5A.1 (continued)

	At validation		Request registration		Registered		Total		
	Number	kCERs	Number	kCERs	Number	kCERs	Number	Percentage	kCERs
MENA	**30**	**3134**	**1**	**455**	**20**	**6242**	**51**	**1.7%**	**9831**
Egypt	4	387	1	455	3	1685	8	0.3%	2527
Israel	20	1988	0	0	10	1113	30	1%	3102
Jordan	1	354	0	0	0	0	1	0.0%	354
Morocco	1	89	0	0	4	256	5	0.2%	345
Qatar	0	0	0	0	1	2500	1	0.0%	2500
Tunisia	0	0	0	0	2	688	2	0.1%	688
UAE	4	316	0	0	0	0	4	0.1%	316
Less developed World	**1988**	**235541**	**146**	**25236**	**948**	**192525**	**3082**	**100.00%**	**453302**

6. The energy sector in Mediterranean and MENA countries

Marcella Nicolini and Simona Porcheri

6.1 INTRODUCTION

The Middle East and North Africa (MENA) region has about 57 per cent of the world's proven oil reserves and 41 per cent of proven natural gas resources and the upstream potential of many countries in the region is still underexplored. The area is also endowed with large solar resources. However, the political upheaval that took place in several Arab countries in 2011 has raised some concerns about the stability of this area. Important political changes are taking place and some observers fear that this might affect energy policies and production. Neighbouring countries, especially those in the northern shore of the Mediterranean, which are dependent on energy imports, are looking for opportunities to reinforce the links with the southern shore. Indeed, the Mediterranean is characterized by a gap between countries rich in natural resources in the South and countries dependent on such resources, mainly in the North. The commercial bundle is strong: in 2010 the MENA region accounted for 32 per cent of EU natural gas imports, slightly more than the 28 per cent recorded in 2000 (Darbouche and Fattouh, 2011).

As for energy policies, EU countries have high requirements in terms of energy efficiency and renewable energy production, while non-EU countries on the northern shore are moving in the same direction. However, in many MENA countries the situation is completely different: fuel prices are distorted by subsidies and thus energy intensity is artificially higher. Moreover, the efficiency of supply is poor.

The aim of this chapter is to describe the energy sector in the area. First, we present some descriptive statistics on energy production in the northern and southern shores of the Mediterranean and MENA countries. Section 3 discusses the energy policies implemented, both to stimulate renewable energy production and to subsidize fossil-fuels consumption. Section 4 discusses the avenues for cooperation across the Mediterranean, while section 5 discusses the estimated consequences of the Arab Spring on energy production in the area. Finally, section 6 concludes.

6.2   ENERGY PRODUCTION AND CONSUMPTION

Energy demand is mainly driven by economic and population growth. The economy has grown at a yearly 2.2 per cent in the 1990–2009 period in the area. Notice, however, that great disparities in living standards occur between the two shores: the northern shore accounts for three-quarters of the Mediterranean's GDP. As for population, there are around 492 million inhabitants in the region and more than half are concentrated in four countries: Egypt, Turkey, France and Italy. The population has grown at a 1.1 per cent annual rate in the last 40 years and estimates suggest it will be 582 million by 2030. This growth is expected to take place mainly in the southern shore of the Mediterranean (OME, 2011).

Total primary energy production in the Mediterranean has increased on average by 1.3 per cent per year since 1990, reaching 636 Mtoe (million tonnes of oil equivalent) in 2009. However, the energy demand has increased more rapidly (2.5 per cent per year over the last twenty years), reaching 988 Mtoe in 2009. The primary energy demand is reported in Figure 6.1, which distinguishes North and South Mediterranean: this is split unevenly, with the northern shore demanding around two-thirds. Primary energy demand has been increasing in both areas over time: the recent crisis has, however, reduced primary energy demand in absolute terms in the northern shore for the first time in 2009.

As for the power generation capacity installed in the Mediterranean, this amounts to 496 gigawatts in 2009 (OME, 2011): natural gas is the main source (33 per cent) followed by hydropower (18 per cent), nuclear (14 per cent), coal (13 per cent), oil (12 per cent) and non-hydro renewables (10 per cent). Energy production is not sufficient to satisfy energy demand in the area, thus the region imports it from outside. All North Mediterranean countries are net fossil fuel importers, while the situation in the South is more varied. There are producing countries such as Algeria, Libya and

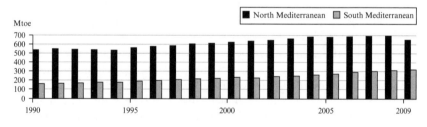

Source: OME (2011).

Figure 6.1   Primary energy demand in the Mediterranean, 1990–2009

Egypt which are large exporters, as well as countries such as Morocco, which are net fossil fuels importers from neighbouring countries. Fossil fuels dominate the energy mix in the region (oil is 41 per cent, natural gas 28 per cent, coal 12 per cent for a total of 81 per cent), followed by nuclear (12 per cent), and renewables (hydro is 2 per cent and other renewables are 6 per cent). Several factors, such as population growth, rapid urbanization and economic growth, are putting pressure on existing infrastructure. This in turn implies a relatively high demand for new investments. Over the next 30 years, the total investment needed in the energy sector in MENA is estimated to be more than US$30 billion a year, which is about 3 per cent of the region's total projected GDP (World Bank, 2010).

Fossil Fuels

The production of fossil fuels across the Mediterranean has steadily increased since 1990 to reach 436 Mtoe in 2009 (the average yearly growth rate is 1.2 per cent). In 2011, the proven oil reserves in the Mediterranean area were around 67 billion barrels, mostly (94 per cent) located in Libya, Algeria and Egypt. As for oil production estimated in the Mediterranean, this amounted to 5 million barrels per day in 2010. Oil has been the dominant fuel in the Mediterranean energy mix since the 1970s. Its demand increased over time at an average of 1.3 per cent per year (1990–2009 period); nonetheless, its share in the energy mix decreased from 50 per cent in 1990 to 41 per cent in 2009, mainly because of an increase in the use of natural gas in electricity generation. Looking at the world's production data for 2010 (reported in the first column of Table 6.1), we find that the largest producers of oil are the Russian Federation, followed by Saudi Arabia and the USA. However, Saudi Arabia is the largest exporter, as of 2009. Interestingly, some Mediterranean countries, such as Italy, France and Spain, are among the largest importers.

The Mediterranean region also has large natural gas reserves: more than 8.9 trillion cubic metres (tcm) are located in Algeria, Libya and Egypt. In the 1970s, natural gas was little used but nowadays it is widely used: its demand increased at an annual average growth rate of 5 per cent (from 108 Mtoe in 1990 to 274 Mtoe in 2009), reaching a significant share of the fuel mix in the region (28 per cent).

As for the larger MENA region, the endowment is consistent, but its global share in terms of exports remains below its potential. Indeed, the overall gas production of the MENA region represented in 2010 only 20 per cent (669 bcm) of the world's total gas production. Table 6.2 reports some statistics on the world's gas production: Iran, Qatar and Saudi Arabia are among the top 10 producers in 2010. Iran is the second largest gas

Table 6.1   The largest producers, net exporters and net importers of crude oil

Producers	Mt	% of world total	Net exporters	Mt	Net importers	Mt
Russian Federation	502	12.6%	Saudi Arabia	313	USA	510
Saudi Arabia	471	11.9%	Russian Federation	247	China	199
USA	336	8.5%	Iran	124	Japan	179
Iran	227	5.7%	Nigeria	114	India	159
China	200	5.0%	United Arab Emirates	100	Korea	115
Canada	159	4.0%	Iraq	94	Germany	98
Venezuela	149	3.8%	Angola	89	Italy	80
Mexico	144	3.6%	Norway	87	France	72
Nigeria	130	3.3%	Venezuela	85	Netherlands	57
United Arab Emirates	129	3.2%	Kuwait	68	Spain	56
Rest of the world	1526	38.4%	Others	574	Others	477
World	*3973*	*100.0%*	*Total*	*1895*	*Total*	*2002*

Notes:
Data relative to crude oil, NGL, feedstocks, additives and other hydrocarbons.
Data for production for 2010, data for exports and imports for 2009.

Source: IEA (2011a).

reserve holder in the world. However, since the Islamic revolution in 1979, gas production has mainly been devoted to meeting domestic demand. The country is the third largest gas consumer in the world: the sustained economic growth of the last decade has increased energy demand at a 6.8 per cent annual average. Qatar has the third largest gas reserves in the world, but, in contrast to Iran, is strongly developing exports: the country has invested in liquefied natural gas (LNG) technology and in the last decade has become by far the world's largest supplier of gas through this channel. Indeed, we find Qatar as well as Algeria among the top exporters. While Qatar invested in LNG, Algeria exports mainly through pipelines. In 2010 Algeria exported natural gas mainly to Italy (28 billion cubic metres, bcm), Spain (12 bcm), France (6 bcm) and Turkey (4 bcm). Around 70 per cent of the commercial gas production (80 bcm in 2010) is exported, while 30 per cent is consumed domestically. Again, we observe among the largest net importers some EU countries.

Table 6.2   The largest producers, net exporters and net importers of natural gas

Producers	bcm	% of world total	Net exporters	bcm	Net importers	bcm
Russian Federation	637	19.4%	Russian Federation	169	Japan	99
USA	613	18.7%	Norway	101	Germany	83
Canada	160	4.9%	Qatar	97	Italy	75
Iran	145	4.4%	Canada	72	USA	74
Qatar	121	3.7%	Algeria	55	France	46
Norway	107	3.3%	Indonesia	42	Korea	43
China	97	3.0%	Netherlands	34	Turkey	37
Netherlands	89	2.7%	Malaysia	25	UK	37
Indonesia	88	2.7%	Turkmenistan	24	Ukraine	37
Saudi Arabia	82	2.5%	Nigeria	24	Spain	36
Rest of the World	1143	34.8%	Others	165	Others	253
World	*3282*	*100.0%*	*Total*	*808*	*Total*	*820*

Notes:
Net exports and net imports include pipeline gas and LNG.
Data for production for 2010, data for exports and imports for 2009.

Source: IEA (2011a).

In spite of the large proven gas reserves, some MENA countries are facing gas shortages. This is due to the sustained economic growth of the area, which increases electricity demand and thus local consumption: today around 70 per cent of the gas produced in the region is consumed locally, which explains why the MENA region plays a relatively modest role in international gas trade (Glachant et al., 2012). All MENA countries endowed with fossil fuels have been following a similar path in recent years: an increasing domestic demand, amplified by artificially low prices (an issue discussed in detail in section 3), which puts a strain on exports. In the last years there has been a shift from oil to natural gas, in order to free oil for exports. However, the lack of infrastructure prevents further increases in production. As will be discussed in section 5, the recent turmoil might imply delays in investment in infrastructure.

For example, Libya's proven natural gas reserves are estimated at 1.5 tcm (trillion cubic meters) and recent discoveries are expected to raise these figures. Natural gas production has grown substantially in the country in the last few years, reaching a level of 15.8 bcm in 2010 and it now accounts for 45 per cent of the country's generated electricity. However, past projects to increase the production in order to free up oil for exports are likely to be delayed. Another country whose infrastructure has been severely damaged is Iraq. With proven natural gas reserves estimated at 3.2 tcm in 2010, the country's production has decreased substantially over the last decade because the conflicts have seriously impaired Iraqi infrastructure. Indeed, over 40 per cent of the production in 2008 was flared due to a lack of sufficient infrastructure to utilize it for consumption and export.

The Mediterranean has around 18 billion tonnes of coal reserves, which are almost entirely found in five countries: Serbia, Bosnia and Herzegovina, Greece, Turkey and Spain. Coal production in the region is around 44 million toe (tonnes of oil equivalent) and 40 per cent is produced in Turkey alone. Coal's share in total primary energy production in Mediterranean countries has been declining since the 1990s and is now 7 per cent of energy production. It has been replaced by natural gas, especially in power generation. There are, however, different patterns across the Mediterranean: coal demand has declined strongly in the North over the past 20 years while increasing in the South. As a consequence, total coal demand in the region is rather stable at around 108 million toe (close to 1990 values), and it accounts for 11 per cent of the energy mix.

Nuclear energy production has expanded from 1973, following the nuclear development programme in France. Power generation from nuclear plants has been rather stable in the last 20 years and accounted for 24 per cent of generation in 2009. France is the largest producer in the area with an installed capacity of 62 763 megawatts. There are no nuclear power stations in the MENA area but some countries, such as Turkey and Egypt, have announced plans. Indeed, nuclear power generating costs are less volatile than those of hydrocarbons, and nuclear power is seen as an option that could help alleviate energy security issues as well as CO_2 emissions. However, the Arab Spring in 2011, jointly with the Fukushima Daiichi nuclear power accident in Japan in the same year, are likely to delay these plans.

Renewable Sources

The Mediterranean has a large renewable energy potential. Nonetheless, renewables account nowadays for a limited share of the region's primary energy supply (8 per cent in 2009) and production (12 per cent). The most exploited renewable sources have historically been biomass and hydropower. Additionally, geothermal energy has been quite developed in a few countries (for example Italy). More recently, wind and solar, both for electricity and heat production, are increasing their share in the energy mix:

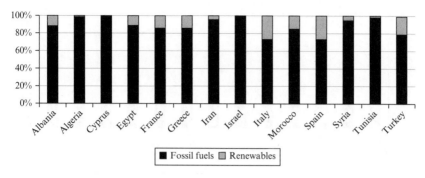

Source: Own elaboration from EIA (2012).

Figure 6.2   Electricity production in 2009

non-hydro renewables more than doubled their installed capacity in the period of 2005 to 2009, mainly with wind turbines. The electricity production from renewables (primarily from hydropower) has reached 18 per cent of electricity supply, almost 340 terawatt-hours in 2009. Figure 6.2 reports the breakdown of electricity production in 2009 between fossil fuels and renewable sources: fossil fuels are still largely predominant everywhere.

EU countries are investing in these sources, notably Italy and Spain. There are a few other countries that produce significant levels of renewable energy: Turkey produces around 10 Mtoe, followed by Morocco and Egypt, while in the other countries there is barely any production.

Two trends describe the development of renewables in the area. Although renewable generation is growing at a sustained pace (compound annual growth rate (CAGR) 1.95 per cent for the period 2000–09), total power generation is growing more rapidly (CAGR 6.3 per cent over the same time period): non-renewable generation increased by 248 TWh since 2000 (almost doubling), while renewables grew by only 3 TWh. Second, among renewables, non-hydro are growing more rapidly than hydropower. The breakdown between hydropower and other renewable sources is reported in Figure 6.3.

The largest source of hydropower in the MENA area is the Aswan Dam in Egypt, inaugurated in 1971. It has a capacity of 2100 MW and produces about 13–14 TWh per year. Non-hydro renewables have grown at an average rate of 25.2 per cent since 2000, however from negligible levels. As for non-hydro renewable sources, their growth is concentrated in Egypt, Morocco, Tunisia and Israel. As of 2009, the other countries in the region did not report any non-hydro generation.

Egypt has seen a strong deployment of non-hydro renewables, in

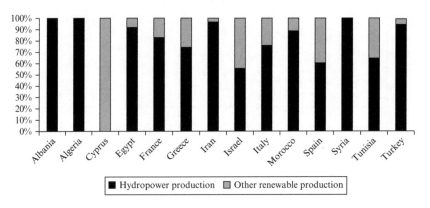

Source: Own elaboration from EIA (2012).

Figure 6.3   Renewable electricity production in 2009

the form of wind, especially along the Red Sea coast, in the past years. Although it is an exporter of fossil fuels, the issue of resource depletion is becoming more important: domestic demand for energy is increasing and blackouts are more frequent, especially in the summer period. Egypt has developed its wind resources with the support of international institutions, notably the World Bank, with the aim of facing the resource problem.

Israel shows surprisingly little production of renewable electricity. The abundant solar resources have been adopted on a large scale since the 1970s for heat. A mass development is, however, missing and a possible explanation is the small internal market which does not allow economies of scale to be realized. However, as solar photovoltaic (PV) is becoming a less expensive technology and concentrated solar power (CSP) is being commercialized in Spain and the United States, an increase of solar energy production might take place in the future.

Morocco and Tunisia have made some efforts to develop renewable energy, notably wind and hydropower, over the past years. As for the other countries, no efforts to develop solar and wind resources have been made so far and renewable energy production is almost absent. This attitude is slowly changing (see more in section 3), but an increase in renewables would require international support, as in the case of Egypt. The EU can play a key role in this respect, as will be discussed in section 4.

As already mentioned, increasing income per capita is likely to imply a problem of resource depletion in the future. Thus, countries are slowly taking steps towards renewables. For example, the United Arab Emirates now hosts the International Renewable Energy Agency (IRENA), and their state-owned power company is working on the Masdar City project, with 90 000 residents, which is intended to be completely supplied by renewables.

Per capita consumption in the residential sector in the South Mediterranean is currently low by regional and international comparisons, being less than half that of the northern shore. This reflects relatively poor living conditions for large parts of the population. Many countries in MENA have close to 100 per cent access to electricity, but an estimated 28 million people still lack access to electricity, especially in rural areas, and about 8 million people rely on traditional biomass for their energy needs (World Bank, 2010). This gap in consumption is expected to shrink and economic development is expected to increase cooling demand considerably. The penetration rates of cooling installations are already rising to high rates in Israel, United Arab Emirates and Saudi Arabia. Indeed, the climate of the countries in the area could lead to very high penetration rates: estimates for Egypt are for a possible 95 per cent penetration rate, compared to the actual 10 per cent share. However, demand for cooling is high where renewable heat is available, that is when it is hot outside. Thus synergies might emerge.

6.3   ENERGY POLICIES

Policies for Renewable Energy

Energy subsidies are increasingly being introduced to promote the use of renewable energy sources as the market alone fails to capture all the costs of producing and using fossil fuels. Support to renewables is necessary to offset these external costs. In order to reach this result governments have used mainly two types of instruments: the Feed-in Tariff (FiT) and the Green Certificate (GC). The first is a tariff that pays the value of energy plus an incentive for the costs of production while the second is a mechanism that sets targets of renewables production, giving the chance to the producers to purchase it through a GC from other suppliers. These policies are generally integrated with tax incentives, investment subsidies and special loan programmes. Even in countries relying mainly on GCs, FiTs are becoming increasingly popular to support small-scale generation, as for example in Italy.

The eight EU members in the Mediterranean follow common policies under the umbrella of the Union directives and regulations. The directive on promotion of the use of energy from renewable sources (EU, 2009) imposes on all member countries binding targets for the share of renewable energy in gross final consumption. The overall EU target by 2020 is

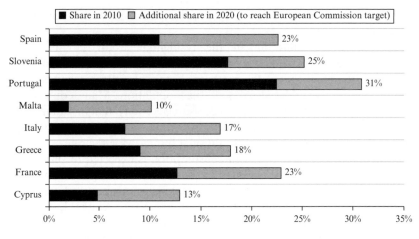

Source: OME (2011).

Figure 6.4   Renewables' share in final energy in EU countries

20 per cent of gross final energy consumption (it was 13 per cent in 2011) and 20 per cent of energy savings. As for renewable energy in transport, by 2000, a number of EU countries have introduced biofuels targets. These measures are driven by environmental and energy security concerns, as well as the aim to promote economic growth and job creation in the agricultural sector. The increase in biofuels has been supported by a 2003 European Directive that requires 5.75 per cent of the transport energy demand to come from biofuels by 2010. The 2009 directive imposes a 10 per cent target for 2020.

However, the overall target for renewable energy production is divided among member states according to the current level of penetration. Data reported in Figure 6.4 show that considerable progress is needed to achieve these targets. Renewables need to double in almost all EU Mediterranean countries and a drastic change is needed in Malta, where renewables need to increase from 2 per cent to over 10 per cent of final energy consumption.

In order to obtain these targets, GC and FiT are in action in most EU countries. Data on the actual estimated amount of subsidies for renewable electricity production granted in three large EU Mediterranean countries are reported in Figure 6.5.

Also, the target of 20 per cent energy savings by 2020 is likely to be missed. Indeed, in spite of significant progress, the actual measures are likely to achieve only a 10 per cent saving.

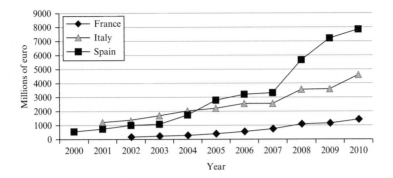

Source: Own elaboration based on countries' reports.

Figure 6.5   Total subsidies for renewable electricity production (2000–10)

The emphasis on biofuels in the EU is expected to continue. The plans require 21.250 Mtoe/y of biodiesel and 7.121 Mtoe/y of bioethanol by 2020. Trade will be necessary: estimates suggest imports of 26 per cent of biodiesel and 25 per cent of the bioethanol to meet the national plans (Muller et al., 2011).

The non-EU countries in the northern shore of the Mediterranean are implementing the *acquis communautaire* in order to conform to the EU requirements and expand their market opportunities.

In comparison with policies for renewable electricity or biofuels for transport, policies to encourage the development of renewable energy in heating have been neglected. However, an analysis by IEA (2008) has shown that the effectiveness of these policies is limited. Nowadays, the most widely adopted financial mechanism to support renewable heat is direct subsidies for the purchase of a renewable heating system. They are generally more effective in the prototype and demonstration phase, but persist when the technology is mature. This might be due to the perceived lack of alternative policies available: the heat market is different from the electricity market in the sense that allocating the additional costs of renewable heating technology among all heating fuel consumers according to the 'polluter-pays' principle appears to be more complicated.

MENA countries in contrast do not have stringent obligations. Indeed, in this area the impetus for the development of renewables comes mainly from international cooperation and multilateral initiatives (see more in section 4). The MENA region is lagging behind in implementing reforms in the electricity sector and lacks private sector investment. There is thus much scope for improving the efficiency of energy supply and energy conservation, as well as the development of renewable energy resources. MENA has begun to exploit its renewable energy potential on a large scale with the support of international institutions such as the World Bank, which supervised 17 investment projects in 2010 totalling about US$2.1 billion. Additionally it launched the Clean Technology Fund, which has allocated a total of US$1.2 billion for MENA, of which US$750 million is to design and implement a MENA Concentrated Solar Power (CSP) plan, US$275 million is to develop wind energy in Egypt and US$200 million is to develop wind energy in Morocco.

The World Bank is also carrying out analytical and advisory energy work in most countries of the region, on issues such as developing energy/electricity sector master plans and reforms (Djibouti, Lebanon, Morocco and Syria) or energy efficiency (Jordan, Tunisia and Yemen), developing a financial and institutional framework for energy or specific frameworks for wind power (Egypt and Morocco). Many of the above activities are also carried out in close partnership with donors in the region.

All North African countries and Israel have introduced financial support mechanisms for renewable electricity, contrary to Saudi Arabia and United Arab Emirates. Nonetheless, in practice, the financial incentives have not been implemented and thus they have not encouraged a renewable electricity market to date. Indeed, most of the non-hydro renewable development has been driven by international funding from international donors or Clean Development Mechanisms (CDM) revenues (UNEP Risoe, 2010).

In the last few years a number of large projects started, aimed at increasing the integration of the electricity market among the shores of the Mediterranean. These include the Mediterranean Solar Plan (MSP) and the Desertec industrial initiative and will be discussed in depth in the next section. These investments will help MENA countries to increase renewable energy production. The projects to strengthen network interconnections among the MENA countries and between the two shores of the Mediterranean will also facilitate the integration of markets.

Algeria established dedicated renewable energy actors in the past twenty years. Although these institutions have large resources, opposition from entrenched interests from the oil and gas sectors is undermining their effectiveness. A FiT has been introduced in 2004; however, there is no effective implementation.

Egypt founded the National Renewable Energy Authority (NREA) in 1986 but there is no actual financial support mechanism for renewable electricity generation, apart from guaranteed grid access, priority dispatch and some reduction in import duties for technology equipment. International development cooperation has supported renewable generation and is currently shifting to financing an extension of the grid because an infrastructure upgrade is crucial for a large-scale deployment of wind resources: the best are located along the Red Sea coast, quite far from the bulk of the demand, along the Nile and in the capital.

Israel has introduced a FiT in 2009 to meet its targets of 5 per cent renewable electricity generation by 2014 and 10 per cent by 2020, but the mechanism has only been implemented marginally. Large solar demonstration projects, co-financed with the European Investment Bank, have started in the Negev Desert. These are part of a development plan to build 10 large CSP plants in the Negev between 2010 and 2020.

In Morocco the 2007 energy efficiency and renewable energy law includes provisions for an incentive mechanism; however, no support scheme for renewable energy is actually implemented. Since 2009, the government has accelerated its renewable energy promotion efforts in order to attract foreign capital. Again, these efforts are also driven by increasing energy security concerns: the country's electricity imports (primarily from Spain) have quadrupled from 2005 to 2007. In 2009 a new renewable energy law established a renewable energy and energy efficiency fund with the aim of helping leverage public–private partnerships for the development of five large-scale projects within the 2GW solar programme to 2020, which was announced in 2009.

In Tunisia the National Fund for Energy Conservation (FNME) provides financial support for renewable electricity installations. The Tunisian Solar Plan (PST) was launched in 2009 with a budget of US$2.2 billion and encompasses 40 projects to be implemented between 2010 and 2016 under public–private partnership arrangements. National public sector financing to leverage private investment will amount to 25 per cent, while the rest is expected to be covered from multilateral development cooperation, bilateral cooperation and CDM revenues.

Saudi Arabia does not have an official target or policy instruments, but announcements from the government suggest a possible target of 7–10 per cent peak electricity generation from renewables by 2020, which would be equivalent to around 5GW capacity, mostly from solar. The aim is to dedicate some of this production for export.

Finally, United Arab Emirates aim at establishing Abu Dhabi as a global R&D and manufacturing hub for renewable energy technologies, especially solar. The government in 2006 started the above-mentioned Masdar City project, which aims to be the world's largest carbon-neutral urban development. However, this demonstration project may not be sufficient to achieve the 7 per cent target, which implies an estimated installed capacity of at least 2GW of renewable energy.

Fossil-fuel Subsidies

Subsidies to the consumption of fossil-fuels lower prices to consumers and are now rare in most OECD countries, but still present in many other regions, including MENA. Subsidies to production, in contrast, are measures that seek to expand domestic supply and are still widely adopted in both OECD and non-OECD countries, although many subsidies in this category have been reduced.

Both kinds of subsidies encourage excessive production or consumption, naturally leading to an inefficient allocation of resources and market distortions. However, subsidies to production are difficult to quantify as they are often offered through indirect mechanisms, for example tax concessions. While they are absent in the northern shore of the Mediterranean, fossil-fuel consumption subsidies are widely adopted in the MENA region.

Subsidies that artificially lower energy prices have a number of shortcomings. They encourage unnecessary consumption, which leads to faster depletion of energy resources and discourages rationalization and efficiency improvements in energy-intensive industries. There is a strong empirical link between low energy prices and excessive consumption. Extremely high rates of electricity consumption in MENA can be shown to derive from cheap electricity tariffs. The resulting subsidy, in certain cases, has over-burdened government resources at the expense of social and economic expenditures (Khatib, 2010). Additionally, these subsidies can encourage fuel adulteration and the substitution of subsidized fuels for more expensive fuels (Shenoy, 2010). For example, subsidized kerosene for households might be diverted for unauthorized use as diesel fuel, due to the wide price differentials. There is an incentive to sell subsidized products in neighbouring countries with higher prices, thus leading to fuel smuggling. These subsidies undermine the competitiveness of renewable sources. Additionally, they impose a significant fiscal burden on countries' budgets. Moreover, they have negative effects for producers as they quicken the depletion of resources and can thereby reduce export earnings in the long run. Finally, once introduced, they are difficult to reform or eliminate.

Historically, the rationale for the introduction of energy subsidies has been manifold. A first justification is the need to alleviate energy poverty: these subsidies might improve the living conditions of low-income populations by making cleaner and more efficient fuels affordable: for example, liquefied petroleum gas (LPG) in place of traditional biomass. Secondly, in energy-producing countries, they are seen as a means to share the value of national resources. Finally, they are used to stimulate regional employment and economic development. Nowadays there is a general consensus on the necessity to cut these subsidies as they have often proven to be an unsuccessful or inefficient mean of achieving these goals.

Fossil-fuel consumption subsidies worldwide amounted to US$409 billion in 2010. The annual level fluctuates widely following changes in international energy prices, domestic pricing policy, exchange rates and demand.

In a period of high prices, these subsidies impose unsustainable costs on the budgets of those countries that import energy at world prices and sell it domestically at lower, regulated prices. As a consequence, many such countries seized the opportunity offered by the fall in prices after the second half of 2008 to reduce subsidies without impacting much on inflation.

A related motivation for phasing out these subsidies is that in the absence of offsetting compensation payments to companies they reduce companies' revenues and thus limit their investments in infrastructure. This problem is particularly relevant in the electricity sector (leading to blackouts or low levels of electricity access), but is also present in the oil, natural gas and coal sectors.

Energy subsidies are often intended to redistribute income to the poor; however, the greatest beneficiaries are the individuals that consume more energy, that is, owners of motor vehicles and electrical appliances. The IMF has estimated that 80 per cent of the total benefits from oil subsidies in 2009 accrued to the richest 40 per cent of households (Coady et al., 2010). Nonetheless, removing these subsidies needs a careful implementation as the adverse impact on poor households can be disproportionally large.

Over time, these subsidies may even reduce the exports that earn essential revenues for governments. Furthermore, a number of major oil exporters, including Iran, rely on imports of refined petroleum products, as low domestic prices undermine investment in refining capacity. This problem is particularly acute if governments do not reimburse refiners for their losses. Without new measures to phase out subsidies the increase in domestic oil demand to 2020 in Middle East countries is projected to absorb 24 per cent of the growth in crude oil production (IEA, 2010).

The largest subsidies in absolute terms are granted by those countries with the largest resource endowments. Iran was the largest subsidizer in the world in 2010 with US$81 billion, followed by Saudi Arabia, at US$44 billion and Russia, with US$39 billion.

Subsidies accounted for around 20 per cent of GDP in Iran and 10 per cent in Saudi Arabia in 2009 (IEA, 2010). This under-pricing has strained the Iranian economy, forced reliance on refined product imports and led to widespread energy inefficiency. To reduce the fiscal burden, Iran enacted a subsidy reform law in 2010 which would increase prices to market-based levels over the period from 2010 to 2015 and use the savings to replace price subsidies with targeted assistance to low-income groups. Current plans call for oil-product prices to rise to at least 90 per cent of the average Persian Gulf export price and for natural gas prices to be raised to 75 per cent of the export price. Saudi Arabia instead plans minor electricity tariff increases for industrial and commercial users.

Of course, these reforms are likely to be postponed in countries that have faced recent political turmoil (that is, in Egypt, the world's sixth largest subsidizer with around US$20 billion). In September 2009, G20 leaders committed to phase out and rationalize inefficient fossil-fuel subsidies. Many countries are now pursuing these reforms, which would have a dramatic effect on supply and demand in global energy markets. A universal phase-out of all fossil-fuel consumption subsidies by 2020 would cut global primary energy demand by 5 per cent. Such an amount corresponds to the current consumption of Japan, Korea and New Zealand (IEA, 2010).

6.4   COOPERATION IN THE MEDITERRANEAN

The high dependency on foreign gas in the EU causes serious concerns for the security of supply: for example, in January 2009 18 European countries reported major cut-offs of their gas supplies from Russia, as a consequence of a Russian dispute with Ukraine. There is a thus a large potential for the MENA region to help the EU in its efforts to diversify among suppliers.

Cooperation across the Mediterranean is meant to span from fossil fuels to renewables. Efforts towards energy efficiency and renewable energy could represent the key elements of an EU foreign energy policy towards the region. An approach based on these two priorities would provide the double dividend of promoting sustainable economic development in the MENA countries and, at the same time, enabling more gas to be exported. Indeed, it is more efficient if North Africa's solar potential is first devoted to satisfy the increasing domestic electricity demand, thus liberating additional gas exports to Europe. Transporting gas is cheaper than transporting electricity and it is more accepted by the public (pipelines are not visible, in contrast to overhead power lines).

The two shores of the Mediterranean Sea have historically been linked by hydrocarbons trade, which contributed to building long-term partnerships for decades. Now there is an increasing focus on regional cooperation in the electricity sector, particularly for renewables-based generation. Additionally, large schemes to develop electricity interconnections are under consideration. The European Union policy aims at strengthening energy sector integration and stimulating investments in efficient and low-carbon energy technologies in the South Mediterranean. It is also considering the integration of the southern shore of the Mediterranean in the European Union internal energy market by establishing an EU–Southern Mediterranean Energy Community. The 'Mediterranean Ring' aims to connect several electricity corridors, according to the technical standards and the need for synchronization. There is complementarity across the Mediterranean in terms of seasonal electricity demand and this provides mutual benefits in terms of energy supply.

Energy has been a dominant issue in European Union initiatives, starting with the EuroMed Partnership initiated in 1995 with the Barcelona Declaration, the European Neighbourhood Policy in 2003 and the Union for the Mediterranean in 2008, as well as many multilateral or bilateral agreements. The European Union's Energy 2020 Strategy (COM(2010) 639) states that strengthening the external dimension of the European Union energy policy is a key priority. This has been reinforced with the EC's Partnership for Democracy and Shared Prosperity with the Southern Mediterranean (COM (2011) 200), issued in 2011. In March 2011, the EC proposed that a group be formed to focus primarily on the development of renewable energy. In the medium term this is expected to lead to extending the Energy Community Treaty to neighbours or establishing a complementary European Union–Southern Mediterranean Energy Community. Among the EU priorities are greater integration of energy markets by completing the Mediterranean electricity and gas rings.

A New Response to a Changing Neighbourhood, a joint communication from the EC and the High Representative of the Union for Foreign Affairs and Security Policy in May 2011, states that the EU is to step up energy cooperation with European Neighbourhood Policy partners with the aim of further market integration and increased energy security based on converging regulatory frameworks.

Fossil Fuels

As for fossil fuels, the infrastructure in the Mediterranean is quite developed. Algeria has a well-established pipeline transport system linking its gas fields to Italy, Spain and Portugal. Moreover, the new deepwater Medgaz pipeline, commissioned in March 2011, allows Algeria to serve the Spanish market without transit through other countries. The Galsi pipeline from El Kala to Sardinia, if and when completed, will provide direct access to the Italian market. Libya has only one direct pipeline to export gas to Sicily (Greenstream). Also, the Arab gas pipeline connects Egypt with Jordan, Syria and possibly Europe through Turkey. Another pipeline allows Egypt to transport gas to Israel. In addition, the Greece–Turkey inter-connector pipeline allows Europe to receive Caspian gas through

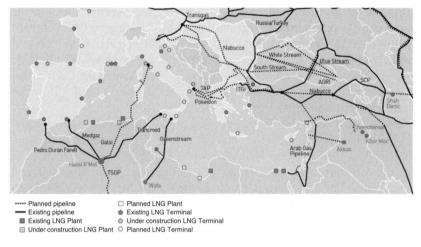

Source: OME (2011).

Figure 6.6   Natural gas pipelines in the Mediterranean

Turkey. There are several other pipeline projects that aim to bring Caspian gas to Europe through Turkey, which are reported in Figure 6.6.[1] Besides pipelines, there are several existing and planned liquefied natural gas plants in the South Mediterranean that allow gas exports to Europe and other markets.

Electricity and Renewable Energy

A prerequisite for cooperation in this field is an improvement of the existing grid. South–North HVDC (high voltage direct current) links across the Mediterranean basin allow the buffering of electricity price rises in Europe. More interconnections will help to promote an electricity market in the MENA region and facilitate integration over time of the South into the European electricity market. This contributes to increased security of supply for the North Mediterranean, particularly for Italy, as these interconnections could avoid the heavily congested corridors across the Alps. Currently there are four main routes under consideration for HVDC South–North interconnection projects, as reported in Figure 6.7: Tunisia–Sicily; Algeria–Sardinia; Algeria–Spain; and a more unlikely Libya–Sicily route. Only the first is progressing and is planned to be operative in 2016.

To take additional power, an Italian grid upgrade in Calabria and Sicily would be necessary to reduce congestion and allow additional flows from North Africa.

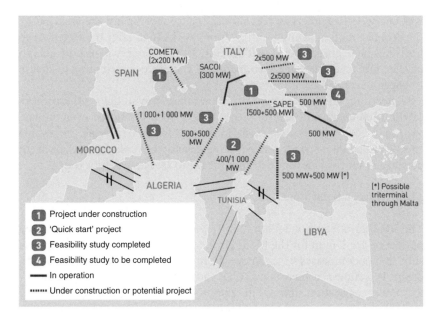

COMETA
(2x200 MW)

SPAIN **1**

ITALY 2x500 MW **3**

SACOI
(300 MW)

2x500 MW **3**

1

.... **4**

SAPEI 500 MW
(500+500 MW)

1 000+1 000 MW **3**

3

500+500
MW

MOROCCO

500 MW

2

400/1 000
MW

3

500 MW+500 MW (*)

ALGERIA

(*) Possible
triterminal
through Malta

TUNISIA

LIBYA

1 Project under construction
2 'Quick start' project
3 Feasibility study completed
4 Feasibility study to be completed
— In operation
······ Under construction or potential project

Source: OME (2011).

Figure 6.7   HVDC transmission links in the Mediterranean

The selection of submarine routes for the South–North corridors is complex: a technical analysis is necessary to identify the optimal sending and receiving ends of the new corridors, as well as their size and the required reinforcements in the terrestrial transmission grids. An environmental study is necessary to provide an analysis of the morphology of the Mediterranean Sea depth to assess the most viable submarine interconnection alternatives. Finally, economic analyses are necessary to assess the profitability of the new corridors (the expected cost is around 1 billion euros per corridor). The analyses will investigate the impact of the electricity imported from the South on prices in the European integrated electricity market.

In the South Mediterranean countries, more cross-border electricity trade can be a catalyst for growth, as the sector's liberalization would attract foreign capital. However, an obstacle is the level of subsidies for electricity in many countries in the South: domestic tariffs are too low to offer profitability for producers.

All southern and eastern Mediterranean countries have embarked during the last years – with the support of the European Union – on an energy pathway focusing on an increased development of renewable energy and energy efficiency. The EU should try to accompany the creation of the broader economic and political frameworks that, after the recent Arab uprisings, new governments will develop. In this way it will also be able to have an impact on the energy cooperation, therefore contributing to ensure European energy security.

Concerning the development of renewable energy in the southern shore of the Mediterranean, several projects have been promoted over the last two years. We will discuss them in detail. These large-scale renewable energy projects are strictly related to the development of gas markets as an increase in renewables production is meant to free up gas for export.

Mediterranean Solar Plan

The Mediterranean Solar Plan (MSP) was launched in 2008 and is a key project of the Union for the Mediterranean (UfM), a multilateral partnership that encompasses 43 countries from the EU and the Mediterranean basin. It is aimed at increasing solar and other renewable energy sources for power generation, improving energy efficiency, developing electricity grid interconnections and encouraging the transfer of know-how and technology to emerging economies. The objective is to achieve the development of 20GW of new renewable energy installed capacity in the MENA countries by 2020 along with the necessary electricity transmission capacity and interconnections between the two shores of the Mediterranean. This will require total investment of around 60 billion euros. Additionally, it aims to obtain significant energy savings by 2020.

This plan needs to address a number of issues such as new interconnections across the Mediterranean, investment in new grids and reinforcement of existing interconnections.

By contributing to the development of solar and other renewables generation capacity and green electricity trade between the Mediterranean countries and the EU, the MSP intends to address the challenges of internal energy demand in the participating countries. During the first Joint Committee of National Experts in July 2011 the European Investment Bank (EIB) presented proposals for the creation of new financial instruments to support the MSP process.

The European Commission is accompanying this initiative through capacity-building projects such as 'Paving the Way for the Mediterranean Solar Plan', aimed at contributing to the establishment of harmonized legislative and regulatory frameworks for renewable energy, improving knowledge transfer and enhancing capacity-building across all the southern Mediterranean partner countries. The indicative budget is around 5 million euros for the period 2011–13. The Medgrid initiative, launched in

2010 under the umbrella of the MSP, aims to create a network of energy enterprises to realize a large network of underwater electric interconnections in the Mediterranean. The estimated budget is 8 billion euros.

Transmission grids in the South are weak or already saturated: they were designed to serve systems based on fossil fuel generation along coastal lines or hydropower on the Nile. However, new large renewables generation projects are largely based in areas far from existing grids and thus transmission systems will have to be expanded and reinforced. Also, the current structure of the European Union transmission grid needs to be improved as it does not allow the injection of several GW from the South, because of congestion.

Desertec Industrial Initiative

The Desertec industrial initiative (Dii) was launched in July 2009 by 12 companies, mainly from Germany, with the aim of delivering the framework for large-scale use of desert solar and wind energy resources to replace fossil fuels and nuclear energy, while also promoting development in North Africa. It involves the construction of concentrating solar power systems over 17 000 sq. km of the Sahara desert in order to generate 50GW of installed CSP capacity by 2050, which would be distributed to Europe and North Africa through a high voltage super grid.

The objective is to meet local demand first and allow these countries to also export energy to Europe. Several individual projects are to be created in cooperation with local subjects (governments, companies), aiming to produce and transfer power generated from renewable resources. In this process, Desertec tries to be a facilitator, catalyst and coordinator.

Among the Dii's main goals are the drafting of business plans and starting industrial preparations for building a large number of networked solar power plants distributed throughout the MENA region. Again, a reinforcement and expansion of the electricity grids locally and in connection to the European grids is one of the prerequisites. Dii expects a super-grid development across the continents, connecting the major renewable sources with demand areas. The target is to produce and export power sufficient to meet around 15 per cent of Europe's electricity requirements and a substantial portion of the energy needs of the producer countries by 2050.

This initiative has the support of the European Commission, through the project 'Paving the Way for the Mediterranean Solar Plan' and through the financial support of the European Investment Bank's Facility for Euro-Mediterranean Investment and Partnership (FEMIP) and the Neighbourhood Investment Facility (NIF).

6.5   THE ARAB SPRING

The recent Arab uprisings may have an important impact on the MENA energy markets' prospects. The domestic social tensions suggest that reforms, including fossil-fuels subsidies reforms, will be delayed, leading to an increase in domestic energy consumption and thus to a constraint of gas exports in the near future.

The IEA (2011b) projects that MENA will contribute more than 90 per cent to the required growth in oil production expected for 2035. For such an increase, upstream investment in MENA needs to average US$100 billion per year from 2011 to 2020 and US$115 billion per year from 2021 to 2035 (in year-2010 dollars). However, the recent uprisings might delay some of these investments. Indeed, governments might choose to develop production capacity more slowly: they might prefer to hold back resources for future generations or to support the oil price in the short term. Moreover, they could give priority to spending on other public programmes rather than upstream development. Legal changes, renegotiation of existing agreements and increased political instability are all factors that could possibly contribute to a delay in investment.

The IEA has produced a scenario which incorporates this hindrance and assumes that upstream oil (and gas) investment will be reduced by one-third in all MENA countries, compared with a business-as-usual scenario without delays over the period 2011 to 2015. The shortfall in investment will affect oil and gas markets directly and have indirect effects on the other energy markets. In this scenario oil and gas production capacity falls progressively short of that projected in the scenario without delays. The shortfall in oil production in MENA reaches over 6 million barrels per day (mb/d) in 2020: this is large enough to have a significant impact on global oil markets and increase oil and gas prices.

The upward part of the price trajectory in this scenario is similar to that which occurred in the last decade, resulting in a spike in 2008, which was also the result, at least in part, of insufficient investment. The downward slope is comparable to the decline after the second oil shock in 1979–80, which saw the same kind of market reaction with a demand decrease through increased efficiency, fuel switching and increased investment in exploration and production in other regions. This is reported in Figure 6.8.

Gas and coal prices are expected to react to the increase in oil price and the reduction in investment in gas supply capacity in MENA, though to a different extent across regions. In the period of high oil prices, gas and coal prices are expected to decouple from oil prices. Notice that the loss of gas supply, as a proportion of global supply, is significantly less than that of oil supply.

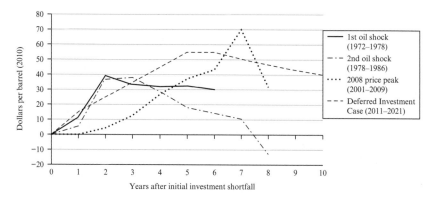

Source: IEA (2011b).

Figure 6.8   Change in crude oil price assuming a delay in investment in MENA

With sharply higher prices, global oil demand is assumed to remain rather constant in the medium term. However, sustained high prices at the level expected make the production of biofuels competitive (IEA, 2010).

MENA investment is assumed to recover gradually after 2015 but, due to the decline in production from existing fields, total MENA production continues to fall until 2020. After 2020, MENA production starts to increase again, reaching its 2010 level by 2023. The recovery of production in the MENA region after 2015 is comparable to that observed after past supply disruptions, as shown in Figure 6.9.

6.6   CONCLUSIONS

The MENA region has large fossil fuel resources and is thus crucial in global oil and, to a lesser extent, gas markets. Moreover, its geography gives to the area a huge endowment of solar resources, which are still largely undeveloped. On the other side of the Mediterranean, the EU includes some of the largest energy importers in the world and is thus extremely sensitive to the issue of security of supply.

We discuss the policies implemented in recent years: while EU countries have stringent requirements regarding renewable energy production and energy savings, the MENA countries lack such policies and additionally face the problem of fossil-fuel consumption subsidies, which are costly and extremely difficult to phase out. We also present a number of

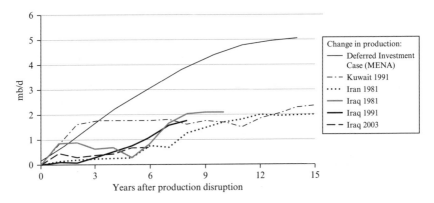

Source: IEA (2011b).

*Figure 6.9   Oil production recovery assuming a delay in investment in
             MENA*

joint projects across the Mediterranean. These range from new pipelines
for gas to an improvement of the HVDC links across the sea. Much
attention is devoted to renewable energy production in the southern shore
of the Mediterranean (such as the Mediterranean Solar Plan and the
Desertec industrial initiative), as this would yield the double dividend of
an increase in renewable energy production to satisfy the increasing local
demand in a sustainable way and freeing natural gas for export to the
northern shore.

The recent political turmoil that took place in some Arab countries is
adding uncertainty to this scenario. This could be an opportunity for EU
countries to strengthen cooperation with new governments in the fields of
energy supply and transmission, both from fossil fuels and from renewable sources. The most likely effect, however, is a delay in the investment
in infrastructure. This will probably imply a loss of production, which is
expected to be initially small, but to become larger in the longer term. As a
consequence, the crude oil price is expected to increase.

NOTE

1.   A detailed North Africa pipelines map can also be found at: http://www.theodora.com/
     pipelines/north_africa_pipelines_map.jpg.

REFERENCES

Coady, D., R. Gillingham, R. Ossowski, J. Piotrowski, S. Tareq and J. Tyson (2010), 'Petroleum product subsidies: costly, inequitable, and rising', IMF Staff Position Note, SPN/10/05, Washington, DC: IMF.

Darbouche, H. and B. Fattouh (2011), 'The implications of the Arab uprisings for oil and gas markets', MEP2, Oxford: Oxford Institute for Energy Studies.

EIA (2012), 'International energy statistics', available at: http://www.eia.gov/cfapps/ipdbproject/IEDIndex3.cfm.

EU (2009), Directive 2009/28/EC of the European Parliament and of the Council of 23 April 2009 on the Promotion of the Use of Energy from Renewable Sources and Amending and Subsequently Repealing Directives 2001/77/EC and 2003/30/EC, Brussels: European Commission.

Glachant, J-M., M. Hafner, J. De Jong, N. Ahner and S. Tagliapietra (2012), *A New Architecture for EU Gas Security of Supply*, Deventer: Claeys & Casteels.

IEA (2008), *Deploying Renewables: Principles for Effective Policies*, Paris: OECD/IEA.

IEA (2010), *World Energy Outlook 2010*, Paris: IEA.

IEA (2011a), *Key World Energy Statistics*, Paris: IEA.

IEA (2011b), *World Energy Outlook 2011*, Paris: IEA.

Khatib, H. (2010), 'Electricity subsidies in Arab countries', paper presented at Arab Energy Forum, Doha, 13 May.

Muller, S., A. Marmion and M. Beerepoot (2011), 'Renewable energy: markets and prospects by region', in IEA (ed.), *Deploying Renewables 2011: Best and Future Policy Practice*, Paris: IEA.

OME (2011), *Mediterranean Energy Perspectives 2011*, Nanterre: OME.

Shenoy, B.V. (2010), *Lessons Learned from Attempts to Reform India's Kerosene Subsidy*, Geneva: International Institute for Sustainable Development.

UNEP Risoe (2010), 'UNEP Risoe CDM/JI pipeline analysis and database', available at: http://cdmpipeline.org/.

World Bank (2010), 'Energy in MENA', available at: http://web.worldbank.org/WBSITE/EXTERNAL/COUNTRIES/MENAEXT/0,,contentMDK:22307440~pagePK:146736~piPK:146830~theSitePK:256299,00.html.

7. Innovation performance of MENA countries: where do we stand?

Maria Giovanna Bosco and Roberto Mavilia

7.1 THE INNOVATION PERFORMANCE OF MIDDLE EAST AND NORTH AFRICAN COUNTRIES: A SLOW PACE TOWARDS CONVERGENCE

Since the pioneering studies of Robert Solow, the origins of economic growth have been pinpointed in innovation. Superior technologies provide gains in productivity and allow for a positive economic growth even in a world whose steady state would imply a long-term null economic growth. Therefore, the ability of countries to produce or import new technologies lies at the heart of the so-called process of convergence, which supposedly leads laggard countries (in terms of economic development) toward the best performing, industrialized countries. Once upon a time, this last definition referred mainly to OECD countries, but today, as BRIC (Brazil, Russia, India, China) countries are stepping faster on the technological scale and the economic and political crises are spreading across industrialized countries, this definition alone does not apply any more.

The position of the Middle East and North African (MENA) countries lies somehow in the middle between the fastest growing countries of Asia and South America and the slowest growing countries of Old Europe. Notwithstanding, Europe remains the dream and the main reference partner for most MENA countries.

In the last decades, the growth performance of MENA countries has only been moderate, if compared with other emerging countries, particularly in Asia. In practice, from 1961 to 2011, the annual average growth rate amounted to 5.56 per cent in MENA countries or to 4.99 per cent if we don't consider GCC countries (World Bank, 2012). These rates approach those registered for some Latin American countries, which generally exhibit more than 6 per cent annual growth. Among MENA countries, Egypt and Turkey were included in the HSBC bank 'CIVETS' list of favored nations for having a diverse and dynamic economy and a young, growing population, as well as in the 'NEXT ELEVEN' Goldman Sachs list of countries having the potential of becoming, along with the BRICs, the world's largest economies in the twenty-first century.

Although the average growth performance of MENA countries is slightly greater than that of EU15 countries (about 3 per cent), several authors argue that some MENA countries have not clearly started their convergence process toward EU per capita levels (Guétat and Serranito, 2009; Péridy and Bagoulla, 2009), except Tunisia, Turkey, as well as Egypt to a lesser extent.

The positive average GDP growth rate has been basically due to the favorable global economic trend characterized by growth in the oil market, the development of tourism, an increase in foreign investment and immigrant remittances (with the exception of Lebanon, the Palestinian Territories and, to a lesser degree, Syria).

Nevertheless, if the figures related to per capita income are examined, a picture emerges which varies widely and is characterized by large disparities. Indeed, per capita income expressed in purchasing power parity for 2009 ranged from US$2380 for Yemen to US$24810 for Israel (World Bank, 2012).

The innovation performance of MENA cannot be stated as homogeneous. Israel represents a case more similar to Western Economies, outperforming EU countries in many sectors and indicators; if Gulf Cooperation Council countries are considered, their innovation and GDP performance follow another, completely different path as their industrial base is almost non-existent, as the service sector is the engine for prospective growth and as the oil reserves are due to be exhausted in 50 years or less.

The economic literature has traditionally neglected to study in depth the causes and origins of such a disappointing innovation pattern for most of the remaining MENA countries, while focusing more on trade and foreign direct investment (FDI) issues on the economic side, and on the peace, stability and migration issues of the political side. Despite the plethora of scholarly articles and international organizations' publications on economic growth in various countries and regions of the world, the contributions on economic growth performance in MENA countries, focusing on the role of innovation and TFP (total factor productivity) growth remain limited.

Abu-Qarn and Abu-Bader (2007) have investigated the sources of MENA growth and have attempted to determine the key factors that led to economic growth in MENA countries over the period 1960–98. They found that MENA growth performance was essentially determined by physical capital accumulation and, to a lesser extent, by the accumulation of human capital. The contribution of TFP to economic growth was negligible; all six Arab MENA countries exhibit negative TFP growth. Nabli and Véganzonès-Varoudakis (2007) address the empirical link between economic reform, human capital, physical infrastructure and MENA economic growth. They find a strong positive impact from advances in physical infrastructure and human capital, and a negative impact from structural reform on growth in six MENA countries over the period from 1970 to 1999. A very recent study also points to a severe lack of technological capacities and innovative activities in the MENA region and shows that region-specific features such as rent- and continuity-oriented political economy structures are simultaneously important determinants and hampering factors to economic development in the MENA region that can partially explain an economically inefficient allocation of resources (Brach, 2009). The importance of availability of down-scale indicators and surveys to monitor and evaluate the innovation performance is discussed in Arvanitis and M'Henni (2010), who also underline the importance of reshaping the interaction of public and private actors to boost knowledge creation and diffusion and cope with the world crisis. The pervasiveness of the public sector and the inefficient scale of private initiatives are also at the heart of the more general interpretation given by Malik and Awadallah (2011).

In this chapter we draw on a few existing works on the innovation performance of the area and on the recent Knowledge Assessment Methodology (KAM) indicators from the World Bank to provide an updated picture of the classical indicators such as R&D expenditure, human capital, patents, high-tech employment and high-tech exports for the MENA countries. We will also present the current policy initiatives in the area and focus on some success cases of innovating businesses.

7.2   STATISTICS AND PERFORMANCE IN FOCUS

When looking at innovation indicators, both at input and output level, we find that the figures for MENA countries are disappointing. For the period 2006–09, the figures ranged from 0.21 per cent for Egypt to 0.63 per cent for Morocco and 0.84 per cent for Turkey and 1.13 per cent for Tunisia. Israel, where this percentage comes in at 4.8 per cent, is an exception. During the same period, the United States spent 2.7 per cent of GDP on research and development, Germany 2.8 per cent, Brazil 1.08 per cent, China 1.4 per cent and India 0.75 per cent. On average, around 90 per cent of spending on research and development comes from the public sector as against around one third in the European countries. All MENA countries rank below the world average (Figure 7.1), except for Israel. From the point of view of the diffusion of new technologies (such as telephone lines,

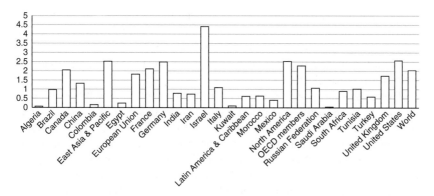

Note: Morocco figures are for 2006.

Source: World Bank (2012).

Figure 7.1 Research and development expenditure (% of GDP), 2005

mobile phones and internet usage), the situation seems slightly better, demonstrating the efforts made in the MENA region over the last 15 years to improve their position in the area of technological supply and telecommunications, with the aim of providing infrastructure for sustained growth. A characteristic feature of MENA countries is that the research and innovation sectors are quite distinguished and separated.

Actually, we find concrete and positive examples of high-level academic research carried out on one side by traditional institutions such as ministries, research councils, universities or public centers, often hindered by modest resources, and on the other side, technological innovation is brought about through operational activities supported by the Ministry for Industry or for the Economy, with cooperation between engineering schools, technology centers (incubator centers and technology parks) and technical and professional centers.

When trying to map technology centers in the Mediterranean area (ANIMA, 2005), we get a picture where the South is characterized by more recent institutions, with fewer financial resources and less staff than in the North. Moreover, in contrast with the North where activities are implemented in a vast range of spheres (such as the environment, renewable energy, logistics, aeronautics, multimedia and so on), in the MENA there is a heavy concentration of activities in the information technology sector, followed by the biotechnology sector. This is a major issue in the creation of employment thanks to the spreading of technological poles and innovation hubs. When compared to the successful Asian experiences of regional innovation in Bangalore, Karnataka, India and of the Pudong district, Shangai, China, there is really not much more that can be discussed. However, the creation of new businesses, of new linkages and the building of social capital is often the key to success in many regional innovation stories.

If one then looks at the impact on the creation of new business start-ups, on average in the European countries the technology centers service five times more businesses than in the South, while the 'business nurseries' and incubators generate up to two and a half times more businesses. In the MENA group of countries, the GCC members are outperforming the others in terms of start-ups and business creation. The number of start-ups in the MENA region increased eight times in 2011 as compared to 2005. Jordan, Lebanon, Egypt and the UAE attracted most early-stage investments in the same period. More specifically, the UAE attracted 17 per cent of these start-ups during 2011, according to a report released by Dubai Internet City (DIC) in collaboration with global business research and consulting firm Frost & Sullivan. The report indicates that government-backed initiatives to encourage entrepreneurship, as well as the development of universities offering programs for entrepreneurs and investors, technology parks, and incubation centers, are some of the reasons behind the surge in the small and medium-sized enterprise (SME) sector (AfricanBrains, 2012).

A definite shortcoming is the financial system attitude and involvement in innovative activities (so-called venture capital). Reasons for this weakness include the existence of commercial risks inherent in the launch of new initiatives, of high country risks, the absence of guarantee systems, a 'family' type business management system which is suspicious of external investors and the narrow outlook of local stock markets which is not conducive to the mobilization of investments.

But also on the financial side, each country stands on its own. On one side there is Israel, a pioneering state in the field of new business development financing, while on the other side there are countries such as Morocco, Turkey and Tunisia and, to a lesser degree, Egypt, Lebanon and Jordan, where the venture capital market has begun to develop. Finally there are Algeria, Syria and the Palestinian Territories, where this market is still at an early stage.

On the northern shore of the Mediterranean, however, the venture capital market is more developed, reporting annual investments that in 2004 were worth around 10 billion euros. Nevertheless, these countries are lagging when compared with the Northern European countries (for example, in 2006, private equity investment as a percentage of GDP was 0.61 per cent in France, 0.34 per cent in Spain and 0.31 per cent in Italy,

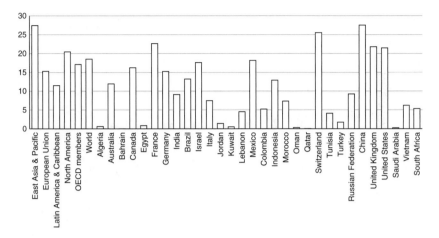

Source: World Bank (2012).

Figure 7.2 *High-technology exports (% of manufactured exports), 2009*

as against 1.258 per cent in the United Kingdom and 1.437 per cent in Sweden, while the European average was 0.596 per cent).

The percentage of high-tech exports over total exports provides an indicator of results in the field of innovation (Figure 7.2). Israel is the country with the highest percentage value on average (14 per cent) between 2005 and 2010 and is in line with the OECD average. The other countries in the area have much lower figures, though it is worth mentioning the performance of Tunisia, which ranges between 4 per cent and 6 per cent, and especially of Morocco, which has gone from almost zero to 10 per cent. In these latter two countries, it is the electrical components sector which has played a significant role, recording percentages with respect to total exports of 10 per cent for Morocco and 11 per cent for Tunisia in 2000.

Another interesting indicator in relation to innovation and technological development is technology-oriented FDI. According to ANIMA-MIPO figures for the period of January 2003 to February 2005, technology-oriented FDI to MENA countries represented 14 per cent of the total in terms of the number of projects (almost double the FDI directed towards the new member states of the EU). The investments mainly comprised financial transactions (such as start-up acquisitions, purchase of phone network licenses and the creation of venture-capital funds) and, secondly, the creation of private centers for research and development.

In terms of sectors, the ICT (Information and Communication Technologies) sector received the lion's share with around two-thirds of

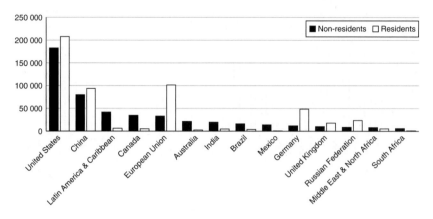

Source: World Bank.

Figure 7.3a   Patent applications, 2005

projects, followed (with much lower shares) by the financial or business services sector (11 per cent) and by the pharmaceutical and biotechnology sector (10 per cent). The source countries of this FDI were the United States and France (with 31 per cent and 26 per cent of the total respectively) while the most significant beneficiary countries were Israel (33 per cent), Morocco (21 per cent) and Algeria (13 per cent).

FDI as a whole is commonly seen as a vehicle of hard and soft knowledge, likely to produce spillovers and channel know-how, technologies and innovative practices. According to the latest data available from ANIMA, in 2010 FDI in the area experienced some kind of sectoral rotation, with a relative loss in industries such as ICT (which used to be until recently a main attractor), agri-food, tourism and chemicals, and with an increase in aerospace, engineering and general public electronics and logistics. In terms of number of projects, the energy sector comes first with 123 projects, followed by banking (88), software (77), electrical and electronic equipment (51), engineering (51), tourism (45), building and public works (41), automobile (38) and agri-food (37) (ANIMA, 2011).

The standard, common indicator for innovation performance, patenting activity, remains quite low for the whole area, with the usual exception of Israel. Figures 7.3a and 7.3b report some figures to grab an idea of the deep differential with other developed and emerging countries, hinting at a technology gap and a wide backwardness in terms of stepping up the technological ladder. The great majority of patents filed in MENA countries up to the past decade have a non-resident origin (Aubert and Reiffers, 2003).

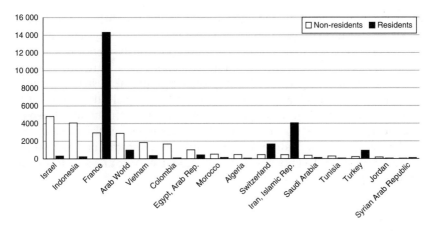

Source: World Bank.

Figure 7.3b   Patent applications, 2005

In recent years, there have also been considerable efforts made to create innovation-friendly infrastructure, such as technology parks, incubator systems, venture capital funds and SME and young entrepreneur training services (particularly in Tunisia and Morocco). As regards the creation of technology parks and incubator systems, for instance, certain practical initiatives are currently in the process of being set up in various countries such as in Morocco, Jordan and Tunisia.

Tunisia is a particularly interesting case, since it is the country in which innovation has been most widely placed at the top of the political agenda, especially in President Ben Ali's program for the period 2004–09. Among the various activities, the Ministry for Industry, Energy and SMEs is responsible for the development of technology centers. According to forecasts, there should be 12 established by 2009. As at 2006, there were two operational, six were being built and the others were at the study stage. The Tunisian technology centers are positioned at the regional level and their objective is that of bringing together businesses, research laboratories and training institutions and centers that operate within the territory in accordance with the model for regional innovation systems.

The existence of such experiences in countries on the southern shores of the Mediterranean is undoubtedly positive from the perspective of developing networking systems for the various parties involved in innovation processes (such as local institutions, research centers, businesses and so on). In general, however, while there is quite significant potential (such as the existence of sectors of excellence in certain countries, a good qualitative level of human resources in the scientific and technical fields, a spread in large cities of new communications systems, and so on), there are considerable lags due to the previously-mentioned scarce resources allocated to research and development, an insufficient qualitative level of the existing technology centers, cultural mistrust towards innovation, the weakness of technical and financial support institutions and a still insufficient development of entrepreneurship. Despite a good qualitative level of human resources in the technical field, the weakness of the innovation systems leads to a substantial brain-drain of researchers and hence an impoverishment of resources in terms of human capital.

7.3   THE KAM INDICATORS

A recent initiative by the World Bank gave birth to a project to track and compare the performance of a country's knowledge economy. The KAM website allows for the investigation of the level and ranking of countries in terms of a series of knowledge-related indicators: Economic Incentive and Institutional Regime, Education, Innovation, and ICT. In practice, the KAM is an interactive benchmarking tool created by the Knowledge for Development Program to help countries identify the challenges and opportunities they face in making the transition to the knowledge-based economy. Specifically, two indicators were elaborated to compare countries' performance: the KAM Knowledge Index (KI) and the Knowledge Economy Index. The KAM Knowledge Index (KI) measures a country's ability to generate, adopt and diffuse knowledge. This is an indication of overall potential of knowledge development in a given country. Methodologically, the KI is the simple average of the normalized performance scores of a country or region on the key variables in three Knowledge Economy pillars – education and human resources, the innovation system and information and communication technology (ICT). The Knowledge Economy Index (KEI) takes into account whether the environment is conducive to knowledge being used effectively for economic development. It is an aggregate index that represents the overall level of development of a country or region towards the Knowledge Economy. The KEI is calculated based on the average of the normalized performance scores of a country or region on all four pillars related to the knowledge economy: economic incentive and institutional regime, education and human resources, the innovation system and ICT. Refer to the website www.worldbank.org/kam for details on how the indicators are computed.

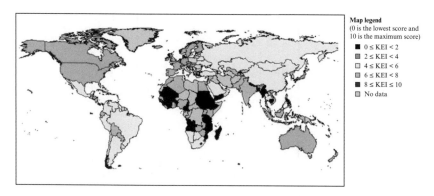

Figure 7.4a   Knowledge Economy Index, 2000, world map

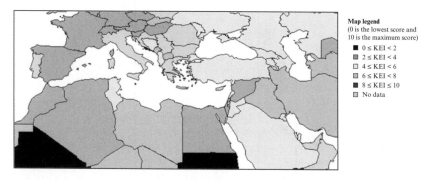

Source: KAM, World Bank (2012).

Figure 7.4b   Knowledge Economy Index, 2000, Mediterranean basin

The maps (Figures 7.4a and 7.4b) of the Knowledge Economy Index give an idea of the positioning of MENA countries with respect to the rest of the world and to the Mediterranean basin in particular. Notice how Tunisia, Lebanon, Jordan and Turkey outperform Morocco, Algeria, Egypt and Syria. Apart from Israel, whose indicator is aligned with the most advanced Northern European countries, only Malta and Cyprus are in line with the other Southern Mediterranean EU countries such as Italy, Portugal and Greece.

While considering country groupings, we see that MENA countries' performance according to the KAM indicators did not change their ranking in 2012 with respect to 2000, while East Asia and the Pacific, South Asia and Latin America did (Table 7.1). Africa as a whole lost one position, while North America remains firmly in the first position. Note, however,

Table 7.1 *KEI and KI Indexes (KAM 2012), world regions*

Rank	Change 2000	Regions	KEI	KI	Economic Incentive Regime	Innovation	Education	ICT
1	0	North America	8.8	8.7	9.11	9.45	8.13	8.51
2	0	Europe and Central Asia	7.47	7.64	6.95	8.28	7.13	7.5
3	1	East Asia and the Pacific	5.32	5.17	5.75	7.43	3.94	4.14
4	1	Latin America	5.15	5.31	4.66	5.8	5.11	5.02
5	−2	World	5.12	5.01	5.45	7.72	3.72	3.58
6	0	Middle East and N. Africa	4.74	4.51	5.41	6.14	3.48	3.92
7	1	South Asia	2.84	2.77	3.05	4.23	2.17	1.9
8	−1	Africa	2.55	2.43	2.91	3.95	1.44	1.9

Source: KAM, World Bank (2012).

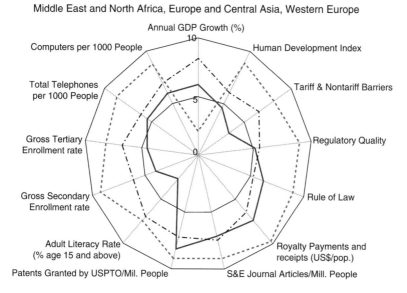

Figure 7.5a   Macro areas comparisons

that the best performing countries in the world in terms of global KAM indicators are the Scandinavian countries, with Sweden, Finland and Denmark ranking respectively first, second and third. To find MENA countries, one has to look on the lower part of the ranking (apart from Israel), among the 75th and 115th position.

A graphical analysis of KAM indicators helps us further understand the relative positioning of the MENA countries with respect to the major geographical areas in terms of Knowledge Economy and Innovation Indicators, as well as ranking countries within the areas of Maghreb and Mashreq (Figures 7.5a, 7.5b and 7.5c).

7.4   PARTNERSHIPS, PROJECTS AND SUCCESS STORIES TOWARDS INNOVATION

In spite of the fact that the innovative performance of MENA countries remains disappointing if compared with other emerging economies, we shall notwithstanding underline that these young, growing economies do present at the moment opportunities and perspectives far brighter than many developed, Western European countries. In a post-crisis world economy which will favor sustainable approaches, the Mediterranean

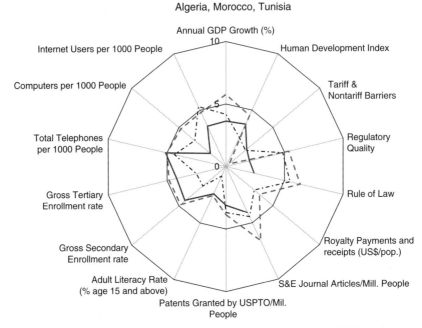

Comparison Group: All Countries; Type: weighted; Year: most recent (KAM 2009)

Figure 7.5b   Maghreb countries

partner countries have the assets to take their place both as a production base for Europe and as a laboratory of the future on certain questions of universal interest – notably, the management of water, cities or energy. Most countries of the region have today committed to important reforms so that their economies evolve towards a greater opening-up to private enterprise. And the future of several sectors in the European Union relies on southern partners – joint production units, new regional branches or headquarters, commercial agreements, foreign investment, technology partnerships, and so on.

Therefore, investment initiatives focused and leading to accrued innovation capacity are increasing on the southern and eastern shores of the Mediterranean Sea. Many success stories can help understand in which sectors foreign partners are investing, such as those provided by the consortium MedAlliance.[1] We report here some of the success stories from the initiatives more related than others to aspects of innovation creation and diffusion. In the IT and telecommunications (TLC) sector, Egypt has created a small 'Silicon Valley' in Cairo for IT service providers, helping it to become one of the top ten offshore countries for IT services. The

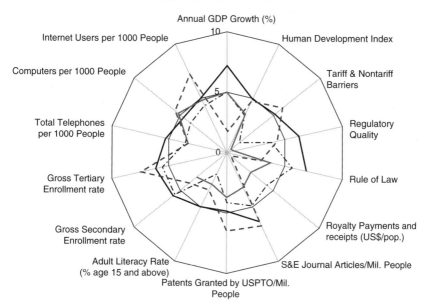

Figure 7.5c   Mashreq countries

German-based SQS Software Quality Systems chose Egypt to build a platform and serve European markets. While the company's offshoring centers in South Africa and India principally deal with Anglo-Saxon and international customers, the focus of the services performed in Cairo is on domestic companies in Germany, Austria and Switzerland. Besides the language skills, the cultural affinity and time difference of just one hour also contribute to the close fit between SQS Egypt and its customers. The SQS subsidiary in Cairo has experienced a successful and rapid start. By the end of its first business year in 2008, employee numbers had risen to 51, and in April 2009, they had increased to over 70.

Stonesoft Corporation from Finland is a network security solution provider. They established the Tunisia office in August 2003 and chose Tunisia because of its political stability, favorable economic situation and good relationship with Europe. From the Tunisia office they expanded operations into other North African countries such as Algeria, Morocco and Egypt, at the beginning working intensively with Tunisie Telecom and Orascom Telecom Tunisia (Tunisiana).

The G.ho.st (Global Hosted Operating System) team is a unique Palestinian–Israeli collaboration. It aims to bring employment, skills and hope to a troubled area and to increase dialogue between Palestinians and Israelis. G.ho.st has launched a Peace Foundation which is donating IT equipment in underprivileged Palestinian and Israeli communities.

In 2000, the France Telecom Group acquired a minority share and agreed to invest in the overall management of the then Jordan national telecom company. Knowledge transfer was then and still is a key driver for France Telecom's investment in Jordan. With a constructive relationship secured with the Government of Jordan, France Telecom went on to acquire the majority shareholding of the company and integrated fixed, mobile, internet and content activities under Jordan Telecom Group in 2006.

In the transport sector, Fokker Elmo, part of Stork Aerospace, specialists in wiring and interconnection systems for aircraft and aircraft engines, chose the Aegean Free Zone in Izmir for their Turkish facility, because of the good conditions that have been created for international companies in terms of business development, labor, set-up time, and environment. The facility in Izmir manufactures wiring systems for aircraft programs of major Fokker Elmo customers such as Boeing, EADS/Airbus and Lockheed Martin. The facility has been fully operational since the third quarter of 2008. The facility's size is approximately 8000m^2 and there are expected to be 300–500 employees and a 50 million euros turnover in five years.

In the energy sector, various oil-related business activities opened up plants and set up collaborative projects with the local governments. Not only oil, but also the solar potential is targeted by firms such as Abener from Spain. In 2007, Abener started construction of the first hybrid plant in the world in Hassi R'Mel (Southern Algeria). This uses ISCC (Integrated Solar Combined Cycle) technology and has 150 megawatts of power. Innovation and sustainability clearly define this project with a time horizon of 2010. It represents a global pioneering experience which integrates a solar field of CCP (parabolic trough collectors) with an area of 180000m^2 of reflective surface.

Success stories can also be related to the effects of former emigrants coming back home to exploit their experiences and know-how at home. In 2010, a study was produced to assess the effects of returning migrants on the economy of their home countries (MedAlliance, 2010). In the high-tech area, at least three initiatives took place thanks to returning emigrants: Protenia, the first Moroccan biotechnological firm; RedFabriq, specialized in IT services in Algeria; and Oxia, a software engineering firm in Tunisia.

The Medibtikar Project

From 2006 to 2009, and in the framework of the Regional Cooperation of the Euro–Mediterranean Partnership,[2] in the MENA area the Medibtikar project collected funds (with a budget of over 9.2 million euros) from the EU Commission to sustain SME competitiveness and technology transfer. The name Medibtikar is derived from MEDiterranean and *ibtikar* (Arabic for innovation) and the beneficiary countries involved were Algeria, Egypt, Israel, Jordan, Lebanon, Morocco, Syria, the Palestinian Authority, Tunisia and Turkey. The beneficiary organizations were public and private enterprises concerned with increasing the competitiveness of SMEs. The mission was to provide the MEDA countries with new and improved instruments to stimulate innovation at the firm and country levels. The project was also meant to stimulate networking across the MEDA region, and between the region and the countries of the European Union.

The statutory objectives were:

- to encourage good practice in technology and knowledge transfer by administrations, enterprises, industry federations, chambers of commerce, etc;
- to support the creation and/or improvement of intermediary organizations in charge of implementing support policies for SMEs (Innovation and Technology Centers (ITCs), TechnoParks, Incubators);
- to support innovation management, from the development of a national innovation strategy to the identification of services to provide to SMEs;
- to provide support to specific sectors facing common challenges in the MEDA region;
- to develop national and regional networks supporting innovation stakeholders and connecting key players across the Euro-Mediterranean countries.

In 2006, Medibtikar produced a series of reports on the innovation performance of the MENA region. According to the results, in order to assess the innovation performance, the key factor lay in the demographic dynamics of the area:

Most Med-Zone countries either have gone through or are now going through a demographic transition. The usual pattern is one in which high mortality and high birth rates associated with agricultural or pre-industrial societies are replaced first by low mortality rates leading to a population surge, and then by low birth rates in which growth returns to normal and the population starts to age. This process will have an important impact on regional demographics and will lead to an increased and urgent need for job creation. In 1960 the total labour force of the 8 Med-Zone partners was just shy of 20M people. By 2000 this had grown to almost 58M. Based on data published by the World Bank the population is expected to exceed 79M by 2010 and 98M by 2020.

Apart from this focus on labor and demography, the valued-added produced by the project has been to provide a snapshot of some of the MENA countries' innovation systems, highlighting strengths and weaknesses.

We are therefore able to grasp the quality and depth of the innovation policies of these countries, based on the reports of Medibtikar. Syria has an innovation policy. This concerns all ministries but there is no coordination structure and no system for policy evaluation. The policy prioritizes IT, manufacturing and agriculture as areas for development. Delivery is left up to the research institutes. Syria has one incubator, MAWRED, established in 2003. This is a women's business incubator with offices in all regions of the country. It focuses on services such as design and recruitment. The rate of incubation is low and many of the tenants are NGOs. In 2005 MAWRED will implement an awareness road-show visiting most parts of the country. The European Investment Bank (EIB) is currently helping to establish the country's first venture capital fund. Industry–academia linkages are very weak.

Egypt has an innovation policy implemented via measures to stimulate investment, venture capital, business incubators, industrial modernization, SME development and entrepreneurship. There is no formal coordination body. The delivery of innovation policy is carried out via the programs of the relevant ministries, often implemented with assistance from donor organizations. An important point of reference is the SFD (Social Fund for Development), which finances business centers and incubators, the IMP (Industrial Modernization Program) and GAFI (the General Authority For Investment).

In Jordan policy discussions emphasize issues such as entrepreneurship, learning and creativity, as well as the creation and application of knowledge for the benefit of industry and society. Although there is no specific innovation policy, elements of programs dealing either with enterprise transformation or human resource development contribute to the overall goal of developing an innovative society and can be thought of as implementing an innovation strategy: Support for innovation comes from a variety of sources and in at least three flavors:

- programs entirely financed by Jordanian funds such as the IRADA program or the Industrial Scientific Research Fund;
- programs run with assistance from donors such as the JJIDP program supported by JICA of Japan, the AMIR program supported by USAID as well as the EJADA and JUMP programs supported by the European Commission;
- Public–private partnerships such as the JEI or Jordan Education Initiative.

Key ministries are:

- MHESR – the Ministry for Higher Education and Scientific Research;
- MoPIC – the Ministry for Planning and International Cooperation;
- MoI – the Ministry of Industry.

MoPIC coordinates international cooperation initiatives with the EU and EU member states such as France, Germany, the UK, Italy and Spain as well as with the US, Japan, Canada and organizations such as the UNDP, UNICEF and the World Economic Forum. It manages programs such as the SETP (Social and Economic Transformation Program). The SETP includes a range of initiatives that address human resource development, basic government services, rural development and poverty alleviation as well as regulatory and policy reform. There is a good culture of evaluation at MoPIC and it has its own 'Department for Programs, Projects Monitoring and Evaluation'. Perhaps the most relevant MoPIC activity, however, is the work of the JNCT (Jordan National Competitiveness Team). Established in 1997 as part of a regional development initiative funded by the Dutch government, the team is now supported by USAID. Their initial work focused on the mapping of industrial sectors and clusters. This was followed by an assessment and evaluation of the sectors and clusters with a view to improving their competitiveness. Their findings have been published as a series of detailed studies including sectoral studies on IT, tourism, textiles and garments, pharmaceuticals, mining, hospitals and the exploitation of the Dead Sea as a natural resource. The JNCT is now in the process of establishing an observatory on industrial competitiveness. It clearly has the potential to provide important inputs to national industry and innovation policy.

Morocco has a clear policy for innovation drawing upon the competencies of several ministries, in particular the Ministry with competence for Industry and that with competence for Scientific Research and Technological Development. This policy is a result of initiatives taken by the Ministry for Industry to develop a dialogue on innovation-related issues with the Ministry responsible for Higher Education and Scientific Research, as well as with the CNRST (the National Council for Research in Science and Technology), OMPIC (the national intellectual property organization) and R&D Maroc (the Moroccan R&D Association). Each organization has now incorporated innovation in its own strategy implemented via its own institutions. The Ministry responsible for Industry and its agencies, for example, are busy with initiatives to develop incubators, encourage the emergence of a private equity sector, and support the development of new business in traditional and emerging sectors alike. The Ministry responsible for Research and Higher Education, acting through the CNRST, has clearly aligned its strategy with the goal of creating an environment to support innovation. It has implemented a program of radical change intended to provide industry with access to facilities, know-how and information. This program involves the development of new university–industry interfaces, the introduction of 'innovation' as an action line in PROTARS, Morocco's framework program for RDT, as well as a network of university-based incubators. High-level coordination of innovation policy is assured by the Permanent Inter-ministerial Committee for Scientific Research and Technological Development.[3] This was established in 2000 and is chaired by the Prime Minister. It meets annually or in extraordinary meetings if needed. At a more operational level, innovation-related programs such as EUREKA or the FSP[4] have their own steering committee. Innovation-related networks such as the RDT,[5] RGI,[6] RIE[7] and the National Business Creation Initiative all have their own coordination committees. The government is now in the process of developing a new network entitled the 'Network for Innovation and Creativity'.

Algeria has neither an RDT nor an innovation policy. An RDT strategy is being developed and the 'Agence Nationale de la Valorisation des Resultats de la Recherche' tries to link research with business development. Some elements of an innovation infrastructure are now being developed. Algeria has one venture capital fund, FINALEP. It is drafting legislation to create better conditions for private equity players. Plans exist to boost the availability of venture capital and to provide financing for SMEs. A technology park is under construction, measures are being taken to promote entrepreneurship and plans exist to develop a national fund for RDT and innovation. The main actors are the Ministry for Small and Medium Sized Enterprise and the Ministry for Higher Education and Scientific Research.

Tunisia has a range of policies that emphasize new enterprise development or new business creation, although there is no formal mechanism for coordination on innovation. It has made good progress in the last five years on building up a private equity sector as well as a system of incubators and technology parks, but much remains to be done.

An especially detailed, although not up-to-date, analysis of MENA countries' innovation systems was realized in 2002 by the World Bank. In particular, the countries were grouped according to their features:

> Three categories of countries can be identified in the MENA region. A first category (Algeria, Egypt, for example) seem to have made serious attempts to integrate S&T into economic development and have accumulated some non-negligible experience. This experience, considered the richest in terms of technology acquisition, appears to have started laying down the basis for an S&T policy and NSI, though not explicitly, in the early seventies. A study conducted in 1996 under the auspices of the Egyptian Ministry of Scientific Research and funded by the World Bank has identified several strengths of the Egyptian S&T system: tremendous human resources with a large number of highly educated and specialized personnel, a considerable number of R&D institutions in various disciplines, many examples of success, particularly in agricultural research and other well focused industries, long tradition of S&T and Government commitment towards S&T institutions. The main driving vectors of this policy included: engagement in programs of scientific research, both fundamental and applied, massive transfer of up-to-date technologies from various advanced countries and substantial investments in education and training, locally and abroad.
>
> A second category, more oriented towards market-driven growth and the contribution of foreign capital to industrialization (Morocco and Tunisia in the Maghreb, and Jordan and Kuwait in the Mashrek for example) were left with little elbow room to link up S&T policy to economic development policy. The technological decision was to a large extent in the hands of foreign firms, at a time when the industrial base of the country was being laid down. Although these countries have managed to develop local industries of small and medium size type, they were no clear bodies in charge of S&T policy and the level of awareness of the fundamental role of S&T in development was relatively low. Thus the basic ingredient for setting up the basis for NSI was missing.
>
> A third category of countries (Libya and Mauritania for example), which lack a sufficient industrial base and are small both in terms of population and markets, had S&T policy and its integration into economic policy low on their agenda. Current potential and infrastructure are unlikely to provide the basis for an NSI (World Bank, 2002).

Recently another ambitious project was included in the file of actions of the Unions for the Mediterranean: the MIRA (Mediterranean Innovation and Research Coordination Action) project. MIRA is a large platform joining policy makers and the European Commission for the observation, analysis and promotion of shared science and technology policies in the MENA region and is devised as a policy discussion forum between EU members and Southern Mediterranean partners. One of the main tasks is to collect indicators according to homogeneous criteria and to support the monitoring of innovative projects and initiatives.

7.5   THE KNOWLEDGE ECONOMY FOR GROWTH AND EMPLOYMENT IN MENA PROGRAM

The Marseille Center for Mediterranean Integration (CMI) was created in 2004 and is a World Bank administered platform for multi-partner programs, aiming to enhance the convergence of sustainable development policies by providing a platform for knowledge sharing and joint learning.

A pillar among the projects undertaken is the implementation and support of the Knowledge Economy. The Knowledge Economy for Growth and Employment in MENA program brings together the World Bank's MENA region, the World Bank Institute (WBI), the European Investment Bank (EIB), and key regional partners, such as the Islamic Educational, Scientific, and Cultural Organization (ISES CO). The program, described in the 2011 Annual Report of the CMI, uses the wealth of knowledge assembled by the partners, and focuses on the 'how to' of making an effective transition to the KE. Its design has incorporated substantive advice from key CMI counterparts, especially Egypt, Jordan, Lebanon, Tunisia and Morocco.

The work will include analysis of the four KE 'pillars' (a favorable economic and institutional regime, a dynamic innovation system, a strong ICT infrastructure, and a reformed education system). Recent events in the region provide an opening to emphasize the importance of tackling governance issues in the transition to the KE, and making improvements that can promote trust-based, open, and change-friendly societies. Many, if not most, of the countries that have made rapid progress on the KE, such as South Korea and Finland, have staged nationwide KE-inspired programs of change. Ambition should be high – Tunisia has what it takes for a modern knowledge economy just as, for example, Estonia did. Moving forward means acting on the four KE pillars while implementing pragmatic policies customized to country specificities and making institutions more responsive to KE needs and opportunities.

The development of this work is being complemented with consultations, beginning with a workshop to foster dialogue among stakeholders in MENA countries in November 2011. The ensuing KE report will integrate the key findings from analytical work and the consultations, and highlight ways in which MENA countries can develop modern knowledge-based economies that are more agile, internationally networked, and constantly learning. The report will be presented at a high-level conference to take place at the CMI with policy makers and change agents in 2012. Other innovation-related programs led by CMI include the program on Supporting the Promotion and Financing of Innovation in the Mediterranean.

7.6 CONCLUSIONS

In April 2012, a high-level conference was held by the European Commission's Research and Innovation DG, in consultation with other departments, the European Parliament, the EU Member States and the Mediterranean countries. The scope of the conference was to highlight the Research and Innovation challenges and perspective for the EU MENA countries, even in a politically troubled situation such as the current one. Participants agreed on a series of conclusions that we chose to share here in that they perfectly conclude our analysis (Ayache and Brach, 2012).

The main problems shared by all countries in the Mediterranean are the uncertain economic perspectives and the devastating job situation. A large share of the youth population is currently unemployed, as are, increasingly, highly skilled and trained graduates from universities and technical higher education institutions. In this context, innovation and research are facing two central challenges: first, to keep up and further support excellent research and teaching institutions. In economic and politically difficult times, this becomes an even more difficult task. Cutting down education and research budgets is often a consequence; however, this must not happen. The second challenge is to find the balance between excellent and frontier-pushing basic research on the one hand, and the development of marketable ideas and innovation on the other. This balance is essential in order to create new knowledge that future generations will be able to draw on and to (further) develop the urgently needed innovative and entrepreneurial skills that will help the young generations to be able to create new jobs.

With respect to these challenges, the Arab Mediterranean (MED) countries face two main problems: limited technological and innovative capacities (Brach, 2009; Brach and Naudé, 2012), and a weak culture of innovation (Pasimeni et al., 2007). Despite the fact that Euro–Med cooperation in the past never explicitly concentrated on strengthening innovation and research, different initiatives have dealt with and supported these topics. However, the participation of Mediterranean countries in scientific cooperation with the EU has been very low. Less than 1 per cent of the allocated contributions and only 10 out of 220 contracts were signed with MED countries in the Fifth Framework Programme (FP) (European Commission, 2005). Only three MED countries, Tunisia, Morocco and Algeria, were involved. The range of countries was significantly expanded in the FP6 (2003–05) to include eight countries (the three North African countries plus Egypt, Jordan, Lebanon, Syria and the Palestinian Territories) and yet the participation of MED countries remained low in an international comparison (cf. Pasimeni et al., 2007). However, the documentation and availability of coherent data is very difficult to access. To the best of our knowledge, no systematic overview of the evaluation of key figures of interest such as the number of contracts and contracting partners or the share of the funds allocated by developing region was available. The same is true for innovation and research indicators, as for example business enterprise expenditures for research and development, number of publications, the number of researchers and others that are regularly compiled by the Commission's joint research center which are not available for the MED countries (Joint Research Center, 2012).

Several reasons are partially accountable for the low participation and success rate: a lack of tailor-made policy instruments that are fitted to the situation that these countries are facing and that are directed at solving central problems. As a result of a lack of capacities and skills as well as a low prioritization of research and innovation by the political actors in the MED countries, there seems to be very little strategy for directing the innovation towards developing new capabilities and entering new, more sophisticated markets based on the existing know-how. The argument concerning a lack of feedback and evaluation mechanisms applies here too. Only rarely is relevant data available, and if it is, this knowledge is rarely used.

The conference pointed out three key elements in order to develop research and innovation in the MENA countries:

1. Bring research and innovation closer together and align existing programs and initiatives at the level of the European Union, at the level of Euro–Mediterranean relations, and at the level of the Mediterranean countries.
2. Unleash the innovative potential in the MED region and make direct use of research and innovation for socio-economic development in MED region in the medium and long term. Innovation is widely and correctly considered as the key driver of sustainable economic development.
3. Fit research and cooperation to strengthen innovation and marketable knowledge in the Mediterranean region. Research is the art to question, analyze and reflect the status quo and to push the knowledge frontier. As such, research is an important ingredient and determinant of the innovation process. Innovation always needs research.

NOTES

1. MedAlliance is a consortium managed by ANIMA and financed at 75 per cent by the European Union running the program Invest-in MED, whose aim is to develop busi-

ness relations, investments and partnerships between the two opposing shores of the Mediterranean, http://www.invest-in-med.eu/.
2. The Union for the Mediterranean promotes economic integration and democratic reform across 16 neighbors to the EU's south in North Africa and the Middle East. Formerly known as the Barcelona Process, cooperation agreements were relaunched in 2008 as the Union for the Mediterranean (UfM). The relaunch was an opportunity to render relations both more concrete and more visible with the initiation of new regional and sub-regional projects with real relevance for those living in the region. Projects address areas such as the economy, environment, energy, health, migration and culture. Along with the 27 EU member states, 16 Southern Mediterranean, African and Middle Eastern countries are members of the UfM: Albania, Algeria, Bosnia and Herzegovina, Croatia, Egypt, Israel, Jordan, Lebanon, Mauritania, Monaco, Montenegro, Morocco, the Palestinian Authority, Syria, Tunisia and Turkey.
3. Comité Permanent Interministériel de la Recherche Scientifique et du Développement Technologique.
4. Fonds de Solidarité Prioritaire, a French development tool.
5. The 'RDT' stands for 'Reseau de Diffusion de Technologie' or 'Technology Transfer Network'.
6. The RGI stands for 'Réseau de Génie Industriel' or 'Industrial Engineering Network'.
7. The RIE is the 'Réseau d'Incubation et Essaimage' or 'Spin-off and Incubation Network'.

REFERENCES

Abu-Qarn, Aamer S. and Suleiman Abu-Bader (2007), 'Sources of growth revisited: evidence from selected MENA countries', *World Development*, **35**(5), 752–71.
AfricanBrains (2012), 'Start-ups in the MENA region grow eight-fold since 2005 with UAE attracting 17 per cent of new enterprises', available at: http://afri canbrains.net/2012/10/18/start-ups-in-mena-region-grow-eight-fold-since-2005-with-uae-attracting-17-per-cent-of-new-enterprises/.
ANIMA (2005), 'Innovation, technology centres and investment attraction in the Mediterranean', Notes & Documents no. 9, November.
ANIMA (2011), 'The Mediterranean between growth and revolution: foreign direct investments and partnerships in MED countries in 2010', available at: http://www. animaweb.org/uploads/bases/document/AIN_FDIPartnerships-2010_Public_ Eng_23-5-2011.pdf.
Arvanitis, R. and H. M'Henni (2010), 'Monitoring research and innovation policies in the Mediterranean region', *Science, Technology & Society*, **15**(2), 233–69.
Aubert, J. and J. Reiffers (2003), 'Knowledge economies in the Middle East and North Africa', Washington, DC: World Bank.
Ayache, C. and J. Brach (2012), 'Report on the Euro-Mediterranean Conference on Research and Innovation', Barcelona, 2–3 April, available at:
http://ec.europa.eu/research/conferences/2012/euro-mediterranean/pdf/euro-med_ conference_consolidated_report.pdf#view=fit&pagemode=none.
Brach, J. (2009), 'Technology, political economy, and economic development in the Middle East and North Africa', *Review of Middle East Economics and Finance*, **5**(3), 1–23.
Brach, J. and W. Naudé (2012), 'International entrepreneurship and technological Capacities in the MENA Region', UNU-MERIT Working Paper no. 2012-20.

European Commission (2005), 'International scientific cooperation with developing countries', Brussels: Directorate General for Research.

Guétat, I. and F. Serranito (2009), 'Convergence et rattrapage technologique: un test par les séries temporelles dans le cas de pays de la région MENA', paper presented at the DREMM CNRS conference, 21–23 May, Istanbul.

Joint Research Center (2012), 'Erawatch Statistical Tools', European Commission, available at: http://erawatch.jrc.ec.europa.eu/erawatch/opencms/data_analysis/.

Malik, A. and B. Awadallah (2011), 'The economics of the Arab Spring', CSAE Working Paper no. WPS/2011-23, available at: http://www.csae.ox.ac.uk/workingpapers/pdfs/csae-wps-2011-23.pdf.

MedAlliance (2010), 'Diasporas: passerelles pour l'investissement, l'entrepreneuriat et l'innovation en Méditerranée', study no. 20, December.

Nabli, M.K. and M. Véganzonès-Varoudakis (2007), 'Reform complementarities and economic growth in the Middle East and North Africa', *Journal of International Development*, 19(1), 17–54.

Pasimeni, P., A. Boisard, R. Arvanitis and R. Rodríguez-Clemente (2007), 'Towards a Euro-Mediterranean innovation space: ideas for research and policy making', paper presented at the 2007 Conference on Corporate R&D (CONCORD), Brussels: European Commission, Directorate General for Research.

Péridy, N. and C. Bagoulla (2009), 'An analysis of real convergence and its determinants: evidence from MENA countries', paper presented at the DREMM CNRS conference, 21–23 May, Istanbul.

World Bank (2012), 'World development indicators database', available at: http://databank.worldbank.org/data/home.aspx.

World Bank (2002), 'Knowledge economy for the MENA region: national systems of innovation in the MENA region', available at: www-wds.worldbank.org.

Index